Small Town Sustainability

Paul L. Knox
Heike Mayer

Small Town
Sustainability

Economic, Social,
and Environmental Innovation

Birkhäuser
Basel

A CIP catalogue record for this book is available from the Library of Congress, Washington D.C., USA

Bibliographic information published by the German National Library
The German National Library lists this publication in the Deutsche Nationalbibliografie;
detailed bibliographic data are available on the Internet at http://dnb.d-nb.de.

This book is also available in a German language edition
Kleinstädte und Nachhaltigkeit (ISBN 978-3-7643-8579-8)

© 2013 Birkhäuser Verlag GmbH
P.O. Box 44, 4009 Basel, Switzerland
Part of De Gruyter
Copy Editing: Anda Divine, Boones Mill, Virginia, USA
Typography and layout: Paul L. Knox

Printed on acid-free paper produced from chlorine-free pulp. TCF ∞

Printed in Germany
ISBN 978-3-03821-251-5

9 8 7 6 5 4 3 2 1

www.birkhauser.com

Contents

Preface

Away from the bustling global cities are the small towns that planners, architects and politicians often forget. These small towns are neither the hubs of the global financial industry nor are they the high-tech centres of their countries. They are towns where ordinary residents experience the vagaries of the global economy and the impacts of global climate changes. But they are also towns from which we can learn how to develop a sustainable future.

We have been on a journey to discover innovative approaches to small town sustainability and have encountered the tremendous enthusiasm and vigour with which ordinary residents, mayors, planners, and architects are shaping the future of their towns. Many towns are connected to others and are engaged in a global dialogue about sustainability and what it means to their future. In this book, we discuss approaches to sustainable small town development and present a set of case studies that illustrate some of the best and most innovative practices. We hope in this way to contribute to a better understanding of a little-discussed urban type. In this second edition, we have added a review of the challenges of sustainable development for small towns in emerging economies. During a time when most discussions in urban planning centre around the ideas of metropolitan regions, mega-regions, and global cities, we see a need to critically reflect upon the role and potential of smaller places: places that often play a pivotal role within regional economies, that lend character and distinctiveness to their regional landscapes, and that, collectively, account for a significant fraction of the population in many regions.

In bringing our work together in this book, we have been helped enormously by our colleagues, friends, and students. Their thoughts, comments, and skills have been invaluable. We would especially like to recognise the contributions of Mariela Alfonzo, Kelly Beavers, Petra Bischof, Whitney Bonham, Elisabeth Chaves, Cherry Chen, Aida Cossitt, Herwig Danzer, Ashley Davidson, Bin Dorim, Daniel Fäh, Jessica Fanning, Mary Fisher, Susan Flack, Johann Jessen, Graeme Kidd, Dale Medearis, Johannes Michel, Elizabeth Morton, Pier Giorgio Olivetti, John Provo, John Randolph, Joe Schilling, Dehyun Sohn, Bernhard Steinhart, Anne-Lise Velez and Fang Wei. We have also been fortunate in receiving financial support for our work from the College of Architecture and Urban Studies, the School of Public and International Affairs, and the Metropolitan Institute at Virginia Tech. Finally, we would like to acknowledge the professional expertise and assistance of Karoline Mueller-Stahl and of our copy editors, Anda Divine and Sabine Rochlitz, together with Werner Handschin, Katharina Kulke, Elke Renz and Robert Steiger at Birkhäuser.

Blacksburg, Virginia, and Berne, Switzerland
June 2013,
Paul Knox and Heike Mayer

1. Ludlow, England. Protest poster.

1

Introduction

Why Focus on Small Towns?

Small towns can be extraordinary places – towns that have their own identity and a sociable and enjoyable way of life for their inhabitants. They can be towns where pedestrians can stroll untroubled by roaring traffic and car alarms – towns with abundant green spaces in which people can breathe clean air. Their municipal councils can insist upon renewable energy and recycling. They can encourage and promote local arts and crafts, as well as traditional eating establishments that serve local cuisine and shops that sell local produce. They can be havens in a fast world, places whose inhabitants think globally but act locally.

Yet globalisation undermines the distinctiveness of many smaller urban places and threatens their vitality and culture. In this book we illustrate small-town responses to the challenges of the fast-paced, globalised world, highlighting movements, programmes, and policies that support local cultures and traditions, conviviality and hospitality, and sense of place and sustainability. We explore the issues of economic, social, and environmental sustainability for small towns in detail, emphasising how the character of towns derives from their history; how their cuisine derives from their regional setting; and how their policies and initiatives are contributing to their economic development, their environmental quality, and their community well-being. By leveraging these attributes and building on comparative advantages, small towns can develop sustainable niches within regional, national, and global economies. Small towns are urban places with no more than about 50,000 residents. Although they are challenged to find a place in the global economy, they have environmental, cultural, and economic assets they can use in developing their sustainable futures.

Small towns account for a significant fraction of the total population in many regions of Europe, North America, Australia, New Zealand, and Japan. In Europe as a whole, small towns are home to one-fifth of the population. Beyond the broad metropolitan core region bounded by London, Milan, and Berlin, the figure is often closer to one-third and, in some regions such as Central and Eastern Scotland, much of Scandinavia, Central and Southern Italy, and Southern Ireland, at least half of the population lives in small towns. In the United States, the fastest-growing places in the country over the past two decades have been towns of between 10,000 and 50,000 inhabitants, which together account for just over 10 percent of the U.S. population.

This book reviews how, in small towns, citizens, planners, architects, and policymakers can work together to develop a sustainable future. We examine grassroots efforts to enhance sustainability in small towns and demonstrate how collaboration and networking within and among small towns can help overcome their inherent disadvantages of small size and lack of resources. Selected case studies illustrate how small towns can proactively shape their social, economic, and environmental future.

The Diversity of Small Towns

There is great variety in the history, morphology, and economy of small towns in the developed countries of the world, though the great majority of them were established as traditional market towns. They have remained small in size because they were bypassed by the transportation systems and agglomeration economies of the industrial era. Many others grew initially as small manufacturing towns during the early industrial era but did not have sufficient comparative advantages to remain competitive in the face of changing technologies and the logic of scale and agglomeration associated with the "Fordist" economies of the mid twentieth century, or with the changing international division of labour associated with the globalisation of the late twentieth century.

As a result, many small towns have experienced decades of economic and demographic stagnation. Outmigration has typically accounted for a disproportionate share of the brightest, most energetic, and best-educated young people, leaving aging populations that tend to become provincial and parochial in outlook, lacking in vision and leadership. When this happens, communities lose the capacity to understand and deal with the many internal and external influences on their well-being. With declining economies and limited capacity to manage change, problems of environmental degradation and social malaise become chronic. Meanwhile, economic rationalisation and globalisation have led inexorably to a decline in locally owned businesses, with a consequent loss of local distinctiveness, character, and sense of place. In the public sector, fiscal retrenchment and the widespread trend toward a neoliberal political economy – in which progressive notions of the public interest and civil society have been eclipsed by a grassroots resistance to taxation – have resulted in cutbacks and closures of schools, hospitals, clinics, post offices, and bus services; a reduction in investment in physical infrastructure and public utilities; and cutbacks in redistributive welfare programmes.

Nevertheless, some small towns are attracting both population and investment. In most of the more highly urbanised regions of the developed world there has been a selective movement of both jobs and households away from metropolitan areas to small towns: *counterurbanisation*. One explanation

for this counterurbanisation is that it has been a consequence of improvements since the 1970s to rural infrastructure, new communications networks, improved water supplies, and better television reception, thus making small towns and rural settings more attractive to both employers and individuals. This idea, in turn, is related to a second broad explanatory theme: *corporate reorganisation and decentralisation*. Small-town settings offered, along with their improved infrastructure and accessibility, relatively inexpensive land and cheap, non-union labour. Many of the jobs and workers involved in the counterurbanisation process, therefore, have been in branch plants – subsidiary factories responsible for standardised, routine production or assembly. There have also been several contingent reasons for counterurbanisation. One was the movement of counter-culture Baby Boomers to small towns in search of alternative lifestyles. Another was the retirement of increasing numbers of workers with enough financial security to enable them to move out of metropolitan areas to resort or retirement areas.

Market towns and hill towns that had previously been regarded as dull and restrictive have come to be seen as picturesque, peaceful, and affordable by many of the key professionals whose employers have moved there. These towns, along with others whose combination of house prices, pace of life, and physical attractiveness have drawn in retired households, teleworkers, long-distance commuters, and second-home owners, have become "gentrified," with upgraded residences, stores, cafés, and restaurants (Fig. 2). While this has brought significant increases in the overall prosperity of towns, it has also brought problems of social inequality and environmental sustainability. It has also contributed to an increasing uniformity of appearance and experience, and an increasing emphasis on competitiveness and place marketing on the part of small towns.

Different kinds of small towns, in different settings, have different needs, challenges, and opportunities (Table 1.1). Their well-being is often critical not only to their inhabitants but also to the economic and social cohesion of metropolitan regions and deep rural areas. Yet they are very often neglected in national policy, slipping through the net between urban policies and policies for disadvantaged rural regions. For the past 20 years or more there has been a relative lack of research into small towns, with researchers' attention being drawn more to the effects of globalisation and technological change on large cities and city regions. Nevertheless, as the effects of globalisation have become increasingly imprinted on small towns of every description, grassroots movements have emerged to address the needs, challenges, and opportunities of small-town communities. Many of these grassroots movements involve partnerships among local community groups, local businesses, and local governments. They are often framed in terms of the sustainability of their community, with an emphasis on liveability and quality of life. These movements and organisations, and their challenges and responses, are a recurring theme in this book. Our emphasis is on collaborative and networked approaches, highlighting the best practices that are emerging in response to the challenges of globalisation and structural economic change.

Table 1.1: A typology of small towns

Growth/Decline	Challenges & Issues
Growing small towns	*Equity* Housing affordability Land use pressures *Environment* Environmental degradation Politics of growth and environmental quality Encroachment on cultural landscape *Economy* Increasing service reliance Homogenisation of retail sector Dependence on other communities for jobs *Culture & Community* Threatened sense of place Commodified identity and culture Increasing community capacity
Declining small towns	*Equity* Decline in public service provision *Environment* Neglect of cultural landscape Vacant land use *Economy* Resource-based/old economy in decline Lack of growth opportunities *Culture & Community* Vacant and abandoned housing Diminishing tax base Lack of animation in politics Isolated indigent population Social isolation Ageing demographics

2. Flagstaff, Arizona, USA. Formerly a lumber, railroad, and mining centre, Flagstaff is now a prosperous town, its old quarters gentrified and its fringes ringed with new development.

Globalisation and Small Town Development

Over the past three decades, people and places everywhere have been confronted with change on an unprecedented scale and at an extraordinary rate. Economic and cultural globalisation has resulted in a "network society" dominated by flows of capital, ideas, and people. Some cities have become "world cities" or "global cities," capturing key economic roles in the global economy. Small towns, on the other hand, have captured few of the benefits of globalisation. They have not been immune, however, to many of the negative consequences of globalisation. Global economic interdependence and reorganisation have undermined and disrupted local economies and exposed them more than ever to external control. The social and cultural forces associated with globalisation have overwritten local social and cultural practices, and globalisation has generated a world of restless landscapes in which the more places change the more they seem to look alike and the less they are able to retain a distinctive sense of place.

The pivotal moment in globalisation was the "system shock" to the international economy that occurred in the mid-1970s. World financial markets, swollen with U.S. dollars by the U.S. government's deficit budgeting and by the huge currency reserves held by the Organisation of Petroleum Exporting Countries (OPEC), quickly evolved into a new, sophisticated system of international finance, with new patterns of investment and disinvestment that led to some radical socioeconomic changes. New social formations emerged as part of new, postindustrial societies in most Organisation for Economic Co-operation and Development (OECD) countries. New urban forms began to develop in response to the new economic logic and the new social structure. A new, transnational material culture emerged around the consumption of globally branded luxury products. Other products themselves became "McDonaldised" – standardised, predictable, franchised, and, in George Ritzer's terms, "nothing," meaning that they are centrally conceived and controlled, and comparatively devoid of distinctive substantive content.[1] Still other products became "glocalised" as a result of the cross-fertilisation of global trends and tastes with local ideas and practices. And, as money accelerated around local, national, and international circuits of capital, so the pace of everyday life quickened, everywhere.

3. Castleton, England. Like many of the textile towns in the Greater Manchester area, Castleton has suffered economic decline, social deprivation and environmental degradation as a result of structural economic change.

The Fast World

Within the fast world of the global economy there is now an intense connectedness that ties together a billion or so of the world's people through global networks of communication and knowledge, production, and consumption. Because capitalism is an inherently competitive system, there is an endless race to seek out new markets and reduce the turnover time of capital (i.e., the amount of time it takes for money that is invested in new ventures to be returned with a profit through the sale of goods and services). In the global economic system, time costs money, and the inevitable result is a steady acceleration in the pace of life. The centres of gravity of the fast world are the big city regions of Europe and North America, but the fast world also extends around the globe to the more affluent regions, small towns, neighbourhoods, and households that are "plugged in" to the contemporary world economy – whether as producers or consumers of its products and culture.

The connections between rapid industrialisation, the acceleration of everyday life, and the decline in the quality of collective life that were first noted by Walter Benjamin[2] have been intensified as postindustrial society has become fragmented and reorganised by the accelerating powers of information technology and transmission. In addition, the number of hours worked per week has actually increased in many countries, making people's home life that much more harried. An increasing number of households depend on more than one income, which means not simply a matter of working more but also a matter of integrating schedules.

These pressures are closely connected with the materialism of postindustrial society. People's notions of self-worth, social position, and well-being are all organised through consumption. As a result, a work-spend cycle has become fundamental to the economic and social dynamics of contemporary society. Speed has become a hallmark of many aspects of consumption, as reflected – and, indeed, prompted – by advertising. In advertisements, the pace of people's consumption is often linked to the pleasure they appear to be experiencing. Speed and busy-ness of schedules are transformed from negatives into symptoms of laudable, well-adjusted, and fulfilling lifestyles. There is emphasis on speed of delivery, speed of

service, speed of cook time, speed of bill paying, speed of opening cans, and speed of gratification. Paradoxically, consumer surveys routinely reveal that people want more relaxed, less consumption-driven lifestyles but in practice they behave differently, adhering increasingly to the work-spend cycle.

4. Schiphol airport, Amsterdam. A fast-world hub.

5. Sydney, Australia. Office workers on their way to work.

Economic Displacement

Just as in previous phases of economic development, globalisation has its own spatial logic. Some places are well situated to benefit from the new transnational, postindustrial, information economy; others less so. Small towns everywhere, however, face intensified challenges in maintaining economic viability as intense competition constantly modifies the variable geometry of commodity chains and consumer markets.

For some small towns, economic development has rested on the ability of business interests and public policymakers to attract investment from large, transnational corporations – often at the price of costly incentives and concessions. Elsewhere, in the absence of such large-scale investment, local economic development has typically reflected structural shifts in the overall economy of the fast world, resulting in a proliferation of office parks, retail malls, supermarket chains, and franchised fast-food and clothing chains. Big superstores and chain retailers have been allowed to spread by planners, town councils, and governments desperate to sustain the local tax base (Figs. 6 and 7). But the chains have become the economic equivalent of invasive species: voracious, indiscriminate, and often antisocial. In small towns it does not take long for superstores, supermarkets, and cloned shops to dominate and suffocate the local economic ecosystem. Their big, centralised logistical operations are driving the homogenisation of business, shopping, eating, farming, food,

the landscape, the environment, and people's daily lives. Town centres once filled with a thriving mix of independent butchers, newsagents, tobacconists, bars, book shops, greengrocers, and family-owned general stores are fast being filled with standardised supermarket retailers, fast-food chains, mobile phone shops, and the downmarket fashion outlets of global conglomerates.

Fast-food restaurants have become icons of this trend. McDonald's alone has some 34,000 restaurants worldwide serving approximately 69 million people in 119 countries each day, and has been opening new ones at the rate of almost 2,000 each year. It is the largest purchaser of beef, pork, and potatoes and the largest owner of retail property in the world. In the United States, 40 percent of meals are eaten outside of the home, most of them at fast-food restaurants. One in four adults visits a fast-food restaurant every day. Not surprisingly, the majority of the population is overweight and the frequency of health problems associated with obesity – such as early-onset diabetes and high cholesterol – is rising rapidly. The cost of these problems to personal well-being and to health care systems is already daunting. Meanwhile, fast food's low-paying service sector has become an increasingly significant component of the economy of the fast world.

Supermarket chains have become even more influential in the economic profile of small towns. In the United Kingdom, for example, the growth of the top four supermarket chains – Tesco, Asda

6. Edge-of-town supermarket. This example, in Belper, England, is typical of the large new supermarkets that have drawn business away from town centre locations. Centralised supply chains mean lower prices but also a high degree of interdependence with agribusiness and big food processing companies.

(owned by Wal-Mart), Sainsbury, and Safeway – has come to dominate the retail environment of small towns with out-of-town superstores and convenience supermarkets such as Tesco Express, Tesco Metro, and Sainsbury's Local along high streets. As a consequence, they have killed off small general stores in the United Kingdom at the rate of one a day and specialist shops – such as butchers, bakers, and fishmongers – at the rate of 50 per week.[3]

Together, the standardised menus of fast-food restaurants and the centralised supply chains of supermarket chains have not only killed off small local businesses but also impacted local farmers. Both the fast-food industry and supermarket chains rely on big suppliers in agribusiness – national and transnational firms that are often highly subsidised and whose global reach depends heavily on monoculture and extensive husbandry that, in turn, require the extensive use of antibiotics in animals and pesticides, fertiliser, and genetic engineering for crops. As a result, small farmers and fishermen have been squeezed from the market. And with them many traditional local foods have disappeared or are in danger of disappearing: aged artisan Gouda cheese in the Netherlands, for example; Ganxet beans and Jiloca saffron in Spain; Cornish pilchards and Old Gloucester beef in England; Mangalica sausage in Hungary; Pardailhan black turnip and Saint-Flour Planèze golden lentil in France; and so on.[4] Meanwhile, supermarket shelves are lined with highly processed foods, out-of-season fruit and vegetables, and produce that has travelled a long

way and, often, been stored for a while. When the average North American or European family sits down to eat, most of the ingredients have typically travelled at least 2,000 kilometres between farm, processing, packing, distribution, and consumption.

The economic dominance of fast-food franchises and supermarket chains in small towns is paralleled by the dominance and homogenising influence of national and international corporate chains in other spheres, including pharmacies, clothing stores, book stores, music and entertainment stores, coffee shops, and even undertakers. The trend is not just an erosion of small local businesses: it also narrows consumer choice, diversity, and innovation. For example, whereas independent local newsagents typically carry a broad range of magazine titles, supermarkets and chain stores typically concentrate on only the 100 (or fewer) titles with the biggest turnover, in order to maximise profit. The same is true for the sale of CDs and DVDs. So, not only do corporate chains reduce the range of shops available in small towns, they also reduce the choice of goods readily available.

The external control of corporate ownership also brings the prospect of closure through rationalisation. In Britain, traditional community pubs are increasingly under threat because of this. According to the Campaign for Real Ale, an average of 48 pubs close in Britain every month as the ownership of pubs becomes concentrated in fewer and fewer hands.[5] Corporate chains such as Greene

7. **Big-box retailing.** A Wal-Mart supercenter in Chandler, Arizona.

King, Punch Taverns, and Enterprise Inns each own thousands of outlets and constantly acquire more in the cause of market penetration and economies of scale. Smaller pubs that do not fit into their business model are sold to a developer to be converted into apartments or restaurants. Following a similar pattern, the number of local bistros in France has fallen to 35,000 from around 225,000 in the 1970s. Many of the surviving local bistros are in danger of having to transform themselves into theme bars, of being swallowed up by large chains, or of going out of business altogether.

The homogenisation of the retail environment in small towns in Britain has been documented by the New Economics Foundation, which has developed an index to identify "clone towns": places "where the individuality of high street shops has been replaced by a monochrome strip of global and national chains, somewhere that could easily be mistaken for dozens of bland town centres across the country."[6] In contrast, a "home town" is a place that retains its individual character and is instantly recognisable and distinctive to the people who live there as well as those who visit. Of the 117 towns surveyed in 2009 by the New Economics Foundation, only 36 percent had sufficient numbers of locally owned businesses to qualify as home towns; 41 percent had so few independent stores that they were tagged as clone towns; and the rest, 23 percent, were somewhere in between. These results confirmed those from an earlier survey, in 2005, and also found that economic recession, just beginning to bite in 2009, was hitting local, independent stores hardest, leaving national chain stores with an increased share of the consumer market.

Examples of clone towns include Kirkaldy, Penzance, St Austell, and Tunbridge Wells. Best among the home towns in the survey was Whitstable, in Kent, famous for its Oyster Festival and bourgeoning food culture, with a growing artistic community and a wide variety of independent shops. Other examples of home towns include Berwick, Haslemere, Hebden Bridge, and St Andrews. In general, places with a larger population size – Cambridge, Reading, Exeter, and Carlisle, for example – are more likely to be clone towns and places with a smaller population size, home towns. This is probably a reflection of the demographic profile necessary to trigger the interest of chain retailers. The survey also found that home towns provided a significantly broader range of goods and services than did clone towns. Clone towns tend to be dominated by certain categories, such as apparel. Home towns average nearly 18 different types of stores and generally have more retailers selling food, hardware, and other everyday goods.

8. Stafford, England. A national chain store with its standardised façade, inserted into the historic fabric of the Greengate Street.

Winchester, England

The first Clone Town report (2005) by the New Economics Foundation placed Winchester (population 40,000) high on the list of towns where retail multiples and microformat supermarkets have displaced the diversity of local shops and services that formerly lent the towns a good deal of their character.

Winchester began as a Roman town, around 70 CE. It was a *civitas* or regional capital, built with its streets laid out in a grid pattern and a *forum* that served as a market place lined with shops and public buildings. The town seems to have been abandoned after the last Roman soldier left Britain in 407, but reclaimed as a military stronghold in the late fifth to early sixth century, the era of the legendary warrior King Arthur and his Knights. In the late ninth century Alfred the Great revived the town, making it his capital and an important ecclesiastical city, the centre of Wessex and England. The streets were again laid out in a grid pattern. By the end of the eleventh century the great cathedral had been completed, along with the *Domesday Book* (also known as the *Book of Winchester*), kept in the royal treasury. In the Middle Ages the main source of wealth in Winchester was making wool cloth. The population of the town never exceeded 5,000 or 6,000 but it remained an important royal and ecclesiastical centre even after the capital had shifted to London. In 1554, for example, Queen Mary Tudor married Prince Philip of Spain in the Cathedral, and in 1603 Sir Walter Raleigh was tried for treason in Winchester's Great Hall.

9. Winchester town centre.

10. Winchester town centre from the East.

11. Winchester Cathedral.

For the most part, though, Winchester continued to function as a small market town. In 1724 Daniel Defoe wrote that Winchester was a "place of no trade, no manufacture, no navigation,"[7] but within a few decades the town had acquired permanent shops and a small professional class; much of the town was rebuilt and some old houses were given a Georgian façade. Real prosperity came to Winchester in the nineteenth century, largely because of the railway that reached the town in 1840. This added a significant amount of Victorian buildings to the town's fabric, along with a certain amount of industry. By 1891 the population of the town had reached more than 17,000. Since then the town's population has more than doubled, its role as the county seat for Hampshire ensuring a prosperous administrative and commercial role. The town centre was redeveloped in the 1950s and 1960s, marking the beginning of the invasion of branches of national retail chains. By 2005, High Street had been pedestrianised in an attempt to retain its attractiveness to shoppers, but few of the shops were local in character.

The town itself is acutely aware of the importance of retaining its heritage, identity, and distinctive sense of place. The town's web site noted in 2008 that "We do not want to become a bland and branded shopping centre, a 'clone town.' We intend to retain our distinctive character and personality [...] We have over 350 shops, restaurants and café bars with a strong leisure and cultural mix. We are a high quality heritage destination. Winchester must continue to develop the quality of what we offer for local people and the visitor, with new facilities alongside our historic attractions."[8] For better or worse, Winchester was not included in the 2009 Clone Town survey conducted by the New Economics Foundation.

12. Winchester High Street, south side, showing part of the Pentice, an arcaded walk beneath overhanging buildings.

13. Winchester High Street and the Butter Cross, a 15th century landmark built with a tax levied on people caught eating butter during Lent.

14. Winchester High Street, north side.

15. Emsworth, England. Typical of the kind of 'home town,' described by the New Economics Foundation, in which a high percentage of the businesses are locally owned. Originally a small fishing port with an important local oyster industry, the town is now a residential centre within the Portsmouth city region, its harbour used almost exclusively for recreational sailing. Since 2001, Emsworth has held an annual Food Festival, one of the largest events of its type in the United Kingdom.

16. Emsworth, England. Emsworth has retained a wide range of independent shops and services, including two greengrocers, two butchers, a fishmonger, two newsagents, three florists, five hairdressers, a Co-op store, and this travel company.

17. Emsworth, England. More independent, locally-owned stores, on High Street.

Marketing and Consuming "Place"

In societies where the commonalities among places are intensifying, the experience of spectacular and distinctive places, physical settings, and landscapes has become an important element of consumer culture. The fast world, with its transnational architectural styles, dress codes, retail chains, and popular culture, is increasingly associated with a sense of placelessness and dislocation, a loss of territorial identity, and an erosion of the distinctive sense of place associated with particular localities. In response, developers have created theme parks, shopping malls, festival marketplaces, renovated historic districts, and neotraditional villages and neighbourhoods. But the more that developers have sought to provide distinctive settings, and the larger and more spectacular their projects, the more inauthentic the result.

Globalisation has meanwhile prompted communities in many parts of the world to become much more conscious of the ways in which they are perceived by tourists, businesses, media firms, and consumers. As a result, places are increasingly being reinterpreted, reimagined, designed, packaged, and marketed. Sense of place can become a valuable commodity through place marketing. Seeking to be competitive within the global economy, many places have sponsored extensive makeovers of themselves, including the creation of pedestrian plazas, cosmopolitan cultural facilities, festivals, and sports and media events – the "carnival masks" and "degenerative utopias" of global capitalism.[9] Almost every place of any size now has home pages on the Internet containing maps, information, photographs, guides, and virtual tours in order to promote themselves in the global marketplace for tourism and commerce. The question of who does the reimagining and cultural packaging, and on whose terms, can become an important issue for the quality of local life.

Central to most place marketing efforts is the deliberate manipulation of material and visual culture in an effort to enhance the appeal of places. In part, this manipulation of culture depends on promoting traditions, lifestyles, and arts that are locally rooted. The re-creation and refurbishment of historic districts and settings are so widespread that they have become a mainstay of the "heritage industry." This industry, based on the commercial exploitation of the histories of peoples and places, is now worldwide, as evidenced by the involvement of the United Nations Educational, Scientific and Cultural Organisation (UNESCO) in identifying places for inclusion on World Heritage lists. One important consequence of the heritage industry is that urban cultural environments are vulnerable to a debasing and trivialising Disneyfication process. The United Nations Centre for Human Settlements (UNCHS) has noted: "The particular historic character of a city often gets submerged in the direct and overt quest for an international image and international business [...] Local identity becomes an ornament, a public relations artefact designed to aid marketing. Authenticity is paid for, encapsulated, mummified, located and displayed to attract tourists rather than to shelter continuities of tradition or the lives of its historic creators."[10]

Yet the more the built environment of places is overwritten by generic and inauthentic structures and settings, the more valued the remaining structures and settings become. The more people's patterns of consumption converge, the more fertile the ground for countercultural movements. The more transnational corporations undercut the authority of national and local governments to regulate economic affairs, the greater the support for regionalism. The more universal the diffusion of material culture and lifestyles, the more local and ethnic identities are valued. The faster the information highway takes people into cyberspace, the more they feel the need for a subjective setting – a specific place or community – they can call their own. The faster the pace of life in search of profit and material consumption, the more people value leisure time. And the faster their neighbourhoods and towns acquire the same generic supermarkets, filling stations, shopping malls, industrial estates, office parks, and subdivisions, the more people feel the need for enclaves of familiarity, centredness, and identity. The UNCHS notes that "In many localities, people are overwhelmed by changes in their traditional cultural, spiritual, and social values and norms and by the introduction of a cult of consumerism intrinsic to the process of globalisation. In the rebound, many localities have rediscovered the 'culture of place' by stressing their own identity, their own roots, their own culture and values and the importance of their own neighbourhood, area, vicinity, or town."[11]

Liveability and Sustainability

The experience of economic and demographic stagnation in small towns, along with the imprint of globalisation and – for some – the pressures of counterurbanisation, has highlighted the question of liveability and the quality of life. From any perspective, liveability is a complex, multifaceted concept. It is also a highly relative term: What would be considered a "liveable" community in one part of the world might be deemed highly unsatisfactory in another. This might be due to cultural differences or to different standards of living that alter expectations for urban design, transportation and other infrastructure, and service provision. Nevertheless, the idea of liveability remains a powerful one.

In Britain, research carried out on behalf of the Department for Communities and Local Government as part of a State of the English Cities project noted that the political and policy importance of the liveability of places has been rising, with the public placing a greater emphasis on local environmental quality than ever before. This research views liveability as a subset of quality of life, one that is concerned primarily with the quality of space and the built environment. Thus liveability "is about how easy a place is to use and how safe it feels. It is about creating – and maintaining – a sense of place by creating an environment that is both inviting and enjoyable."[12] From this

perspective, liveability is essentially about designing and managing the places where people choose to live and work, and it can be understood as a key competitive element between cities in terms of attracting both people and businesses. At the same time, it is acknowledged that liveability is essentially local in character, with four overarching themes: environmental quality, the physical attributes of places, the functional effectiveness of places, and social behaviour and public safety in places.

In the United States, the National Research Council commissioned a study on community quality of life which concluded that "Livability depends upon three key interdependent spheres of social life: the economy, social well-being, and the environment. The economy, which supplies jobs and income, is fundamental to residents' health (e.g., ability to meet basic needs of food, clothing and shelter), as well as higher order needs including education, health care, and recreation. At the same time, the economy should efficiently utilise raw materials drawn from the environment, so as to ensure sufficient resources for current and future generations. Social well-being relies, in large part, on justice: a social and spatial distribution of economic and environmental resources that is fair, and systems of governance that are inclusive of all residents [...] The environment is the critical infrastructure that provides natural

18. Bellinzona, Switzerland.
Liveability depends a great deal on the quality of outdoor spaces.

resources, the capacity for waste assimilation, and links between people and the natural world."[13]

"Third Places" and Community

For many people, a critical aspect of social well-being and liveability concerns the ambience of places and their ability to facilitate social inter-action. Successful and attractive places – both from the insiders' perspective and an outsider's perspective – not only have the lineaments of good infrastructure and a clean and attractive environment but also an underlying dynamic of activity. Routine encounters and shared experiences make for the common understandings that underpin a sense of place and a sense of community. Thus, among the attributes of successful places we should expect to find plenty of opportunities for informal, casual meetings and gossip; friendly bars and pubs and a variety of settings in which to purchase and/or consume food; street markets; a variety of comfortable places to sit, wait, and people-watch; a sense of ease with changing seasons; and, above all, a sense of belonging, affection, hospitality, vitality, and historical and cultural continuity.

"Third places" are an important component of this. Author Ray Oldenburg contrasts third places with homes ("first places") and workplaces ("second places"), describing them as informal gathering places that are "the core settings of informal public life" that "host the regular, voluntary, informal and happily anticipated gatherings of individuals beyond the realms of home and work."[14] Third places are settings for conversation or reflection; reading or storytelling; places where there are regulars but where everyone is welcome, neutral ground that is easily accessible and open to all. German beer gardens, English pubs, French cafés, Italian bars, coffee houses, and book shops all qualify as third places.

The Lewes Arms, a 220-year-old pub in Sussex, England (Fig. 19), is a good example of a third place as well as a good example of the threat to the sustainability of such places. It has been described as being "like a communal sitting room [...] there's no juke box, no TV, no fruit machines. It's a conversation pub."[15] Cell phones are banned. The Lewes Arms has been host to many local clubs and societies, including angling, chess, and darts clubs, as well as three cricket teams. Its regular customers have always organised their own sports day, harvest festival, and plays. The pub has always served a local beer, Harveys, which has been brewed a few hundred metres away, beside the River Ouse, by an independent family firm since 1790. It was voted best "bitter" (a pale ale with relatively high hop influence) in 2005 and 2006 at the Great British Beer Festival. But in 2006 the popular beer was withdrawn from the Lewes Arms after the pub had been acquired by the Greene King corporation, which hoped to sell more of its own beer, an IPA (India Pale Ale), brewed in faraway Bury St Edmunds, Suffolk. More than a thousand locals signed a petition against the change but the company went ahead, prompting a boycott of the pub by many former regulars and a rupture of its function as a third place.

Small Town Sustainability

Sustainability, like liveability, is about the interdependent spheres of the economy, the environment, and social well-being. This is often couched in terms of the "three Es" of sustainable development, referring to the environment, the economy, and equity in society (Fig. 21).[16] It is a normative view that combines environmental sustainability with notions of economic growth and social justice. The difference between liveability and sustainability is that the concept of sustainability involves a longer-term perspective. The oft-quoted definition of sustainable development from the *Brundtland Report*, which examined the issues at the international scale, is that sustainable development is "development that meets the needs of the present without compromising the ability of future generations to meet their own needs."[17] In fact, this is a relatively small part of the report's concept of sustainability, which extends to reviving economic growth; meeting essential needs for jobs, food, energy, water, and sanitation; ensuring a balance between population and resources; conserving and enhancing the resource base; reorienting technology and managing risk; merging the environment and economics in decisionmaking; and reorienting international economic relations.

When it comes to urban sustainability, people are generally clear about the symptoms of unsustainable small town development: structural economic decline, environmental degradation, outmigration,

19. Lewes, Sussex. The *Lewes Arms*, a traditional local pub that has been taken over by a national chain.

20. Pest, Hungary. The *Central Kavehaz* is an historic and classic coffeehouse popular with writers.

segregation, exclusion, antisocial behaviour, and loss of distinctiveness and sense of place. Specifying just what is – or may be – sustainable is, however, problematic. For many, the salience of environmental issues means that the very idea of sustainability implies a deep anti-urban sentiment. Such bias notwithstanding, it is clear that, in urban settings, the socioeconomic dimensions of sustainability are critical. They include the need to maintain local sociocultural attributes – neighbourliness and conviviality, for example – in the face of global influences and interdependencies. They also include aspects of social development that relate to the incidence of poverty and inequality, and accessibility to health care and education. Finally, they include aspects of social, cultural, and political sensibilities that relate to a community's willingness and capacity to manage change in order to be more sustainable in a biophysical environmental as well as economic sense.[18]

The complexities and ambiguities involved in the interdependencies among economy, the environment, and social well-being within urban settings mean that the subject can be overwhelming, and for local planners and policymakers this can lead to a kind of despairing inertia. Finding a balance between the three Es is not easy in practice because of various conflicts associated with relationships between them. In particular, providing economic opportunities for a wide range of people can often be in conflict with environmental protection. Nevertheless, growing calls for local solutions to seemingly intractable global problems mean that small town sustainability is increasingly seen as important, with more and more communities becoming aware of the "triple bottom line" of the three Es

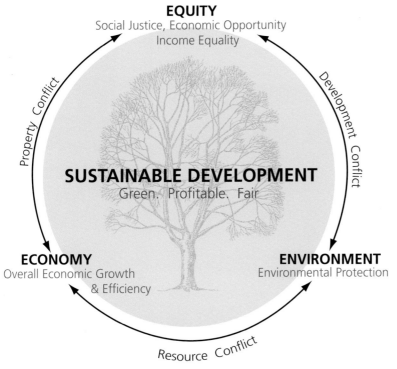

EQUITY
Social Justice, Economic Opportunity
Income Equality

Property Conflict

Development Conflict

SUSTAINABLE DEVELOPMENT
Green. Profitable. Fair

ECONOMY
Overall Economic Growth
& Efficiency

ENVIRONMENT
Environmental Protection

Resource Conflict

21. The Three Es of Sustainability. The circle illustrates the interdependencies between the three goals of sustainability. Considerations of equity, the environment, and the economy can often stand in conflict with each other, but if they reinforce each other, they can lead to sustainable development. Small towns should strive to develop programmes and policies that combine the three goals of sustainability and work toward the goal at the centre of the circle.

Source: Campbell, S., "Green Cities, growing cities, just cities? Urban planning and the contradictions of sustainable development." *Journal of the American Planning Association*, Vol. 92, No. 3, 1996.

22. Orvieto, Italy. Cittaslow headquarters at the *palazzo del gusto*.

2

Mobilising for Change in Small Towns

Interest in sustainability and liveability is in large measure a reaction against the consequences of the far-reaching economic, environmental, and socio-cultural forces associated with globalisation and the work-spend lifestyle that dominates the economic and social dynamics of contemporary society. From this perspective, the idea of sustainability can be seen as a reaction to the skein of interlocking crises that includes energy use and climate change, environmental degradation, food supplies, diets and obesity, traffic gridlock, and social polarisation. In practice, the reaction has been articulated in many ways, from grassroots social movements, nonprofit organisations, and professional bodies to government agencies, supranational agencies, and, increasingly, corporations with an eye toward environmentally and socially conscious market segments.

Mobilisation Against Globalisation

Globalisation and its consequences are embraced, modified, or resisted in different ways in different parts of the world. One striking form of mobilisation against globalisation is old-fashioned popular protest (Figs. 23 and 24). Some of the most vivid examples have been provided by French farmers who, in protest over the European Union's trade liberalisation policies, have regularly taken to tactics such as blocking streets with tractors, with produce, with farmyard manure, or with farm animals. Also very visible have been mass demonstrations at meetings of the G8 countries, the World Trade Organisation, and the World Bank. The principal focus of concern at these events is the neoliberal ideology that has come to dominate economic globalisation. As articulated by the *Association pour la Taxation des Transactions pour l'aide Aux Citoyens* (ATTAC), this ideology emphasises a free-market, speculative logic that supports the interests of multinational corporations and financial markets, undermining local decisionmaking, democratic institutions, and sovereign states and increasing economic insecurity and social inequalities.[19]

Reaction to the unwanted side effects of globalisation has also been condensed through environmental movements. These include nongovernmental organisations such as Greenpeace and Friends of the Earth. They also include movements and organisations whose scope extends beyond the traditional environmental focus of nature and wilderness to human ecology and community well-being. The emergence of the Green movement is a broad reflection of this impulse in the political arena, and it has undoubtedly fostered an increased interest and awareness in urban environments. Urban transportation, for example, has come under scrutiny from a "green" perspective, with an increasing number of towns, cities, and government agencies taking the environmental, social, and economic impacts of transportation into account when making decisions. As a result, initiatives such as car-sharing, bicycle rentals, and pedestrian zones have become widespread. In addition there are many innovative and experimental approaches, such as the programme in Graz, Austria, where, among other things, cooking oil recycled from local restaurants is being used to run the city's fleet of 130 buses. The programme has reduced vehicle emissions and cut fuel costs by 10–20 percent. It is part of an EU initiative, CIVITAS, which has dedicated over €300 million to sustainable urban transport projects in 36 different cities.[20]

23. Montréal, Canada. Demonstrators march in protest against genetically modified organisms.

24. Genoa, Italy. Carabinieri guard a McDonald's franchise during the G-8 meetings in 2001.

25. Organic food. Changing consumer preferences have meant that many supermarkets now offer a basic range of organic fruit and vegetables, sometimes locally sourced.

Local, Organic, Authentic, Slow

At a broader level, an awareness of liveability and sustainability issues has made consumers powerful agents of change. Market researchers have been quick to recognise this, identifying a new market segment of "Lifestyles Of Health And Sustainability" (LOHAS) consumers. Approximately 16 percent of all adults in the United States, for example, are considered to belong to this market segment. LOHAS consumers are people who make conscientious purchasing and investing decisions based on social and cultural values. They are interested in products covering a range of market sectors and subsectors, including green building supplies and energy systems, alternative health care, fitness products, organic food, personal development media, ecotourism, and socially responsible investing and "green stocks." In Japan, the Consumer Marketing Research Institute uses the term "Slow Lifers" to identify one of its most desired demographic groups – typically, middle-aged men who have reached a comfortable point in their careers and who no longer base their life choices on what perceived social or financial betters are doing.[21]

Perhaps the most obvious example of consumer-led change is the trend toward "ethical eating," a development that includes vegetarianism, organic food, Fair Trade products, and direct farmer-to-consumer marketing. Organic food has become the most mainstream component of this trend (Fig. 25).[22] Just what justifies the label "organic" is a matter of contention, but it is generally accepted that organic foods must be produced without the use of chemical fertilisers, pesticides, or genetically modified organisms (GMOs), and that organically produced animals should have access to pasture. Organic foods have slightly higher levels of minerals, trace elements, vitamin C, while small organic farms support more wildlife and biodiversity among insects and birds, use less energy, and cause less pollution than conventional farms.

Nevertheless, the success of the organic food movement underlines the tensions inherent in balancing the three Es of sustainability (environment, the economy, and equity in society). The most striking example, perhaps, is the huge quantity of organic food that is shipped via air freight to supermarkets in Europe and North America from farms in Africa and South America. Meeting consumers' demand for affordable organic products has also brought large-scale production ("industrial organic"), which has undercut the comparative advantage of small, local organic farmers. Large-scale organic farming also tends to stretch the definition of "organic" food. For example, two of the largest dairies in the United States, Horizon and Aurora, raise thousands of cows indoors, where they are fed organic grain rather than grazing in open pasture.

Farmers' Markets

The popularity of organic food, coupled with an increasing demand on the part of many consumers for fresh, locally grown produce, has made direct farmer-to-consumer marketing extremely popular (Figs. 26 and 27). Farm shops and farmers' markets have proliferated. In the United States, for example, there were fewer than 100 farmers' markets in 1974 when the federal government passed the Farmer to Consumer Direct Marketing Act to allow farmers to sell their products beyond their roadside stands. By 1994 there were 1 755 and by 2006 there were 4 385. In the United Kingdom there are over 1,000 farm shops selling local food, and about 550 farmers' markets. Most operators of farmers' markets have some sort of community base and are supported by volunteer organisations or local government. In the United Kingdom the average number of market stalls is 24; the largest, in Winchester, has 100. In some cases, farmers' markets have become so popular that they are perceived to be in danger of becoming victims of their own success, losing their local character as traders come in from outside the area, selling foreign produce and cut-price goods. Increasingly, farmers' markets in many towns have had to develop operating rules that define who are "local" vendors and that forbid or restrict the selling of non-local goods.

Eating Local

Another facet of the same general trend is the "Eat Local" movement, which places emphasis on consuming fruits, vegetables, meats, and other products grown miles, rather than days, away, and consumed in season. Driven in part by the food safety concerns and environmental sensitivities of LOHAS consumers, restaurants and grocery stores have developed partnerships with small farmers to supply at least part of their inventory. In the United States, LOHAS-oriented supermarket chains such as Wegmans and Whole Foods have systematically developed such partnerships for each of their stores. The Eat Local movement has also been promoted by public development agencies, which have supported local and regional festivals aimed at encouraging healthy eating, diversifying farm economies, and stimulating agrotourism as well as reducing food-miles.

26. Spilimbergo, Italy. Local cheeses feature prominently at the annual fair.

27. Orvieto, Italy. Saturday farmers' market in October.

Fair Trade

Meanwhile, people recognise that sustainability is about interdependence across geographic boundaries, and in parallel with the growth of farm shops and local farmers' markets has been the emergence of the Fair Trade movement. This began in Europe in the 1960s and 1970s in order to promote the payment of a fair price and ensure social and environmental standards for producers in disadvantaged regions of the world. By the 1990s a certification and labelling system had evolved, with Fair Trade Labelling Organisations International, an umbrella organisation of 17 national labelling groups, maintaining the standards for the "Fairtrade" label and certifying cooperatives that meet these standards. Goods displaying the Fairtrade label are sold with a guaranteed minimum price that includes a social premium paid by the consumer to the democratically organised cooperatives, to be spent on infrastructure investments – such as processing facilities, schools, and hospitals – for the benefit of members. Fairtrade goods meet environmental sustainability standards and International Labour Office conventions covering workplace practices. The movement has focused in particular on exports such as coffee, cocoa, tea, bananas, cotton, and handicrafts from developing countries to developed countries. The total value of fair trade products – estimated to account for 0.5–5.0 percent of all sales in their product categories in Europe, the United States, and Canada – is minor in relation to the overall flows of international trade, but it is estimated that by 2006 over 1.5 million disadvantaged producers worldwide were directly benefiting from Fair Trade.[23]

Much of the impetus for the movement has come from small towns in Europe as part of a broader approach to sustainability. Some have become Fairtrade Towns, their local councils passing resolutions supporting Fair Trade and committing to serve Fairtrade coffee and tea in their offices and canteens, and working to ensure that a range of Fairtrade products is readily available in the town's shops, served in local cafés and restaurants, and used in a number of local work places and community organisations. The Fairtrade Town movement began in 2000 in Garstang, England (population 4,000), and by 2008 more than 275 localities in the United Kingdom had joined, with another 230 or so in the process of working toward Fairtrade status. In Belgium, one in every three towns in the northern region of Flanders had become Fairtrade Towns; in France there were more than 100 Fairtrade Towns, and there were nascent Fairtrade Town movements in Norway, Sweden, Italy, Ireland, and the United States.[24]

28. Matlock, England. One of the Fairtrade towns in the United Kingdom.

29. Ashburn, Virginia. Much of the food at the American Flatbread pizzeria in Ashburn, Virginia, is organic, but the real emphasis is on local food. The wood-fired oven is made from red Virginia clay. The beer is brewed nearby, and the leaves of the iced tea are grown and packaged on a local herb farm. A hand-painted map of Loudoun County is emblazoned on the restaurant's back wall, delineating the farms and dairies the restaurant pairs with to produce its menu.

30. Lugano, Switzerland. Local produce is featured prominently in the town's main department store.

Going Slow

Underpinning much of this consumer-driven change is a broader philosophical change that has been characterised in terms of a reaction against the negative consequences of the work-spend lifestyles associated with the economic and cultural dynamics of contemporary societies. The shorthand for this change has come to be described as a shift from "Fast" to "Slow" approaches to life (Table 2.1). The label should not be taken too literally. As described by Carl Honoré, "Fast is busy, controlling, aggressive, hurried, analytical, stressed, superficial, impatient, active, quantity over quality. Slow is the opposite: calm, careful, receptive, still, intuitive, unhurried, patient, reflective, quality over quantity. It is about making real and meaningful connections – with people, culture, work, food, everything [...] [T]he Slow philosophy can be summed up in a single word: balance. Be fast when it makes sense to be fast, and be slow when slowness is called for. Seek to live at what musicians call the *tempo giusto* – the right speed."[25]

Authenticity is slow; standardization is fast. Individuality is slow; franchises are fast. Silence is slow; noise is fast. Trees are slow; concrete is fast. Cycle paths are slow; parking lots are fast. The

Slow philosophy has been adopted in a variety of contexts. Slow medicine, for example, promotes a holistic philosophy to health, in contrast to the high-technology, drug-centred approach of conventional medical practice. The vanguard of the Slow movement, however, has been Slow Food.

Table 2.1: Contrasting approaches: fast and slow

Approaches	Mainstream ("fast")	Alternative ("slow")
Characteristics	Homogenised	Idiosyncratic / Asset specific
	Single imperative	Multiple imperatives
	Inequitable	Equitable
	Industrial	Craft
	Standardised	Customised
	Corporate	Grassroots
	Unsustainable	Sustainable
	Copied	Authentic
	Low quality	High quality
	Replicable	Asset specific
	Insensitive to local history, culture	Sensitive to local history, culture
Examples	Urban megaprojects	Community economic development
	Smokestack chasing	Cittaslow
	Industrial food systems	Slow Food

Slow Food

The Slow Food movement was conceived as a direct riposte to globalisation – a cultural barricade to resist the relentless hegemony of McDonald's, Starbucks, Wal-Mart, and other icons of the fast world. Italian journalist and food writer Carlo Petrini, aghast at the announcement of plans to open a McDonald's restaurant in the Piazza di Spagna in the heart of Rome in 1986, was the founder of the Slow Food movement. The name was selected to represent qualities that are the opposites of fast food: sustainable farming; artisanal production; fresh, local, seasonal produce; recipes handed down through generations; and leisurely dining with family and friends. It struck a chord with many others in Italy, who recognised that fast food is culturally invasive and corrosive, a serious threat not only to healthy diets but also to the sociability of eating and to valued patterns and rhythms of life. The Slow Food philosophy is what Petrini calls *tranquillo*: calm, unhurried, and restorative of body and soul. The movement's goal is to protect the "right to taste" by preserving almost-extinct traditional food products, raising the awareness of the pleasures of eating (including the social aspects of sharing a meal), taste education, and paying attention to traditional agricultural methods and techniques, among other initiatives.

The Slow Food movement was officially launched in 1989 with a manifesto that states its aim as "rediscovering the flavours and savours of regional cooking and banishing the degrading effects of fast food." Slow Food's goal is to "counteract fast food and fast life, the disappearance of local food traditions and people's dwindling interest in the food they eat, where it comes from, how it tastes and how our food choices affect the rest of the world."[26] The Slow Food movement touches on important aspects that keep local economies vital. In particular, Slow Food is locally grounded through its goal of maintaining the viability of locally owned businesses such as butchers, bakers, restaurants, and farms. Slow Food also emphasises local distinctiveness through traditional specialties, traditional foods, and ways of producing and growing produce such as wine, cheese, fruits, and vegetables, and traditional ways of preparing and cooking signature dishes.

At the core of the movement is the concept of *terroir*, the way foods and wine express the soil, climate, culture, and tradition of a region. In the words of Carlo Petrini, the concept of *terroir* is a "combination of natural factors (soil, water, slope, height above sea level, vegetation, micro-climate) and human ones (tradition and practice of cultivation) that gives a unique character to each small agricultural locality and the food grown, raised, made and cooked there."[27] The concept has a long history. It was first codified in France in 1855, when Napoleon III established the Grand Cru wine areas of Bordeaux. Subsequently, other wine regions were recognised, as were areas of traditional food production, such as Parma (for prosciutto), and Modena (for balsamic vinegar). In 1992, the EU introduced regulations to protect these so-called designations of origin; by 2008, the EU had identified almost 750 place-based foods. Slow Food's understanding of territory connects the environmental aspects of a place to the culture and the history of people who inhabit the territory and have utilised it for generations for traditional food production.

With more than 80,000 members in over 100 countries, the Slow Food movement has become a well-established part of the culinary scene, with a network of local chapters (*convivia*) organising dinners, wine tastings, and festivals. The Slow Food headquarters in the Piemonte town of Bra, Italy (population 29,000) keeps 130 employees busy producing guidebooks – such as the annually updated *Osterie d'Italia*, a reliable source of information about good, inexpensive Italian restaurants – and organising the movement's two principal strategic projects: the Ark of Taste and Presidia. Promoting *osterias* (taverns or humble restaurants where wine is served as the main attraction and tasty food is prepared to accompany it), it is argued, supports small business owners and preserves local cultures and traditions. *Osterias* serve traditional local cuisine, are mostly family-owned, have simple service and a welcoming atmosphere, serve good-quality food and local wine, and, most importantly, charge moderate prices. Slow Food saw the opportunity to support these smaller restaurants as an alternative to fast-food places.

Connecting the environment with social and economic aspects is the central idea of Slow Food's Ark of Taste programme. The function of the Ark of Taste is to protect endangered foods such as Piedmontese veal, Andean corn, and unpasteurised English cheeses through cataloguing and promoting them. To be incorporated in the Ark's catalogue, a product has to fulfil several requirements: they must be connected to a specific territory (for example, through the use of local ingredients and/or the use of traditional local practices); they also must be linked environmentally, socioeconomically,

and historically to a specific locality; they must be made in limited quantities by small producers; and they must be at risk of real or potential extinction.

One example that highlights the intimate connection between the environment and the local economy is the case of wine production in the Italian region Cinque Terre. The region is known for its steep terraced hills along the Mediterranean coast of northwestern Italy. Wine production on these steep hills became almost extinct and the associated cultural landscape was in

31. Bra, Italy. An annual fair in the "City of Cheese" features Slow Food products and practices.

32. Slow Food publications. Slow Food books and magazines spotlight quality food and wine production, educate consumers about artisan food specialties, crop varieties, animal breeds and food culture, and promote good, clean and fair food products.

danger. Slow Food promoted the protection of the vineyards by emphasising the quality of the locally produced wine, the so-called *Sciacchetrá* wine. Higher quality means higher prices for the wine, which in turn makes it worthwhile for young people in the villages to become wine makers. This made it more appealing to younger generations to continue caring for the vineyards and thereby cultivating the landscape. They were in turn supported by training courses about how to improve the quality of their wine.

Presidia, which means "garrisons" in Latin, are outposts of traditional farming or food production that have been adopted as going concerns by the Slow Food movement. A presidium can involve a single producer, such as a cheese maker who makes a rare mountain variety, or a village that unites to sell a product directly. The first 92 presidia, all Italian, were announced in 2000. In 2001, Coop Italia, the retailing chain with the largest food market share in Italy, signed an agreement with Slow Food, linking its commercial brand to some of these presidia and supporting the educational objectives and agricultural policy strategies of the movement (Fig. 33). By 2007, there were presidia in 43 countries, including 195 in Italy.[28]

33. Milan, Italy. Coop Italia supermarkets now carry Slow Food certified produce.

Meanwhile, the Salone del Gusto, the movement's international festival that is held in Turin every two years, has become a combination of gastronomic event, culinary expo, and giant farmers' market that attracts more than 130,000 visitors.

Networking Toward Sustainability

The increasing success of farmers' markets, organic and local food movements, Fair Trade Towns, and the Slow Food movement is evidence of the significance to people, in a globalising world, of the local dimensions of liveability and quality of life. It follows that strategies for sustainable development in small towns should emphasise endogenous factors – building on local comparative advantages, local resources, local products, and local distinctiveness. We suggest that such an approach can best be propagated through networks of towns, with partnerships among local business leaders, community groups, local governments, and government agencies that can share information, ideas, and best practices. In recent years there has been a proliferation of such initiatives. Some are grassroots organisations and some are sponsored by state or trans-state agencies. Some have a focus on economic development while others focus on environmental sustainability. A few are more holistic, emphasising liveability and quality of life while encompassing the three Es of sustainability.

Networks for Economic Development
For small towns and their residents everywhere, sustainability means developing the capacity to manage change in the face of broad economic forces that operate at regional, national, and international levels. Without the resources to employ a full range of specialised professionals, small towns can easily find themselves at a serious disadvantage. In addition, small towns tend to be overlooked or excluded from many of the programmes at the transnational (e.g., EU), national, and regional levels that are dedicated to one or another aspect of sustainability. For many towns, economic survival becomes a first priority, and the pursuit of economic development often simply takes the form of seeking to attract investment from exogenous sources: "smokestack chasing." For small towns in general, this is of course a zero-sum game. But even when towns can successfully attract inward investment – most commonly in the form of branch-plant factories, call

centres, or chain stores – it is often at the expense of costly incentive packages, while the bulk of the profits are drawn away from the town, back to the parent company. In the medium and longer term, it leaves the towns vulnerable to disinvestment as external companies revise their strategies. Because so many small towns have been experiencing a long secular trend of economic stagnation and decline, many of the emerging networks have a strong focus on local economic development. A good example from the United States is the North Carolina Small Towns Initiative, a nonprofit partnership that gives special emphasis to small towns experiencing hardships posed by business closings and layoffs, devastation from natural disasters, or persistent poverty. The initiative relies on a combination of education and training programmes, research and data gathering, partnership development, Internet-based networking, and project implementation grants for building re-use and restoration, job creation, and planning and policy development.[29]

In Europe, the EU's Regional Development Fund has established a Small Town Network as part of its Northern Periphery Programme. The Network's principal aim is to encourage the regeneration of towns in Greenland, Iceland, the Faeroe Islands, and the remoter parts of Finland, Norway, Scotland, and Sweden, propagating a shared agenda for regional agencies and local groups by supporting voluntary groups drawn from local business and community sectors.[30] The EU also funds the AlpCity project, which focuses on the local development and urban regeneration of small alpine towns, many of which, like the towns of the northern periphery, have undergone protracted socioeconomic decline, have inadequate public and private services, a deteriorating built environment, and aging populations with limited access to culture, and are situated in fragile natural environments. Unlike the towns of the northern periphery, they are islands of disparity in a generally affluent part of Europe.[31]

In contrast, some small towns face problems of coping with sudden economic expansion after long periods of stagnation or decline. Small towns that are now growing as a result of counterurbanisation, gentrification, or exurban development suffer from "growing pains" such as land shortage for business, high levels of car dependency, loss of traditional functions, shortage of community facilities, decrease in community origins and ownership, and often a crisis in identity. The EU's SusSET project ("Sustaining Small Expanding Towns")[32] has been established in order to identify the best "coping strategies" for small traditional yet expanding towns. Among the network's members are Ellon, Inverurie, and Stonehaven in Scotland; Amal, Kungalv, and Stromstad in Sweden; Hel, Lebork, and Puck in Poland; and Aeghio, Messolonghi, and Pyrgos in Greece.

Networks for Health and Environmental Sustainability

One of the first and, now, largest urban networks with a focus on health and environmental sustainability is the World Health Organisation (WHO)'s European Healthy Cities network, launched in 1987 by the European Office of the WHO. The goal of the network is to develop physical environments that promote good health as well as a good overall quality of life. The core strategies of Healthy Cities are set out in Health 21 and Local Agenda 21 (the WHO's main policy frameworks), the Athens Declaration of Healthy Cities, and the Aalborg Charter.[33] These documents aim to engage local governments across Europe in the creation of healthy and sustainable urban settings through a focus on environmental justice and the social dimensions of sustainability, community empowerment, and urban planning. By 2013 there were more than 1,400 European towns and cities designated as WHO Healthy Cities. The programme is now in its fifth phase (2009–2013), during which towns currently involved in the network are working on three core themes: caring and supportive environments, healthy living, and healthy urban design.

Biophysical aspects of sustainability have found expression in the Eco-City movement. Drawing on principles of urban ecology that were established at the first International Eco-City conference in 1990 in Berkeley, California, the movement's goals include:

- Encouraging recycling, appropriate technological innovations, and resource conservation;
- Promoting environmentally sound economic activities among the business community;
- Raising awareness of the local and regional biophysical environment an sustainability issues;
- Restoring unhealthy urban biophysical environments such as waterways and shorelines;
- Reorganising land use in order to encourage compact, diverse, green, safe, pleasant, and mixed-use communities near transit nodes and transport facilities;
- Recasting transportation priorities to encourage pedestrian and bicycle traffic rather than automobiles; and
- Supporting local farming and community gardening.[34]

The Canadian town of Okotoks, Alberta (population 17,145) became one of the first municipalities in the world to establish a development plan based on eco-city principles when, in 1998, it adopted a plan based on growth targets linked to infrastructure development and environmental carrying capacity. The town's water plan includes conservation measures, a new wastewater treatment plant, and cooperation with surrounding areas to maintain the river's watershed. Drake Landing Solar Community, a master-planned Okotoks neighbourhood, utilises a direct energy system to store solar energy underground during the summer months and distribute the energy to each home for space heating needs during winter months.[35]

Translating eco-city principles into the design of new towns has proved difficult. The most publicised and ambitious example is the town of Dongtan, near Shanghai, China. Dongtan was scheduled to open in 2010 with accommodation for 50,000 people, with an eventual population of 500,000. The plan for the town, by Arup Urban Design, London, was designed to deploy a variety of water-saving technologies, to produce few carbon emissions, and to require no landfills. An "energy centre" would have managed power provided by wind turbines, biofuels, and recycled organic materials. Waste would be reused when possible, and organics would be composted or used for biomass energy. Sewage would be treated and used for composting, and greywater would be used for irrigation.[36] The city was to be part of the 2010 Shanghai World Expo as an example of visionary sustainable urban planning, but the moment passed before any of the plan could be realised; today all that exists on the site is a solitary wind farm.

Equally ambitious are plans for Masdar, a zero-carbon, zero-waste city in a Special Free Zone adjacent to Abu Dhabi in the United Arab Emirates. Designed by Foster + Partners, London, the town will be based on the mixed-use, high-density principles of an ancient walled city, combined with modern alternative energy technologies. The six-square-kilometre site will accommodate a population of 50,000 and include a university, an Innovation Centre, the headquarters of the Abu Dhabi Future Energy Company, and economic zones for up to 1,500 clean-technology companies.[37]

Unlike Dongtan, construction of the early phase of the settlement has begun; but critics are concerned that the city will only be symbolic, a spectacle of "starchitecture" that, because of its costliness, will become a luxury enclave for the wealthy.

In Japan, the Ministry of Economy, Trade and Industry and the Ministry of Environment have initiated an Eco-Town programme based on "the three Rs" – reduce, recycle, and reuse.[38] Many of Japan's Eco-Towns are medium-size cities such as Chiba, Gifu, Kawasaki, Kitakyushu, Kochi, Naoshima, Okayama, Suzuka, and Toyama. Smaller towns in the network include Kamaishi, Itsukaichi, Minamata (notorious for Minamata disease, the result of mercury poisoning from industrial effluent discharged into the sea in the 1950s), Oomuta, and Uguisuzawa. The emphasis is on innovation, especially in relation to green procurement, green consumerism, industrial ecology, extended producer responsibility, socially responsible investment, integrated waste management, green labelling, and corporate social responsibility. The programme offers an incentive system whereby one-third of the cost of approved projects is subsidised by the ministries.

Finally, a Transition Towns network has emerged with the objective of developing "energy descent pathways" – strategic plans to reduce dependency on fossil fuels and to become increasingly self-reliant – in response to the twin challenges of peak oil (the imminent decline in the capacity of known oil reserves) and climate change. Based in Britain but with member towns in Ireland, Australia, and New Zealand, the Transition Town initiative is based on the premise that, just as immense amounts of creativity, ingenuity, and adaptability were used on the way up the energy upslope, there should be no reason not to do the same on the downslope. The Initiative centres around a "wiki" collaborative web site that allows members to create, edit, and link their web pages.[39]

Networks for Liveability and Quality of Life

Some small-town networks are broader in scope and aspire, usually implicitly rather than explicitly, to address the three Es of sustainability. The project Lebensqualität durch Nähe ("Quality of

Life through Proxmity"), for example, originated in Austria as a broadly framed approach for small towns in rural regions that were experiencing economic decline and outmigration as well as the loss of vital social and economic service functions.[40] More than 180 small towns are now part of the network and undertake various activities that strengthen small-town liveability. For example, the town of Steinbach in Austria began to focus on quality of life in the mid-1980s. The town lost its local cutlery industry in the 1960s and experienced economic crisis, outmigration, and abandonment of its historic centre. Since joining the Lebensqualität durch Nähe network, the town has created more than 180 jobs. It has begun to protect and market its traditional heirloom apples; more than 40 percent of its citizens volunteer; it has revitalised its historic core; and an empty traditional rural restaurant is now being used as a café and local supermarket. Key to the success of these projects is the proactive engagement of local citizens because the programme is attempting to build consciousness among citizens about their town's quality of life. It is also important that the mayor and council members are on board because each town's involvement has to be ratified by the town council.

In the remainder of this section we focus on two important networks that will provide a number of examples of innovation and best practice in subsequent chapters of the book. The first is the Market Towns Initiative that was established by the central government in Britain, an example of a top-down initiative that has become a locally driven membership organisation. The second is the Cittaslow network, a determinedly grassroots movement that is an explicit reaction to globalisation.

Action for Market Towns

In the United Kingdom a network of "Market Towns" that was initially organised by the central government's Countryside Agency has been taken over by a nonprofit membership organisation, Action for Market Towns. The organisation acts as a central clearinghouse for information and advice about how to develop and share good practice among Market Town partnerships, and provides national representation on policy issues affecting Market Towns. One of the most successful aspects of the organisation's activities has been the dissemination of a "Market Towns Toolkit," which contains advice about community participation, funding for projects, training, transport, and business support. It also includes a 70-page "Healthcheck" handbook (initially developed by the Countryside Agency) that has become an established process for towns to appraise their strengths, weaknesses, and opportunities in relation to their economic well-being, their environmental quality, social and community issues, and the adequacy of their transport infrastructure. In practice, healthchecks have revealed widespread concerns about several dimensions of life in UK Market Towns: limited employment opportunities, especially for young people; narrow ranges of recreational facilities; deteriorating town centres, retail areas, main approaches, and derelict areas; and inadequate transport facilities.[41]

Market Towns' traditional association with local food and agriculture, together with an awareness of the increasing interest in local, organic foods, has prompted Action for Market Towns to develop a structured process by which towns can assess and develop their local food economy. The result is a "Foodcheck" handbook, designed to assist towns in reasserting the linkages between the countryside, traditional farming methods, and the production and sale of distinctive and fresh local food. As a result, Action for Market Towns has been able to facilitate the development of local food business networks, business plans for local food distribution schemes, local branding initiatives, food events programmes such as food festivals, local food directories, and the promotion of local food in schools.

34. Bridport, England. A "Beacon Town" on the Dorset coast, where the focus is on local food.

35. Belper, England. The contraction of the textile and hosiery industry has resulted in a great deal of vacant floorspace. Belper is situated in the Derwent Valley, the site of some of the first textile mills at the beginning of the Industrial Revolution, now recognised as a U.N. World Heritage site.

Meanwhile, the UK's Countryside Agency (now merged into a new government department, Natural England) has sponsored a network of 16 "Beacon Towns" in order to demonstrate the range of different problems and challenges which Market Towns experience and from which other towns can learn. Beacon Towns are not the "best," but are simply those places in which work that is being done by partnerships among local government, business, and community groups can help inform the work of other town partnerships and the development of national policy. Each Beacon Town partnership is charged with addressing a specific challenge. For example, in Bridport, Dorset (Fig. 34), the focus is on local food; in Longtown, Cumbria, it is renewable energy; in Belper, Derbyshire (Fig. 35), it is vacant floorspace; in Richmond, North Yorkshire, it is heritage-led regeneration; in Newmarket, Suffolk, it is affordable housing; and in Uttoxeter, Staffordshire, it is integrated transport.[42] The Action for Market Towns healthcheck has often been the catalyst that has encouraged the formation of these partnerships.

Cittaslow

The Slow philosophy and the Slow Food movement have created the ideological platform for networks of small towns – the Cittaslow movement – that constitute what is arguably the broadest and most grassroots implementation of the principles associated with liveability, quality of life, and sustainability. The Cittaslow movement is closely associated with the Slow Food movement, and the aims of the two movements are complementary. In broad terms, both organisations are in favour of local, traditional cultures, leisurely consideration, enjoyment, and conviviality. Both are against big business and globalisation, though their driving motivation is not so much political as ecological and humanistic.

The Cittaslow movement began in October 1999, when Paolo Saturnini, mayor of Greve-in-Chianti, a Tuscan hill town, organised a meeting with the mayors of three other municipalities (Orvieto, Bra, and Positano) to define the attributes that might characterise a *città lente* – slow city. At their founding meeting in Orvieto, the four mayors committed

themselves to a series of principles that included working toward calmer and less polluted physical environments, conserving local aesthetic traditions, and fostering local crafts, produce, and cuisine. They also pledged to use technology to create healthier environments, to make citizens aware of the value of more leisurely rhythms to life, and to share their experience in seeking administrative solutions for better living. The goal is to foster the development of places that enjoy a robust vitality based on good food, healthy environments, sustainable economies, and traditional rhythms of community life.

These ideas soon led to a Charter with a 54-point list of pledges. The Charter leans heavily toward the enjoyment of food and wine, the fostering of conviviality, and the promotion of unique, high-quality and specialist foods. To be eligible for membership, candidate cities must have no more than 50,000 inhabitants and must pledge to introduce a range of measures from the promotion of organic agriculture to the creation of centres where visitors can sample local traditional food. They must also take steps to protect the sources and purity of the raw ingredients and to fend off the advance of fast food and cultural standardisation.[43]

Promoting local distinctiveness and a sense of place is almost as important as the enjoyment of good local food and wine. This means that the Charter also covers many aspects of urban design and planning. Candidate cities must be committed not only to supporting traditional local arts and crafts but also to supporting modern industries whose products lend distinctiveness and identity to the region. They must also be committed to the conservation of the distinctive character of their built environment and must pledge to plant trees, create more green space, increase cycle paths and pedestrianised streets, keep piazzas free of advertising billboards and neon, ban car alarms, reduce noise pollution, light pollution and air pollution, foster the use of alternative sources of energy, improve public transport, and promote eco-friendly architecture in any new developments. The movement is committed to the management standards embodied

36. Cittaslow. The official logo.

in ISO 9000 and to the environmental management and monitoring standards of ISO 14000.

Achieving the goals of the Cittaslow movement requires, in the first instance, a strong commitment to the principles of the movement on the part of the city mayor. In the longer haul, success will depend on developing a new political dynamic that incorporates an alliance of city leadership, local businesses, and residents in support of Cittaslow ideals.

Membership of the Cittaslow movement is carefully controlled, and cities are admitted to membership only after trained local "operatives" have prepared an initial report on the town's commitment to Cittaslow principles, followed by a detailed audit report covering six key areas: environmental policies and planning; use of infrastructure; integration of technology; promotion of local produce and ways of life; hospitality and the rhythm of life; and sense of place. The movement is governed by an elected assembly of ten city mayors, with a president, three vice presidents, and a chief operating officer – all of whom serve on a voluntary basis.

In 2001, the first 28 Cittaslow towns were certified. All 28 charter members were Italian, the majority of them located in northern and central Italy, particularly in Tuscany and Umbria. By 2008, more than 70 towns had been certified as Cittaslow towns. The majority are located in Italy but towns in Australia (Goolwa, Katoomba, and Willunga), Austria (Enns), Belgium (Silly), Germany (Deidesheim,

Hersbruck, Lüdinghausen, Marihn, Schwarzenbruck, Überlingen, Waldkirch, and Wirsberg), the Netherlands (Midden-Delfland), Norway (Eidskog, Levanger, and Sokndal), New Zealand (Matakana), Poland (Biscupiec, Bisztynek, Lidzbark, Reszel, and Warminski), Portugal (Lagos, Silves, Sao Bras, and Tavira), South Korea (Shinan, Damjang, Wando, and Jangheung), Spain (Lekeitio, Mungia, and Palf), Sweden (Falköping), Switzerland (Mendrisio), and the United Kingdom (Aylsham, Berwick-upon-Tweed, Cockermouth, Diss, Linlithgow, Ludlow, Mold, and Perth) are now certified. More than 300 other towns from around the world have inquired about joining. As the movement has spread and become international, so has its organisation and certification process. Cittaslow members in Germany, for example, have organised a nonprofit group to manage the German network. They have translated the Charter into German and have adapted it to the national context. For example, unlike the Italian charter, the German charter includes an indicator that notes whether a town has a policy in place that bans genetically modified plants and organisms in the local agricultural economies. The town of Überlingen (population 21,300) was the exemplar for this indicator since the town was the first in Germany to ban GMOs within its perimeter. The GMO ban fits the overall ideas of Slow Food and the addition of a new indicator shows that countries are encouraged to adapt the system to their own needs. In general, the six key areas of the Charter remain the same, but the overall number and type of indicators change slightly in the context of each national framework as each country develops its own Cittaslow organisation.

One obvious critique of the Cittaslow movement is that it could all too easily produce enervated, backward-looking, isolationist communities – living mausoleums where the puritanical zealotry of Slowness has displaced the fervent materialism of the fast world. But Cittaslow towns do not want to be stultifying, uneventful places where there is no diversity and nothing for young people to do in the evening. Nor do Cittaslow towns aim to be antithetical to business, innovation, or technology. Aware of the dangers of prescriptive Slowness, the Cittaslow movement hopes to propagate vitality through farmers' markets, festivals, and the creation of inviting public spaces. It aims to deploy technology

37. Chiavenna, Italy. A Slow City where conviviality comes naturally.

38. Überlingen, Germany. A Cittaslow member town, Überlingen has established itself as a "GM-Free" zone. On the left is Cornelia Wiethaler, who initiated the movement to ban genetically-modified crops and food from the town.

in air, noise, and light pollution control systems, modern energy systems, waste-cycling plants, and composting facilities. It seeks to encourage business through ecologically sensitive, regionally authentic, and gastronomically-oriented tourism. Here, though, is another danger: paradoxically, Cittaslow designation might become a form of brand recognition within the heritage industry. Because such cities are so small – 50,000 inhabitants or less – the charming attractions of Cittaslow towns could all too easily be overwhelmed by tourism. So the more they flaunt their gentle-paced

life, the faster they might end up changing. In this scenario, shop prices will rise and cafés will lose their spilled-drink, smoky, messy authenticity. The better-known that Cittaslow towns become, the more Swedes, Germans, Dutch, and Americans will choose to make their second homes in them. House prices will go up and the poor and the young will be pushed out. The only solution to these gentrification trends might be to make the movement ubiquitous.

Table 2.2: Cittalsow's *Tavolo di Progetti.* Examples from Italy, Germany, and the UK

Cittaslow Criteria	Active Cittaslow Members
Environmental Planning	
Urban Design	Italy: Levanto, Chiavenna, San Miniato
ISO Certification	Italy: Levanto, Castelnovo Monti
Recycling, Composting	Italy: Città della Pieve, Castiglione del Lago, Cutigliano, Zibello, San Daniele
Protection of Drinking Water	Italy: Castelnovo Monti
GMO Free Landscape	Germany: Überlingen
Ecological Land Use Planning	Germany: Überlingen
Protection of Cultural Landscape	Germany: Hersbruck
Alternative Energy	Italy: Cutigliano; Germany: Wirsberg, Schwarzenbruck
Climate Change Strategy	UK: Diss
Plastic Bag Free Town	UK: Cockermouth
Organic Food	UK: Perth
Infrastructure Planning	
Planning for Public Transportation	Italy: Città della Pieve
Cittaslow Awareness	
Participatory Local Politics	Italy: Castelnovo Monti, San Miniato, Caiazzo
Cittaslow Working Groups	Germany: Lüdinghausen; UK: Ludlow
Local Food in School Cafeterias	Italy: Bra, San Miniato
Promotion of Family Life and Recreation, and Activities for Seniors	Italy: Francavilla al Mare; Germany: Waldkirch
Urban Quality	
Downtown Revitalisation	Italy: Levanto, Chiavenna, San Miniato; Germany: Lüdinghausen
Historic Preservation	UK: Diss, Berwick-upon-Tweed, Linlithgow
Trash Management	Italy: Casalbeltrame, San Daniele, Trani
Green Buildings	Italy: Città della Pieve, San Daniele del Friuli, Positano, Castiglione del Lago
Social Equity	Germany: Waldkirch
Healthy Region Initiative	Germany: Hersbruck
Buy Local Campaign	UK: Cockermouth, Perth
Conviviality	
Parking Management	Italy: Orvieto, San Miniato
Tourism Strategy	Italy: Levanto, San Daniele; UK: Berwick-upon-Tweed, Linlithgow
Food Festivals	UK: Ludlow, Mold
Cittaslow Publications	Italy: Caiazzo
Special Projects	
Hydrogen Initiative	Italy: Orvieto, Penne
Support for Small and Medium Enterprises in the Fishing Industry	Italy: Francavilla al Mare
Didactic Public Gardens	Italy: Cittaslow Towns in Umbria; Germany: Marihn

Orvieto, Italy

Orvieto (population 21,000) is a founding member of the Cittaslow movement and serves as its headquarters. The town sits high up on a tufa plateau whose 190-metre cliffs are nearly vertical. Its commanding site dominates the valley of the Paglia river, a key strategic location since very ancient times. Orvieto was originally a Roman settlement, built on Etruscan ruins, that was overrun by the Goths and later taken by the Lombards. The prosperous medieval town was in competition with Florence and Siena for access to the sea, torn apart between the Guelphs (the Pope's party) and the Ghibellines (the Emperor's party). It was taken by the church and became a refuge for the popes, relinquished, and then annexed to the Italian kingdom in the nineteenth century. Bypassed by the industrial revolution because of its restricted site, it has more recently become a short stop on the itinerary of tour buses. Situated close by the main north-south *autostrada* and just an hour or so from Rome, Orvieto's picturesque streets and medieval cathedral (c. 1290), with its spectacular polychrome façade, attract more than 2 million visitors each year.

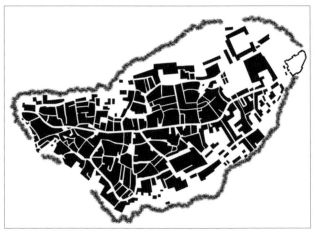

39. Orvieto town centre.

40. Piazza della Repubblica and the town hall.

41. Orvieto skyline.

Conscious of the need to preserve the town's fabric and the lifestyle of its inhabitants, former mayor Stefano Cimicchi was one of the original signatories of the Cittaslow Charter. His successor, Stefano Mocio, serves as vice president of Cittaslow Italia. Between them, they have taken significant strides toward improving the quality of life and sustainability of the town. Cittaslow members contribute to a *tavolo di progetti* – a pool of information about policies and projects relating to different aspects of the Cittaslow Charter (Table 2.2). Orvieto's specialty is sustainable transport. The historic town centre has been closed to all automobile traffic, saving the town not only from traffic but also pollution and noise. Visiting drivers are directed to a huge parking garage hidden beneath a park and piazza below the city centre, and they ride up in elevators inside the town's stone ramparts. On the other side of the town, visitors arriving by train ride a funicular up to the town centre. Small electric buses ferry visitors through town. In 2003 Orvieto hosted the signing ceremonies for the Hydrogen Cities Charter, which commits signatories "to prepare for a hydrogen economy based on renewable energy sources so that the human species may finally become a community fully integrated in the earth's ecosystem and promote a new hydrogen based energy regime that will be more sustainable in relationship to local and regional environmental resources which must be preserved for our future generations."[44]

The gastronomic influence of the Slow Food movement has also heavily influenced Cittaslow in Orvieto. The town has a zoning law proscribing fast food and large supermarkets, and school can-teen menus use organic products and emphasise traditional local dishes. On Friday evenings, a Slow Food-style dinner is served at the Palazzo del Gusto (formerly a monastery, the Chiostro di S. Giovanni), which also functions as the main office for the Cittaslow movement. On the second floor of the Palazzo, a regional culinary school offers courses for both amateurs and professionals. In the cellars are facilities for wine tasting and for educational pro-grammes relating to viticulture and wine making. The superior white wines of the district, from a mix-ture of Trebbiano Toscano, Verdello, and Grechetto grapes along with the mysterious alchemy of the district's volcanic minerals, are highly prized. The town has also introduced *orti sociali* – communal allotments where citizens can keep in touch with the land by growing their own vegetables. This is especially important for the elderly, keeping them active and engaged. Finally, the Cittaslow organisa-tion has dramatically improved and expanded the range of cultural events in the city, with some, such as Umbria Jazz Winter and "Orvieto con Gusto" (a food festival), attracting an international audience.

42. Traffic restrictions in the *centro storico*.

43. Electric-powered community bus service.

44. Wederath, Germany.

3

Environmental Sustainability

The vitality of the natural environment – one of the three Es of sustainability – and the ability to preserve environmental resources for the future are central to small town sustainability. Many small towns are working to decrease their dependence on fossil fuels; they contribute to clean air and water; they limit waste and educate the public about the benefits of recycling; they curb sprawl and apply novel approaches to land use planning; they ensure biodiversity; and they encourage and support green industries and eco-friendly building techniques. In this chapter we highlight the ways in which small towns connect their environmental efforts to economic and equity goals and show how they are leaders in applying a systems-based approach that connects the triad of environment-economy-equity.

Small towns often stand in the shadow of larger cities. Portland, the major metropolitan region in the U.S. state of Oregon with about 2 million residents, or Freiburg, a medium-sized city of about 220,000 residents in southwest Germany, are much-lauded for their environmental efforts and sustainable achievements. While cities like Portland and Freiburg have stood in the sustainability

spotlight for quite some time, small towns across the world are overlooked, despite their innovative and exciting approaches to environmental sustainability. For example, in Europe, as early as the 1980s, small towns in Sweden adopted a systems-based approach to sustainable development and they initiated a national and international movement now known as the eco-municipalities movement. Across the Atlantic, as of spring, 2008, 1,000 communities in the United States, including many small towns, have started to develop action plans to reduce carbon emissions even though national-level policies do not support international climate protection agreements such as the Kyoto Protocol. Many grassroots efforts are emerging and their activities range from biomass district heating systems to eco-friendly kindergartens.

Whether in large metropolises or small towns, a common mistake in planning for sustainability is to pursue environmental efforts on a project-by-project basis or to address only one issue, isolated from its broader context. This approach might work if a community needs to demonstrate sustainability goals through a pilot project but, if systemic changes are required, a more holistic approach is needed. When projects take on a life of their own, they can also conflict and compete with other sustainability objectives.[45] This so-called silo approach divorces considerations about the environment from necessary changes or benefits to the local economy and from the social welfare of a community.

To bring about real change, environmental sustainability efforts must be integrated into the social and economic fabric of small towns. This is usually easy to do because such efforts often have multiple sustainability benefits. For example, cleaning up and protecting local waterways benefits natural water quality, human health, stormwater management, biodiversity, recreation, and aesthetics. By integrating environmental and other objectives in this way, environmental initiatives gain a broader constituency and support. The Natural Step, a sustainability movement founded in 1988 by Swedish clinician and cancer researcher Karl-Henrik Robèrt, takes such a systematic approach to community sustainability.

45. Jökulsárlón, Iceland. This glacial lagoon is one of a kind, it is also the largest and most famous in Iceland. The lagoon is formed by a lake at the end of the glacier called Vatnajökull. The spectacular view of blue and white icebergs in the lagoon was the backdrop for many movies such as the James Bond films *Die Another Day* and *A View to a Kill*. Climate change and global warming lead to a rise in sea levels and the melting of glaciers like this one in Iceland. In 2007, a record high volume of icebergs were floating in the lagoon.

Its four guiding objectives, which were adopted in 2000 by the American Planning Association, are:

1. Reduce wasteful dependence upon fossil fuels, scarce metals, and minerals that accumulate in nature.
2. Reduce wasteful dependence upon chemicals and synthetic substances that accumulate in nature.
3. Reduce encroachment upon nature.
4. Meet human needs fairly and efficiently.[46]

Sustainability Conflicts

Applying the three-E framework to real-world environmental planning problems can expose critical conflicts between economic, environmental, and social sustainability goals. Urban planning scholar Scott Campbell illustrates the tension between environmental protection and economic development when he describes the conflict between the protection of the spotted owl in the forests of the U.S. Pacific Northwest and the need to ensure employment opportunity for timber workers.[47] More recent examples from that region highlight the conflict between salmon protection and retaining hydropower dams for electricity production. Small towns often find themselves in the middle of such conflicts. For example, the unincorporated town of Truckee, California (population 13,864) faced a similar conflict when the public utility board had to vote on a 50-year contract that would help finance a coal-fired power plant in nearby Utah.[48] Proponents of the contract noted the economic benefits from cheap electricity, whereas those against it referred to global warming and the fact that the area, heavily dependent on winter tourism, is already seeing less snow. California's Governor Arnold Schwarzenegger, in line with his efforts to make California one of the greenest states in the United States by 2020 and a law that prohibits such contracts with polluting power plants weighed in on the controversy and urged the board to vote against the contract. Ultimately the board voted 4:1 against signing the contract and today Truckee receives most of its electricity from a biomass (wood chip) heating system.

Another example in which well-intended sustainability goals conflict with existing laws and regulations has to do with the simple, yet essential, daily task of drying laundry and the use of traditional clotheslines. Most homeowner associations (HOAs) in the United States ban or restrict externally mounted clotheslines. According to many HOA rules, they must be hidden and out of sight in order to avoid depreciating neighbourhood property values. Economic gains trump the environmental benefits from drying clothes naturally. Several states, including Vermont and Connecticut – which are dominated by small towns where clotheslines have traditionally been a familiar sight – have developed legislation that would allow air-drying laundry.[49] These examples illustrate how conflicts can arise from different planning objectives and goals. In small towns, such conflicts may be sharper because they may be more visible and the parties that gain and lose may be better known. However, benefiting from their smallness, small towns may be able to uncover potential conflicts and initiate conversations between those affected. Small towns typically have leaner bureaucracies that make working across departments involving economic, social, and environmental considerations easier. Small towns are also advantaged because they are able to develop a culture of sustainability through their social networks and civic capacities (see Chapter 7).

46. Procida, Italy. With a little more than 10,000 residents and about 4 square kilometres in size, the island of Procida is a charming jewel in the Mediterranean sea. It is the smallest island in the Mediterranean and less well known than its neighbours Capri and Ischia. Some of the neighbourhoods, such as the small fishing quarter Corricella, are characterised by a traditional architectural style that emphasises vaults and arches. Balconies are used to dry laundry outdoors.

47. Acting Locally. Nuclear-Free road sign in Lamporecchio, Tuscany, Italy.

Small Town Exceptionalism

Small towns have also shown great exceptionalism and creative responses in the face of national policies that have created sustainability conflicts. Although the United States does not ban nuclear power, some small towns have declared themselves as nuclear-free zones. East Windsor, Connecticut (population 9,818), for example, developed a Nuclear Free Zone Ordinance as a result of a proposal in the early 1990s to locate a nuclear waste dump there. As mentioned in Chapter 2, the town of Überlingen – a Cittaslow since 2004 – declared itself to be free of genetically modified organisms (GMOs). More than 70 farmers agreed to keep 200 hectares free from genetically modified seeds. Germany's major environmental nonprofit group, BUND, is asking municipalities to sign on to its initiative *Keine Gentechnik auf Gemeindeland* (No GMO on Municipally Owned Land), and more than 20 regional parishes decided to keep their land free of GMOs. Similar developments to keep GMOs out of their limits are taking place in small towns in Italy, Austria, Switzerland, and Australia. In the United States, the town of Burlington (population 38,889) is one of 83 towns in Vermont that expressed opposition to genetic engineering. Brooklin, Maine (population 841), declared itself a GMO-free zone even though genetically modified foods and other organisms are widely used elsewhere and are allowed by federal policy. This type of small town exceptionalism is a testament to the vigour of grassroots environmental movements that are concerned about the numerous threats to biodiversity and the natural environment.

Environmental Problems in Small Towns

Even though small towns have in many cases proven to be leaders in environmental sustainability, they experience many problems associated with environmental degradation. Environmental threats in small towns are more severe than in larger cities because small communities typically depend more directly on their immediate natural resources and their cultural and environmental landscape. Farming and agriculture as well as natural resources serving as recreational amenities are often essential to the small town economic base. As a result, environmental degradation has an immediate impact on small-town residents' health and economic livelihoods.

Environmental problems such as noise, water and air pollution, wasteful land use and sprawl, the loss of open space, and natural disasters such as floods or storms are only a few examples of the threats to the environment. For example, the entire small Alaskan village of Newtok (population 321) will be moved because the permafrost upon which the village was built is melting as a result of climate change and global warming.[50] Apart from the environmental threats, the native Alaskan population is already struggling to hang on to their traditional ways of life and their culture of subsistence hunting and fishing. Experts predict that if global temperatures rise due to an increase in carbon dioxide in the atmosphere, many low-lying coastal regions, including large cities and small coastal towns, will face a similar fate as Newtok. The Intergovernmental Panel on Climate Change (IPCC), which was established by the World Meteorological Organisation (WMO) and by the United Nations Environment Programme (UNEP) in 1988, predicts that sea levels will rise between 0.18 and 0.59 metres by the end of the twenty-first century.[51] This will have tremendous environmental implications such as flood damage, saltwater intrusion, erosion of beaches and coastal wetlands, and – on the human side – the new phenomenon of climate refugees.

Small towns are often plagued by air and noise pollution due to their overdependence on specific industries. At one end of the spectrum, towns that have become part of the fast world because of their attractiveness to tourists have seen heavy traffic and demand for public services. Orvieto, Italy, described in Chapter 2, has seen the negative environmental impacts from tourism and decided to restructure transportation and divert traffic from its town centre. Small towns that depend on extractive resource-based industries or host industrial food processing operations, such as large hog or poultry farms, experience higher levels of air and water pollution. Many small towns in the U.S. Midwest are dependent on these types of industries. Besides environmental degradation, workers in industrial food companies are often subject to unhealthy and unsafe working conditions, threats vividly described by author Eric Schlosser in his revealing 2001 book *Fast Food Nation*.[52]

A common threat to small towns in industrialised and developing nations is rapid urban growth. In developing countries, migration to urban areas has led to the hasty expansion of smaller towns that have now grown into larger cities. They need to cope with negative spillover effects resulting from this growth. In Kenya, for example, growth has created environmental risks such as the destruction of environmentally sensitive land along rivers, and informal growth and squatter settlements result in groundwater pollution. In response, Kenya's small towns can participate in an environmental training project called the Green Towns Project. The project was developed in a unique transnational partnership between local authorities, the Ministry of Local Government, the Ministry of Lands and Settlements, the Government Training Institute in Mombasa, and Wageningen Agricultural University in The Netherlands. Community-based workshops and action groups identify and work on environmental problems. This represents a novel approach and has proven successful in mobilising local voluntarism and civic engagement for sustainability.[53]

In industrialised countries, rapid growth of small towns has led to the loss of open space. Often, valuable farmland is converted into lucrative housing developments, golf courses, or recreational facilities. These developments are especially problematic in the United States, where most rural areas and small towns lack appropriate zoning authority to curb sprawl. This leads to leapfrog development (new development located beyond the city's service areas) that literally "skips over empty land"[54] beyond a town's limits where developers do not face any regulations or restrictions. Unlike some European countries where strict land use regulations limit urban growth, most state and local governments in the United States do not yet employ appropriate measures such as growth boundaries or other types of land use requirements. In addition, zoning regulations such as mandatory setbacks, street widths, and requirements to separate commercial from residential uses often work against the desire to develop in more compact and sustainable ways.

48. Water pollution.

In recent years, urban sprawl has also been linked to adverse public health outcomes such as obesity. Researchers have shown that there is a critical connection between the built environment and levels of physical activity. Because most of these studies have focused on large cities and their suburban environments, the applicability to small towns was not clear. In 2006, however, a study conducted by researchers at Saint Louis University in Missouri showed that the environmental characteristics of small towns in Missouri, Tennessee, and Arkansas influence public health.

Specifically, the researchers noted that the lack of nearby recreation opportunities such as trails and fitness centres, the lack of sidewalks, and safety concerns influence inactivity and ultimately result in poor health such as obesity.[55]

49. Aylsham, England. Through traffic of large trucks is a common problem for small towns without a modern by-pass system.

50. Bellinzona, Switzerland. Electronic vehicle access control system.

The Big Picture: Global and Local Action

The pressing need to address environmental degradation and climate change has led to numerous international agreements and local efforts. In 1992, the United National Conference on Environment and Development (generally known as the Earth Summit) was held in Rio de Janeiro. One hundred seventy-nine governments voted to adopt a blueprint for sustainability. Local implementation of the ideas discussed at the summit was seen as essential. As a result, the so-called Local Agenda 21 was developed and local governments pledged to undertake a consultative, grassroots process to discuss sustainability and take action. Discussions in Rio were especially influenced by presentations of several small Swedish eco-municipalities that have addressed sustainability since the 1980s. These presentations helped shape the Agenda 21 and its focus on local implementation.[56] In many countries, the Local Agenda 21 process was seen as a way to create local accountability and engage citizens in discussions about sustainability and quality of life. Implementation, however, has varied widely from country to country. In Germany, for example, observers noted a lack of coordination between the local and federal level.[57] Nevertheless, Local Agenda 21 processes have become important predecessors for other small town sustainability initiatives such

as the Cittaslow activities. In Waldkirch, Germany, for example, the Local Agenda 21 process had already initiated discussions about sustainability long before the town became a Cittaslow member. Some local representatives, however, critiqued the theoretical nature of Local Agenda 21 discussions and praise Cittaslow for its pragmatism and action orientation. In essence, Waldkirch's Cittaslow membership is translating Agenda 21 ideas into a forceful and tangible action programme.

Agenda 21 represents a voluntary programme of action for sustainability. Starting in 1997, the international community became more proactive and forceful when more than 179 nations signed on to the Kyoto Protocol and committed to reducing greenhouse gases. Several countries did not sign on to the agreement, most notably the United States, which is one of the largest emitters of greenhouse gases in the world. In 2006, China surpassed the United States as the largest emitter, underscoring the need to focus on environmental sustainability in newly industrialising countries. In response to federal inaction in the United States, there has been a groundswell of local action. In 2005 the U.S. Conference of Mayors adopted the U.S. Mayors Climate Protection Agreement, and by 2007 more than 355 mayors representing over 54 million Americans in 49 states had signed the Agreement.[58] The Cool Mayors website,[59] a tool

51. Avignonet-Lauragais, France. Renewable energy from windmills. The European Commission unveiled sweeping plans in 2007 to diversify EU energy sources, slash carbon emissions by 20 percent and enforce rules for fuel competition.

for sharing information among local leaders, now lists more than 1,000 large and small towns that have signed on to the agreement. Although most of the cities that have signed on to the agreement are large metropolitan areas, some small towns have shown remarkable grassroots action. For example, the California town of Atascadero (population 28,361) is a big advocate of sustainable land use, known as smart growth, and in 1998 adopted a native tree regulation to protect its oak trees. The town of Frisco in Colorado (population 33,714) signed on to the Climate Protection Agreement in 2007 but, long before, the town had adopted an environmental stewardship policy to incorporate energy efficiency into its municipal operations. In 2007, Frisco switched to wind and other renewable energy for 100 percent of its municipal operations and purchased carbon credits for the municipally owned vehicles. The U.S. Mayors Climate Protection Agreement catalyzed a powerful grassroots network in the United States. Some critics, however, argue that without federal and state support, many of the potential gains from local actions will not materialise.[60]

Sweden's Eko Kommun Movement

One of the most impressive small town environmental movements is the Swedish network of eco-municipalities. The movement encompasses 71 municipalities of varying sizes – more than a quarter of the country's cities and towns. Each Swedish eko kommun works toward a sustainable future and collaborates with others. They are committed to the Natural Step Framework and they understand sustainability as a systemic issue that involves environmental, economic, and social objectives. The towns typically engage study circles in which residents can exchange ideas and develop a common understanding of what it means to develop a sustainable future. The ideas for eco-municipalities originated in the 1980s when a small town close to the Arctic Circle, Övertorneå, began to envision a fossil fuel-free future. Övertorneå became the first eco-municipality in Sweden and in the world. Residents and local leaders were motivated by a crisis in the form of economic and social decline.[61] High unemployment, out-migration, and a lack of social engagement alarmed local leaders and they initiated a grassroots process to discuss the town's future. Today, Övertorneå has achieved 100 percent independence from fossil

52. Allgäu, Germany. Renewable energy from solar panels on a barn.

fuels in its municipal operations. Most municipal buildings use efficient biomass heating systems and the town's fleet runs on biofuels. Fuel consumption dropped substantially, freeing financial resources for other investments. The town built an eco-village to attract new residents. It also rebuilt the town's school using ecological building materials and forgoing any plastic products or plastic furniture. Policymakers, businesses, and residents are engaged in continuous training and education.

In 1995, Sweden's eco-municipalities created an umbrella organisation known as Sveriges Ekokommuner (SEkom). The organisation developed an environmental indicator system that towns can use to monitor progress toward sustainability. SEkom eco-municipality indicators are:

1. CO_2 emissions from fossil fuel (tons per resident).
2. Quantity of dangerous waste from households (kg per resident).
3. Percentage of arable land with organically grown crops.
4. Percentage of environmentally approved forestry [certified by the Forest Stewardship Council (FSC) or the Pan European Forest Council (PEFC)].
5. Percentage of protected environments (nature reserves).
6. Collection of household waste for recycling (responsibility of manufacturer; kg per resident).
7. Total amount of household waste (excluding responsibility of manufacturer; kg per resident).
8. Heavy metals in drainage sludge (mg per kg toxic substance).
9. Percentage of renewable and recycled energy in municipal premises.
10. Transportation energy for business trips by car (tons per employee) and CO_2 emissions from business trips by car (tons per employee).
11. Purchase of organic provisions within the municipal organisation (percentage of the cost).
12. Percentage of environmentally approved schools and day care centres [certified systems such as Green Schools, Schools for Sustainable Development, ISO 14001, Eco-Management and Audit Scheme (EMAS)].[62]

Other countries, such as the United States, Ireland, Japan, New Zealand, and some African countries, are replicating the Swedish eco-municipality model. In the United States, the North American Eco-Municipality Network, formed in 2005, includes representatives from North American towns that have adopted the eco-municipality model. Several small towns, most notably in the states of Wisconsin, Pennsylvania, New Hampshire, and Minnesota, are working toward a sustainable future. Town councils in Ashland and Washburn in the Chequamegon Bay region in Wisconsin passed resolutions to become eco-municipalities, created study circles, and adopted formal sustainability plans. The region has developed a long-term sustainability initiative, the Sustainable Chequamegon Initiative Strategic Plan 2006–2011. In Ireland, a grassroots group formed in Clonakilty, a small town about 50 kilometres south of Cork, and is developing a sustainability agenda modelled after the Swedish eco-municipalities.

Robertsfors, Sweden

The town of Robertsfors is part of the fifth generation of Swedish eco-municipalities, and its ambition is to create a model for sustainable development. Robertsfors is located about 60 kilometres north of Umeå, the capital of Västerbotten County in northern Sweden. It is a small and spatially dispersed community with about 7,050 residents. Two thousand citizens live in Robertsfors town centre and the rest are sprinkled in nine villages and 20 hamlets in the surrounding rural countryside.[63] The region is known for its legacy in the iron works industry and its deep agricultural roots.

Until the late 1990s, environmental sustainability was pursued on a project-by-project basis. In 1999, however, a discussion was initiated about the potential to become a model community for sustainable practices. The town joined SEkom and began to develop a comprehensive grassroots planning process in 2001. "Sustainable Robertsfors" is based on a five-year initiative and the goal is to develop a model process for how to initiate economic, environmental, and social change. The town wants to be "at the cutting edge of what is sustainable development and serve as a living model and prototype for all other municipalities' work on sustainable development."[64] It has developed a sustainability plan that serves as a living document, recognising the need to be able to adjust and change course of action based on the community's needs and achievements.

In terms of environmental sustainability, the town has an ambitious vision. By 2050, Robertsfors would like to:

- Be highly self-sufficient as to foods and other daily needs;
- Have minimised need for transport;
- Have developed closed cycles and non-poisonous sustenance between soil and table and between city and country;
- Use 100 percent renewable raw materials in all energy use;
- Be a leading example in the world of a thoroughly sustainable community; and

53. Robertsfors town centre.

54. Robertsfors. Robertsfors is located in the northeast of Sweden, a sparsely populated area. The town itself has about 2,000 residents and the five smaller villages add another 5,000 residents. The most important industry sectors are forestry, farming, and tourism.

- Have intensive exchanges of knowledge with the rest of the world and with leading experts on sustainable development both within private business and in the public sector.

In order to get there, the town is working to phase out fossil fuels, which is congruent with the Swedish government's goal to eliminate the use of oil by 2020. Efforts include switching the town's fleet to using ethanol fuel. Schools have been environmentally certified. Biomass heating is used. The town has also created a poison-free, organic farmers market and is working to detoxify its waste and sewer management.

Sustainability is not an ephemeral undertaking in Robertsfors: The town revises and updates the Sustainable Action Plan every year. An ambitious goal is to connect the plan with the budgeting process so that decisions to finance certain projects are linked to sustainability goals. The town also employs a sustainability coordinator who makes sure that the various public agencies and depart-ments adopt sustainability ideas and goals.

Even though Robertsfors is a small town that is located in a rather remote region, the town has recognised the global nature of the issues related to sustainability. The town has developed a partnership with another small town in Kenya. The goal is to offer sustainability training and to develop leaders who initiate and guide the efforts. The Kenyan town, Machakos, a rapidly grow-ing town located about 65 kilometres southeast of Nairobi, has adopted the eco-municipality ideas and the mutual visits of Swedish and Kenyan leaders enhance their understanding.

While Robertsfors has made significant progress toward environmental sustainability, several issues remain. Planners are recognising the importance of a strong economy for the continued success of the initiative. In addition, concerns over equity, marginalised groups, and the continued out-migration of people – especially those between 18 and 24 – from the rural areas to urban centres such as Umeå may significantly inhibit the town's comprehensive success.

55. Robertsfors. To develop and implement the project Sustainable Robertsfors, the town used a participatory process and conducted numerous community meetings and events. Information and education of residents – old and young – is viewed as one of the success factors. Schools are now implementing sustainability ideas and children are an integral part of the larger project.

56. Robertsfors, Sweden. The town is building a district heating system that uses wood. To implement the project, the city hall is collaborating with other municipalities and a utility company.

57. Robertsfors. Residents in the village Överklinten agreed to renovate a formerly abandoned mill. The building, in traditional red with white trim, now houses a hotel and a fishing center. The building is equipped with a sauna, a restaurant, 18 guest rooms, and high-speed internet access.

Land Use and Urban Development

An environmentally sensitive approach to land use planning and urban development is key to successful sustainability efforts in small towns. Small towns in growing regions must focus on curbing sprawl and greenfield development, while those towns threatened by decline need to develop tools to encourage infill development and adaptive reuse to keep town centres vital. Three small towns in Germany have developed innovative practices in sustainable land use guidelines and regulations.

The town of Überlingen (population 21,000), the fourth certified Cittaslow in Germany, participates in the ECOLUP (Ecological Land Use Planning) programme, applying the European Eco-Management and Audit Scheme (EMAS II) to the land use planning process.[65] Überlingen cooperates with three other cities located on Lake Constance. The collaborative project is unique, as it tries to find ways to create partnerships across international borders in a densely populated yet ecologically sensitive area. Lake Constance serves as the most important fresh water reserve for the region and many of the cities are built very close to its shores. The region's high quality of life also contributes to steady population growth and to its popularity among tourists.

Besides Überlingen, the German city of Constance and the Austrian towns of Dornbirn and Wolfurt are part of the ECOLUP project, and the model program is supported by the Lake Constance Foundation. In 2004 Überlingen was the first community in the European Union to have developed an EMAS-certified communal land use planning system. In Überlingen, project teams have examined the strengths and weaknesses of the existing land use and environmental planning systems. In community workshops focused on relevant land use topics, residents have discussed ways to implement the system. International workshops are hosted to ensure knowledge transfer among the pilot communities. Through ECOLUP, Überlingen's planners ensure sustainable land use; planning regulations encourage infill development; forest areas and open spaces are protected; and the town is actively encouraging green roofs and the unsealing of areas such as parking lots and

58. Überlingen, Germany. As a spa and resort town, Überlingen benefits from its location along the shores of Lake Constance. The walkway along the lake is publicly accessible and used by visitors and residents alike. The town has experienced steady population growth and planners are concerned with urban growth and its impact on the sensitive ecosystem around the lake. Überlingen's planning approach incorporates environmental sustainability and a strong concern for protecting sensitive riparian buffers.

plazas. Other important aspects include planning for energy efficiency and the protection of watersheds as well as traffic calming. The ecological audit of the land use planning system and civic participation make the Überlingen model stand out.

Another innovative approach to land use development can be found in a small Bavarian town near Munich. The town of Fraunberg (population 3,400) has eliminated the industrial area land use category from its land use plans.[66] Instead, it has developed new plans and concepts to allow for the commercial and residential use of buildings and areas in the town centres and neighbourhoods. It defines these areas as "valuable cultural landscapes" because of their unique small-town characteristics. Threatened by population increases and the development of the nearby new Munich airport, the town wanted to retain its traditional character. But it also faced a rapid decline in family-owned farms (from 1994 to 2002, more than 20 percent of the farms disappeared and now only a quarter of the 240 farm homesteads are used for agriculture). Residents formed a nonprofit

group called *Gemeindeentwicklung Fraunberg e.V.* (Fraunberg Community Development) and helped develop the new land use concept. The idea behind it is to find new functions for farm buildings, which traditionally have been characterized by the unique combination of living space and farming (*Wohnstallhaus*, "stable house"). Formerly empty homesteads now house businesses; other buildings in close-in locations have been torn down to make room for new construction; and public plazas have been beautified. Such efforts help to maintain the vitality and the character of the small towns.

Small towns with deep agricultural roots and heritage face an uncertain future as the traditional use of their built environment does not fit with changed economic systems. They must find ways to ensure their social and economic vitality while also being sensitive to the environment. In Waldkirch, a Cittaslow member, traditional Black Forest farms have been allowed to rent out rooms to tourists in exchange for connecting to the local sewer systems. This has encouraged better environmental management while at

59. Überlingen, Germany. Wooden houses are becoming more popular in Germany.

60. Wirsberg, Germany. Wirsberg actively promotes alternative energies and has installed a photovoltaic system on the roof of the city hall building. One of Wirsberg's districts, Weißenbach, is known as the "Solar Village."

the same time giving farmers and their younger generation additional income opportunities.

The small town Viernheim (population 33,000) in southwest Germany used a two-pronged approach to develop a new neighbourhood. The local land use plan incorporated many ecological building features, and intensive public relations work and education of residents ensured widespread public acceptance of the project.[67] Located near two major autobahns and in close proximity to Mannheim and Darmstadt, the town experienced strong population growth and demand for new homes in the 1990s. When planners developed the land use plan for the new area, they were guided by the objectives to build in eco-friendly ways and to minimise the use of scarce resources. The local building plan (*Bebauungsplan*) incorporates the natural features of the terrain and regulates the location of the buildings so as not to destroy valuable ecological areas. In addition, the number of buildings and size of their footprints are limited. Green roofs and the use of vegetation regulate microclimates and

innovative techniques are used to manage stormwater. A district heating system and passive/active solar building design encourage energy efficiency. Besides these types of formal regulations, planners and policymakers have developed a unique public relations strategy. They have published ecological guidebooks and have offered seminars at the local adult education centre. They credit their success to the combination of environmentally sensitive land use planning regulations with public education.

61. Viernheim, Germany: A planned 5.5 hectare neighborhood "Am Schmittsberg" built in the 1990s incorporating ecological objectives. To limit land use, the town set the maximum amount of land each building could use. Buildings were required to incorporate green roofs, rain water is collected and a small district heating system is used.

Vigorous Small Town Responses

The vigour with which many small towns are working toward creating a healthy and sustainable environment is impressive. The pioneers have traditionally been small college towns with a progressive residential population that is willing to experiment with and change traditional planning practices. Towns with a culture of stewardship for the land and natural resources are also often pioneers in this area. Increasingly, however, progressive ways to protect the environment are emerging from unlikely places. Often, crisis situations such as a decline in population – as was the case in Övertorneå – or a devastating natural disaster catalyse community responses to threats such as global warming and environmental devastation. Such local action is emerging in many different types of places. As mentioned in Chapter 2, Abu Dhabi is building a new city, Masdar (Fig. 62) for up to 50,000 people that will use renewable energy, including solar power. Designed by Foster + Partners, the town will be a sustainable place in the desert. The small U.S. town of Greensburg, Kansas (population 1,574) decided to go green after it was completely devastated by a tornado. Planners in the town of Keene, New Hampshire (population 22,563) are using social pressure to convince residents to change behaviour and become more sustainable.[68] Friends, neighbours, and co-workers will exert peer pressure to encourage more sustainable ways of living. The town of Bahía de Caráquez in Ecuador (population about 30,000) became an "ecological city" in 1999 after it experienced negative impacts from torrential rains and mud slides. Its projects include the planting of native trees for erosion control, the creation of urban "wild corridors," and ecological education.[69]

The few examples highlighted in this chapter illustrate the various ways in which small towns can incorporate sustainable practices to protect the environment. And the vigour with which this is being done is testament to the power of grassroots movements to initiate social change.

62. Masdar City, Abu Dhabi, United Arab Emirates. Masdar City is a planned sustainable town in the middle of a desert in Abu Dhabi. The master plan is designed by Foster + Partners and provides for a town of 50,000 residents. The city will be completely carbon neutral and will use solar power and narrow shaded streets to reduce energy use. Cars will be banned and planners envision a personal rapid transit (PRT) system.

63. Hersbruck, Germany.

4

Inherited Identities: Built Form and Sense of Place

Liveability is a critical aspect of sustainability for small towns and, as we have seen in Chapter 1, it is essentially local in character. Liveability depends on how easy a place is to use, and how it feels. The physical attributes of the built environment – the morphology, form, layout, amenities, and architecture of a town – are important aspects of liveability. But there are also important socio-cultural dimensions of liveability that have to do with identity and sense of place. People's physical well-being, opportunities, and lifestyle choices are all affected, for better or worse, by the particular attributes of specific places. Ordinary places provide the settings for people's daily lives and for their social relations. Even though satellite television and the World Wide Web may claim more and more of people's time and attention, it is still in particular places that people learn who and what they are, how they should think and behave, and what life is likely to hold for them. Ordinary places also contribute to people's collective memory and become powerful emotional and cultural symbols.[70]

The Legacy of Built Form

For most small towns, both the physical and the sociocultural dimensions of liveability are inherited characteristics, hewn from history and the regional cultural landscape. The particular "feel" of a town is a product of its size, geographic location, climate, underlying topography, street plan, building materials, and architectural styles. The character of a town is also a product of the type of local industry or agriculture, with its built form a legacy of periods of prosperity. It is upon these foundations that contemporary residents are able to develop a collective identity and sense of place.

Small Towns in Europe

Many of Europe's small towns have their origins in the early medieval period or before, as ecclesiastical or university centres, defensive strongholds, or administrative centres within regional feudal systems. From the eleventh century onward, however, feudal systems faltered and disintegrated in the face of successive demographic, economic, and political crises caused by steady population growth in conjunction with only modest technological improvements and limited amounts of cultivable land. To bolster their incomes and raise armies against one another, the feudal nobility began to levy increasingly higher taxes. People were consequently obliged to sell more of their produce for cash on the market. As a result, a more extensive money economy developed, along with the beginnings of a pattern of trade in basic agricultural produce and craft manufactures. The regional specialisations and trading patterns that emerged provided the foundations for a new phase of urbanisation based on merchant capitalism. Beginning with the frameworks established by the merchants of Venice, Pisa, Genoa, and Florence and the towns of the Hanseatic League (a federation of city-states around the North Sea and Baltic coasts), a trading system of immense complexity soon came to span Europe, articulated by a dense network of market towns (Fig. 67). Their layout and built form derive in large measure from this initial phase of growth and prosperity, while industrialisation and modernity have added new urban fabric in the form of accretions and replacements, outward extensions, and internal reorganisations. With each successive phase of urban growth, initial forms of house, plot, and street types became hybridized as new buildings replaced old, plots were amalgamated or subdivided, and street layouts were modified.

There is rich variety in the legacy of market towns, but their original prosperity almost always hinged on strategic situations along routeways, at crossroads, or at bridging points on rivers; and on well-chosen sites, usually on ridges for good drainage and close to rivers or streams. The initially dominant structures were castles, palaces, churches, and monasteries; the dominant space was the market place (Figs. 68 and 69). The pattern of a main street – widening in the centre to accommodate a market and narrowing at the ends to allow entry to be controlled – was a distinctive feature in many towns. As historian Mark Girouard notes, most market towns "started off with a single open market, but if they prospered almost invariably ended up with several. Annual fairs and markets, if they started off in the centre, tended to move off to the periphery, to get rid of the inconvenience for everyone concerned of having large numbers of animals trampling through narrow and crowded streets. Covered markets and market halls appeared. The main market place sometimes got smaller because stalls developed into shops and houses, and sometimes bigger because it was enlarged."[71] As towns expanded, secondary streets and cross streets were introduced, often giving rise to complex web-shaped and organic plans. Trade-based prosperity also brought new structures and new spaces. In addition to market halls there were guild halls, almshouses, hospitals, schools, public granaries, and town halls. Streets were widened, paved, and drained; gates and walls were fortified; drainage and water supply systems were installed; and public spaces were opened up.

In much of Europe, the territorial expansion of trade and settlement led to the founding of new towns. Convenience and practicality were their basis. For ease of assigning plots to settlers, towns were laid out in rectilinear grids, though the grid pattern was often skewed or broken to accommodate topography or existing structures. The principal concern

64. Bellinzona, Switzerland. Many small towns in Europe have a legacy of institutional buildings like churches, along with remaining fragments of fortifications. In Bellinzona, the surviving fortifications date from 15th-century improvements undertaken by the ruling Sforza family. They were restored in the 1980s and 1990s and collectively recognised as a World Heritage Site by UNESCO in 2000.

65. St Andrews, Scotland. From medieval times until the Scottish Reformation in the 16th century St Andrews was the ecclesiastical capital of Scotland. Its historic cathedral now in ruins, the town functions as a regional market centre.

66. Winchester, England. The prosperity of market towns in the late medieval period saw the addition of new institutional buildings. These almshouses were rebuilt in 1856 on the site of the 16th century St John's Hospital almshouses.

of the landowners responsible for establishing the towns of medieval Europe was to generate income. As a result, special attention was given to market places, with vendors of different categories of products each allocated set locations, many of which became established as street names or place names. Subsequent phases of growth and development have turned small towns into palimpsests, their streets and buildings recording, on the template of medieval street plans, the imprint of new technologies, new modes of economic and social organisation, new designs, and new fashions. The sixteenth and seventeenth centuries brought assembly rooms, theatres, pleasure gardens, coffee houses, and permanent shops as well as new housing. By the nineteenth century towns had become characterised more by their industrial specialty (or lack thereof), with their market functions receding in importance. Seaports, mill towns, brewing towns, railway towns, manufacturing towns, and mining towns each had their own functional and architectural features, as did the spas and resort towns that grew as a result of the prosperity of the industrial era.

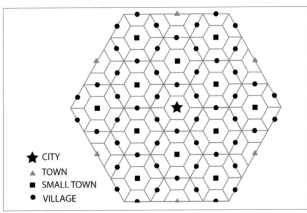

67. Central Place Theory. In many regions of pre-industrial Europe there developed nested hierarchical systems of settlements, with a small number of large central places – cities – offering a wide range of higher-order goods and services and serving an extensive hinterland that also contained many smaller central places – towns, villages, and hamlets – that offered a narrower range of mostly lower-order goods and services to proportionally smaller hinterlands. This was the spatial pattern identified by the famous German geographer Walter Christaller.

Legend:
★ CITY
▲ TOWN
■ SMALL TOWN
● VILLAGE

68. Salisbury, England. A "central place" in southern England, where the original Charter market still takes place every Tuesday and Saturday, augmented by a farmers' market every first and third Wednesday of the month and a French market (featuring a diverse range of French goods and foods, including, cheeses, charcuterie, patisserie and bread) three times a year.

69. Salisbury, England. The market place was kept as an open space as the streets and buildings of the new town were laid out in the 13th century. Oatmeal Row, Ox Row, Butcher Row, and Fish Row were subsequent encroachments of permanent shops that were built to replace the temporary stalls of earlier times. The town's butchers occupied more permanent structures in the Butcher Row, while out-of-town butchers had their stalls on the site of Ox Row.

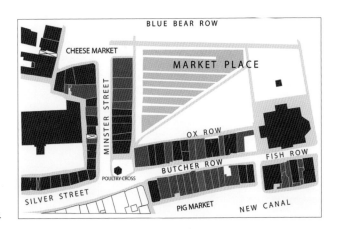

70. Trevi, Italy. Medieval Europe, divided into a patchwork of feudal kingdoms and estates, was largely rural. Towns were mostly small: defensive strongholds of the feudal nobility. Hilltop sites provided secure, strategic settings as in this example: Trevi, Italy, on Monte Serano, overlooking the wide plain of the Clitunno river system.

71. Eger, Hungary. The town's prosperity in the medieval period was a result of its status as an ecclesiastical centre. It became an important border fortress town during Turkish incursions into central Hungary in the sixteenth century but was reclaimed by its bishops when the Habsburgs regained control of the region at the end of the seventeenth century, leading to another prosperous period that has left a legacy of Baroque architecture.

72. Skagen, Denmark. Located at the northern tip of Jutland, Skagen was a remote and inaccessible fishing village until a paved road to the town was completed in the 1940s. Now, counter-urbanisation and tourism, combined with EU regional policy support, have turned it into a prosperous community.

73. Assisi, Italy. Creatures of topography, hill towns have inherited narrow, picturesque streets and alleyways.

74. Trevi, Italy. The topographic restrictions on motor traffic have become a positive legacy of calm pedestrian passageways through the town.

75. Orvieto, Italy. Split levels create an ambience of privacy. Terraces lead down to pleasant grids of cobblestoned streets broadening here and there into piazzas, most of which are named for the churches that dominate them. Along narrow, vertiginous lanes, houses seem to lean together until they almost join overhead. Impractical for motor traffic, hill towns nevertheless offer the prospect of liveability.

Ludlow, England

Ludlow (population 10,500) came into existence as a "planted" town after the Norman Conquest of 1066, one of a series of outposts guarding the Welsh Marches, or borderlands. A planned town was laid out – planted – around the castle, partly to provide essential services for the garrison, partly to stabilise the surrounding countryside (still seething with anti-Norman sentiments) and partly as a source of income – through market fees, tolls, rents, and court fines – for Ludlow's aristocratic rulers. As a planned town, Ludlow's streets were laid out with spacious dimensions in a grid pattern. Like other planted towns, Ludlow was also distinctive for its exceptionally wide market place. As the town grew, the castle was extended and in 1233 a circuit of defensive walls was constructed around the castle and the town.

Like other medieval towns in England, Ludlow was laid out with "burgage plots" – long narrow strips of land with a building fronting onto a main street, the land extending to a back lane that acted as a service road. Burgage plots were allotted by the lord of the manor to freemen who were entitled to practice a trade within the town (and therefore to participate in electing members of the town's ruling council) and who paid a cash rent for the plot instead of (as was previous practice) occupying land by virtue of having given feudal service to the lord of the manor. The nucleus of the planned town was the High Street market place, running eastward from the castle to meet a pre-existing north-south drovers' trackway. The intersection of the trackway and the market place grew into the town's beast market and became known as the Bull Ring. The shops in the market place began as rows of stalls, many of them abutting onto pre-existing walls and buildings, as in Drapers' Row (now King Street). At first the shops were lock-up units, with the shopkeepers living elsewhere. Later, cellars were excavated for storage, and rooms were erected above the shops for residential use.

Ludlow's emblematic timber-framed buildings date from the seventeenth century, when many of the town's medieval town houses were lavishly refronted and decorated, the timber ornamentation getting more elaborate with height. Much of the town was remodelled yet again toward the end of

76. Ludlow town centre. The figure-ground pattern is dominated by the grid layout of the planted town and the principal north-south street, formerly a drovers' trackway.

77. Ludlow from the West.

78. Ludlow is generally regarded as one of the most attractive small towns in England. Its medieval street pattern survives almost intact, along with a splendid fifteenth century church, timber-framed Tudor buildings, handsome Georgian town houses, and elaborate Victorian cottages and villas.

the seventeenth century, but still on the basis of its medieval framework. Half-timbered façades gave way to new brick ones on plot after plot, but the change was usually superficial, with the original timber frame surviving behind the new front. With the turnpike mania of the mid-eighteenth century, improved roads in the region intensified Ludlow's importance as a market town. The period has left its mark most strikingly on Broad Street, where the Georgian buildings were based on the safe, sensible façades of the pattern books of the time. The railway came to Ludlow in 1852 but the town had no comparative advantages within the networked urban system of industrial Britain. It has therefore remained a provincial market town, slowly adapting and refitting in response to new technologies and planning regulations. The most significant development, in fact, has been the active conservation of the built environment. A fad of antiquarianism that became fashionable in Britain after 1900 helped to propagate awareness of Ludlow's heritage, and statutory powers of conservation were enacted by the national parliament in 1947. The Ludlow Civic Society was formed in 1954 and the historic core of the town became a conservation area in 1970, with 469 listed buildings (increased to 502 in 1992, when the conservation area was extended). When a bypass was built to the east of the town in 1978, the town was relieved of the congestion of traffic on the main road between Shrewsbury and Hereford, restoring a good deal of composure to the town. In 2004, Ludlow became the founding member of Cittaslow in the United Kingdom.

79. The Butter Cross building was built between 1742 and 1744 as a Town Hall. Designed in classical style with cupola and clock tower, it also served as a butter market, with a charity school on the upper floor.

80. Ludlow Market, by Louise Rayner, c. 1865.

81. The buildings on Broad Street relate especially well to one another, adjusting to the slopes on which they are built, with eaves, lintels, and sill levels carrying through, so far as possible, to the nearest corresponding feature on the adjoining house.

Small Towns in North America

Small towns in North America have a shorter history than their European counterparts even though the historical roots of urban settlements lie in the early arrival of indigenous people thousands of years ago. Native Americans inhabited the American continent as indigenous people and they built sizable settlements, especially in the Southwest. As European pioneers arrived from the fifteenth century onward, many more small towns appeared, primarily as staging areas to exploit natural resources. Most small towns in New England or the mid-Atlantic states such as Maryland and Virginia served as trading centres for tobacco and cotton, which were shipped to Europe. Small towns, especially those along waterways and ports, flourished because of this mercantilist regime. Most other towns were small central places serving their hinterlands (Fig. 82). In terms of morphology, the dominant pattern was rectilinear, dominated by a Main Street and a central crossroad, but without the market places characteristic of small towns in Europe.

Between the 1830s and 1850s, a vast transportation infrastructure network was constructed and railroads and canals opened up the interior and the western part of the continent. While this created a boom for cities such as Calgary, Chicago, and Kansas City because they served as important trading centres for livestock and other agricultural products,[72] small towns suddenly stopped growing, both in size and number. Consequently, a dense, hierarchical urban system similar to the one found in Europe never developed in North America. Not surprisingly, academic literature and theorizing on urban issues in North America has never placed much emphasis on small towns.

Recently, metropolitan decentralisation and counterurbanisation have led to rapid growth in many of the smaller towns near large cities,[73] but many of the more remote small towns have lost their function and populations. Many single-industry towns that had developed because of the exploitation of natural resources such as lumber and coal have become ghost towns. Others may symbolically hold on to their industrial or agricultural heritage, but their employment base is now primarily in low-wage service industries. Many

small towns have also experienced the arrival of Wal-Mart and other discount chains and the consequent decline of locally owned specialist shops on Main Street. Meanwhile, a few small towns, primarily those with high quality of life and amenities, have become hotbeds for migrants such as young outdoor enthusiasts and highly educated professionals who can work from anywhere.

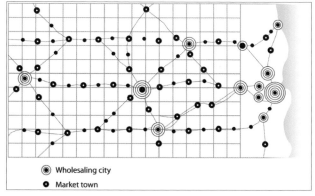

○ Wholesaling city

○ Market town

82. Central Places in North America. The North American urban system developed as a mercantile subsidiary of the European urban system, connected by Atlantic coast ports. As these entrepôts grew, they came to dominate larger and larger hinterlands, within which smaller settlements emerged as local market towns. In time, these market towns became inland gateways that acted as bulking points and provided an array of services for the frontier agriculturalists. Continuing demand for staple exports and increasing colonisation combined to draw settlement further into the interior, requiring the development of long-distance rail routes and the emergence of towns serving as "depots of staple collection" at strategic locations along these routes. After James Vance, Jr., *The Merchant's World: The Geography of Wholesaling.* Englewood Cliffs, N.J.: Prentice Hall, 1970, p. 151.

83. Decorah, Iowa. A central place and agricultural depot on the northern plains.

A Cumulative Legacy

For many of today's small towns in both Europe and North America it is this sort of cumulative legacy that lends character and texture, a collaboration of the centuries that appeals as much to the imagination as to the eye. The most recent inscriptions on the palimpsest of urban development – the standardisation, rationalisation, and homogenisation associated with globalisation – are, however, widely seen as unsympathetic. The physical consequences of the structural economic change of the late twentieth century are all too visible in empty factory buildings (Fig. 84) and vacant land. Gap sites and decaying buildings, particularly if they are in prominent locations, can have a serious blighting effect on the environment of a small town and can reduce confidence in its future. Meanwhile, the rise in automobile ownership, along with the growing reliance on larger cities for employment and services, has led to a significant increase in traffic between many small towns and larger cities. This has often resulted in congestion (Fig. 86). The centres of small towns, especially those that have not been bypassed and where the historic street pattern has remained largely intact, have suffered particularly acute traffic problems. In many towns, standard traffic engineering solutions have proved to be out of scale with the inherited form and character of the area. At the same time, the individuality of high street shops has been overwritten by the invasion and succession of superstores, supermarkets, franchised fast-food and clothing chains, and generic buildings and storefronts. As a result, one of the most important assets of small towns – their distinctive sense of place – has become threatened.

84. Chiavenna, Italy. A derelict textile mill stands as a reminder of structural economic change.

85. Belper, England. Renewal in the 1960s destroyed much of the original fabric of the main shopping street of Belper, a nineteenth-century mill town.

86. Lewes, England. Traffic congestion.

The Social Construction of Space

Nevertheless, sense of place is not simply a matter of bricks and mortar or the aesthetics of the built environment. It is always socially constructed, and a fundamental element in the social construction of place is the existential imperative for people to define themselves in relation to the material world. Places are constantly under social construction by people as they respond to the opportunities and constraints of their particular locality. As people live and work in places, they gradually impose themselves on their environment, modifying and adjusting it to suit their needs and express their values. At the same time, they gradually accommodate both to their physical environment and to the values, attitudes, and comportment of people around them. People are constantly modifying and reshaping places, and places are constantly coping with change and influencing their inhabitants.

The roots of this idea are to be found in the philosophy of Martin Heidegger, who contended that men and women originate in an alienated condition and define themselves, among other ways, through their socio-spatial environment.[74] People's "creation" of space provides them with roots – their homes and localities becoming biographies of that creation. Central to Heidegger's philosophy is the notion of *dwelling*: the basic capacity to achieve a form of spiritual unity between humans and the material world. Through repeated experience and complex associations, our capacity for dwelling allows us to construct places, to give them meanings that are deepened and qualified over time with multiple nuances.[75] Another crucial concept here is that of the *lifeworld*, the taken-for-granted pattern and context for everyday living through which people conduct their day-to-day lives without having to make it an object of conscious attention.[76] People's experience of everyday routines in familiar settings (Figs. 87–90) leads reflexively to a pool of shared meanings. Neighbours become familiar with one another's vocabulary, speech patterns, dress codes, gestures, and humour, and with shared experiences of the physical environment such as streets, markets, and parks. Often this carries over into people's attitudes and feelings about themselves and their locality and to the symbolism they attach

87. Citta di Castello, Italy.

88. Spilimbergo, Italy.

89. Chiavenna, Italy.

to that place. When this happens, the result is a collective and self-conscious "structure of feeling": the affective frame of reference generated among people as a result of the experiences and memories that they associate with a particular place.[77]

The basis of both individual lifeworlds and the collective structure of feeling is *intersubjectivity*: shared meanings that are derived from the lived experience of everyday practice. An important part of the basis for intersubjectivity is the routinisation of individual and social practice in time and space. A positive and distinctive sense of place stems in large part from routine encounters and shared experiences that make for intersubjectivity. This requires plenty of opportunities for casual meetings and gossip; friendly settings in which to eat, drink, or linger; street markets; and a sense of historical and cultural continuity.

Place as Text and Context

Place, then, is much more than urban form. It is both text and context: a palimpsest of recorded history in bricks and mortar and a setting for contemporary social interaction that, among other things, structures the daily routines of economic and social life; structures people's life paths (providing them with both opportunities and constraints); provides an arena in which everyday, "common-sense" knowledge and experience are gathered; provides a site for processes of socialisation and social reproduction; and provides an arena for contesting social norms.[78]

The sense of place in a small town also includes a consciousness of its links with the wider world. The specific and unique character of a town does not depend solely on the internal history of a particular place; it also depends on the relations between it and other places. It results from a distinct mixture of wider and more local social relations, so that an understanding of sense of place can only be constructed by linking that place to places beyond.[79]

Geographer Robert Sack has made the distinction between "thin" places and "thick" places. Thin places are very specialised, have very porous boundaries with the outside world because their people have extensive connections outside, and do not intrude much on people's consciousness. Thick places are populated by people who are more inward-looking and are more aware of the place in their everyday lives. Sack observed, "Thinner places can be [...] liberating, and its opposite – living in a closed and thick place with a rich web of stipulated meaning and routines – can be stultifying [...] But [the freedom of thinner places] can also be unsettling, alienating, and lonely."[80]

90. The social construction of space. We live both in and through places. People's territoriality and sense of "dwelling" are informed by broadly shared notions of social distance, norms of comportment, forms of social organisation, and so on. There is an important dialectical relationship between people's everyday practices and the spaces and places that they inhabit. The inherited settings and intimate spaces of small towns provide many opportunities to foster what novelist Milan Kundera called the "secret bond" between slowness and memory.

91. Lewes, England. A strong sense of identity and sense of place is an important component of liveability. It can be reinforced in many different ways, including memorials to townspeople killed in wars.

Cultural Landscapes

By their nature, small towns are intimately bound up with their regional cultural landscapes: the surrounding countryside can usually be seen from many parts of the town; the town itself draws on the vernacular architecture and building materials of its immediate region; and the landscape itself often reflects the agricultural specialties associated with the town. As such, cultural landscapes are often an important part of the identity and sense of place in small towns. The economy, politics, and culture of a region are all inscribed in fields and fences, farmsteads and hamlets. As the product of economic and social history, landscapes not only echo and embody the fortunes of successive generations – they also reflect our individual behaviour and even the way people think and act collectively. Cultural landscapes, in other words, can be powerful but stealthy backdrops that naturalise and reinforce dominant values and practices as if they were simply given and inevitable. Laden with layers of ascribed meaning, regional landscapes can be powerfully symbolic because they are understood as being associated with particular groups of people. The classical Tuscan landscape, for example, became emblematic of Italy itself with the creation of modern Italy and the *Risorgimento* (political unification, 1815–1861) and has been the subject of landscape painters, romantic poets, and novelists ever since. Similarly, the well-ordered and bucolic landscapes of lowland England have become symbolic not merely of the English countryside but also of traditional rural and small-town social values and cultural norms.

93. Orvieto, Italy. Traditional neighbourhood names and emblems reinforce residents' sense of place.

93. Citta di Castello, Italy. Graffiti (in this case by Fiorentina fans after Liverpool had defeated AC Milan in the 2005 European Cup final) often reflects a town's sense of identity.

94. Cultural landscapes. The Umbrian landscape has the well-groomed, obedient look of earth that has been tended for centuries. Elegant cypress trees stand out against the silvery-green of olive trees on the hills around scattered farms and villas.

95. Umbria, Italy. Regional landscapes are an important component of the identity and sense of place of small towns. Seen from almost every part of Orvieto, the Umbrian landscape, with its patchwork of olive groves, wheat fields and vineyards – the customary Mediterranean trinity of oil, bread, and wine – is stitched together by seams of tall cypresses that shade the tracks leading to the farmhouses hidden from the roads.

Affect and Intersubjectivity

Along with the legacy of built form, then, every town with any depth of history at all inherits the foundation for a subjective sense of place and a complex of intersubjective meanings. As a result, towns are shot through with – and continually generate – *affect*: people's emotional responses to their environment, to each other, to the rhythms of the town's economic, social, and cultural activities. Affect is often overlooked as a component of liveability and sustainability because it is difficult to quantify or classify. Affect is generated not only from the meanings ascribed to buildings and spaces, but also from the happy shouts of children at play (Figs. 96 and 97); the conviviality of a farmers' market; "the way that the sun, low in the east, plays early morning tricks in the streets, gilding unexpected features and casting improbable shadows";[81] the way that moonlight "transforms the town into a backdrop for an opera, accentuating the shadows, making each colonnade a scene for drama, every street corner a romantic trysting place."[82] Affect can be negative, too: generated by the rumble of heavy trucks through the town centre, the antisocial behaviour of groups of teenagers, or the depressing air of a derelict factory.

96. Orvieto, Italy. Small spaces are commandeered by neighbourhood children for impromptu games; the affect is one of vitality.

97. Diss, England. Parks and public open spaces combine relaxation and serenity with playfulness.

98. Bellinzona, Switzerland. Open-air dining and sidewalk cafés lend an atmosphere of conviviality.

Rhythms, Sequences, and Synchronies

The rhythms, sequences, and synchronies of a town are the fundamental regularities through which inhabitants frame and order their experience, which in turn contributes to their quality of life. People's experience of everyday routines in familiar settings leads to a pool of shared meanings – intersubjectivity. The way in which we make sense of our own actions and the actions of others – and the way we generate meaning in the world – is rooted in routinised, day-to-day practices that occupy a place in our minds somewhere between the conscious and the unconscious. Recursivity, the continual reproduction of individual and social practices through routine actions (time-space routinisation), contributes to the development of social systems and social structures in particular locales.[83]

Respect for seasonality and the traditional rhythms of community life propagates recurring and interlocking patterns of events that make for cultural transactions and public sociability in the public realm. Elements of daily rhythms – mid-morning grocery shopping with a stop for coffee, the *aperitivo* en route from work to home, and the after-dinner stroll – are all critical to the density of routine encounters and shared experiences that underpin the intersubjectivity that is the basis both for a sense of place and for a structure of feeling within a community (Figs. 98–99). The same is true of elements of weekly rhythms, such as street markets and farmers' markets; and of seasonal rhythms, such as food festivals, craft shows, and arts festivals. These rhythms, in turn, depend on certain kinds of spaces and places – not only streets, squares, and public open spaces but also third places: the sidewalk cafés, pubs, post offices, drug stores, corner stores, and family-run trattoria that are the loci of routine activities and socio-cultural transactions. The nature and frequency of routine encounters and shared experiences depend a great deal on attributes of these spaces and places. To generate positive affect, urban form should be permeable enough to generate casual encounters and should facilitate solitary as well as informal social activities. Third places should accommodate "characters," "regulars," and newcomers as well as routine patrons and, like public spaces, should facilitate casual encounters as well as settings for sustained conversations.

Life in small towns is framed by daily, weekly, and seasonal rhythms and patterns and sequences of movement that are all underpinned by urban form. On workdays, the regular pulse and steady hum of traffic lays a base rhythm to the town's daily business. The movement of people through the town is regulated by the commonplace rhythms of work, shopping, and school. For some, there are eddies of slowness in otherwise faster-paced routines: the traditional *Stammtisch* in German towns, for example – regular but informal get-togethers

99. Abbiategrasso, Italy. Routine meetings and encounters in the semi-public settings of "third places" help to frame the rhythm of a town. Early evening is a time for pre-dinner drinks and casual conversation.

100. Marktplatz, Waldkirch, Germany. On market days, twice a week, the market place is crowded with tables and stalls. People come from surrounding areas not only to shop but to greet friends and to make business arrangements.

101. Cremona, Italy. On market days the vendors arrive an hour or so early, at about 7:00 a.m., unfolding what seems like whole stores or supermarket aisles from specially made trucks and wagons. Like many contemporary markets, there are extensive sections of housewares and hardware, clothing, footwear, and gardening tools.

102. Aylsham, England. In a large saleyard near the town centre there is a weekly auction market of antiques, books, pictures, furniture, farm equipment, and household goods that attracts people from kilometres around, lending the town an air of urgency and anticipation.

of groups of friends who have a favourite table or booth reserved at their preferred third place. Evenings, especially summer evenings, resonate a little more with the traditional ways and pace of life that lend identity to the town for its inhabitants, narrower streets and small squares and piazzas slowly filling with people for an hour or two. In Italy, there is the evening *passegglata*, which serves as a way to see friends and relatives, put on fine clothes, and meet potential boyfriends or girlfriends. Knots of teenagers gather, disappear, and reappear; men get together in groups of three or four for a coffee or a glass of grappa; couples stroll along the main streets; and dog owners take their companions for a walk.

Weekends bring shopping and recreation, and for many towns Saturday is a market day. Market places are arguably the hearth of affect and intersubjectivity in small towns (Figs. 100–102). During market times, they provide a setting for conviviality and casual interaction, and a direct connection, through the produce stalls, to the surrounding region. Outside of market times, they provide a nodal space and a pivotal point of reference in people's mental maps of their town. In traditional market towns, they connect the present with past. In other towns, they cater to the growing hunger for public spaces that are egalitarian and unfettered by corporate enclosure, places that provide an antidote to themed and commodified spaces of the fast world.

Throughout the year, daily and seasonal rhythms are punctuated by seasonal fairs and festivals. The local traditions, local crafts, and local produce featured in these fairs and festivals have been augmented in many towns by recently established festivals designed to boost tourism and economic development. As a result, there is a seasonal calendar of jazz, blues, rock, folk music, opera, and drama that flickers from one town to another. The seasons themselves add their own rhythm, and for towns that have been able to retain a significant link to regional agriculture, there is the added dimension of the seasonality of cuisine (Figs. 103–107). Take, for example, the towns of Umbria, where the high point of the culinary calendar is the summer season of *scorzone* (black truffles). Summer is also the season for fresh aromatic herbs such as marjoram and fennel and fresh vegetables of all kinds, including arugula, asparagus, aubergine, radicchio, endive,

103. Orvieto, Italy. Saturday is market day and the weekly meeting place of the town's folk. From 7:00 a.m. to 11:30 a.m. the market is in full swing, sprawling out from Piazza Ventinove Marzo. Stallholders sell fruits and vegetables, eggs and cheese, honey, meat, clothes and crafts, fish and flowers, local wines, and breads and pastries still warm from the oven.

104. Orvieto, Italy. Beans are an autumn specialty.

hot peppers, sweet peppers, *fagioli sgranati* (shelled fresh beans), and purple artichokes. After the autumn harvest, Umbria's markets and menus are replenished with hams, salamis, and special sausages prepared in local cellars. Pork is an Umbrian specialty, the hogs traditionally having been fed on the abundant acorns of the region. *Mazzafegati* (sausages made from hog's liver, orange peel, pine nuts, raisins and sugar), *colombaccio* (wood pigeon), and sweet-and-sour ox tongue are particular favourites. Autumn also brings field mushrooms, white truffles, replenishments of lentils and *fagioli*, fresh-pressed olive oil, and flour for the Umbrian *tagliatelle* and *umbricelli* pastas. Late autumn is the season for *fave dei morti* (special cakes with almonds) and *rocciata* (cakes with raisins, nuts, and almonds). With these cakes it is traditional to drink *vin santo* (an aromatic and sweet home-made wine). Local wineries produce white wines made from Trebbiano grapes. A winter specialty of the region is *torta al testo*, a hand-made bread stuffed with ham or sausage and herbs prepared in olive oil, and cooked on a special marble stone in a wood-burning oven. Christmastime brings the appearance of traditional *pinoccate* cakes of

sugar and pine-nuts and *torciglione* cakes with almonds. At Easter there are cheese pies, cakes and *beccicuta* (salted or sweet pasta and cooked in the oven) and *ciaramicola*, a cake with egg icing.

Authenticity

The changing nature of contemporary towns, influenced inevitably by standardisation, rationalisation, and globalisation, tends to give urban dwellers a sense of time that is increasingly linear rather than cyclical or seasonal. Affect and sense of place are also influenced by the more recent impositions of the fast world. The widespread appearance of superstores, supermarkets, franchised fast-food and clothing chains, and generic buildings and storefronts are seen by many as undermining towns' distinctive sense of place and introducing an affect of indifference. Martin Heidegger, writing in the 1920s, anticipated that rationalism, standardisation, mass production, and mass values would attenuate people's capacity for dwelling and for constructing a strong sense of place. Towns become inauthentic and placeless. This can produce feelings of being strangely out of place while in everyday settings – *Unheimlich*, in Freud's terms. Contemporary social science frames the process in terms of "time-space distanciation" – the process whereby remote (rather than face-to-face) interaction has become an increasingly dominant feature of human life. Through time-space distanciation, social systems that were previously distinctive have become connected, interdependent, and convergent. Time and space become "emptied out," with the result that people become "disembedded" from their localities.[84] The inevitable result, it is suggested, is that the authenticity of place is subverted. One consequence of this has been the prominence of nostalgia in postmodern sensibilities. Similarly, the attenuation of the traditional rhythms of town life, displaced by a fast-paced perspective, "our own lives unreeling out behind us like cigarette smoke,"[85] has also been a precondition of nostalgia.

Yet "authenticity" itself is an elusive concept, especially when applied to something as complex and dynamic as a town. Economist Virginia Postrel has pointed to three common interpretations of authenticity. First is authenticity as purity: the original form of something, natural and functional. Second is authenticity as tradition, grounded in custom. Third is authenticity as aura, witness to the wear and tear and adjustments resulting from the passage of time.[86] In contradistinction to these interpretations is the idea of authenticity as referential: relating to or honouring some other period. This is a product of the postindustrial shift toward an "experience economy" based on the commodification, staging, and mediated memorability of places and events.[87] As we shall see in Chapter 5, all of these interpretations of authenticity are relevant to contemporary attempts to address small-town sustainability through urban design.

105. Orvieto, Italy. Artichokes on sale at the farmers' market in autumn.

106. Orvieto, Italy. Chestnuts on sale at the farmers' market in autumn.

107. Orvieto, Italy. Pumpkins, potatoes, and tomatoes on sale at the farmers' market in autumn.

"Wirsberg – seit 2007 Mitglied in der Internationalen Vereinigung der lebenswerten Städte Cittaslow/Slow City"

SLOWCITY

108. Wirsberg, Germany.

5

Sustainability by Design

Urban design is a key component of small town sustainability: It can contribute to liveability and sense of place by enhancing both the aesthetics and the functionality of places. The case is made succinctly by the International Making Cities Liveable organisation (IMCL) – a loose network of city officials, practitioners, and scholars in architecture, urban design, planning, and urban affairs, health and social sciences, and the arts. According to Suzanne Lennard of IMCL, good urban design can not only "enhance the well-being of inhabitants of towns," but also "strengthen community, improve social and physical health, and increase civic engagement."[88] The Making Cities Liveable movement promotes the idea of "True Urbanism," based on "time-tested principles" that emphasise the importance of the quality of public spaces (especially squares and market places); of human-scale architecture with mixed-use structures that accommodate both retail and residential functions; of a compact urban fabric of blocks, streets, and squares; and of outdoor cafés and restaurants, farmers' markets, and community festivals. True Urbanism seeks to create "places of short distances" where balanced transportation planning makes possible commuting via pedestrian networks, bicycle networks, traffic-quietened streets, and public transportation. The Making Cities Liveable movement also places great emphasis on the inherited identity of towns – their "DNA" – and seeks to promote public art and the idea of the built environment itself as a work of art.

Designs for Liveability

The ideal of True Urbanism draws on a broad intellectual platform. Within the design professions there has been a long history of engagement with the notion of liveability. Since the mid-twentieth century the discourse has been framed largely around various reactions to the dominant paradigm of Modernist design. Indeed, as early as the 1920s Lewis Mumford, following Patrick Geddes's writings at the turn of the century, had argued for the preservation of regional architectural traditions in the face of rapid industrialisation. In the 1950s a "Townscape Movement" emerged in Britain as a reaction to the sculptural architecture of Modernism and the lack of urbanity and human scale in British New Towns. The movement stressed the "art of relationship" among elements of the urban landscape and the desirability of the "recovery of place" through pictorial composition: unfolding sequences of street scenes, buildings that enclose intimate public spaces, and variety and idiosyncrasy in built form. These were sentiments that were soon echoed elsewhere, though mostly in the form of "paper architecture."

In 1960 Kevin Lynch, on the planning faculty at the Massachusetts Institute of Technology, introduced the notion of the "legibility" of townscapes, asserting that people's perceptions of the built environment are dominated by a few key elements: landmarks, paths, nodes, edges, and districts (Figs. 109–111). In the 1970s Christopher Alexander, an English architect who taught at Berkeley, California, sought to identify a "language" of patterns among elements of built form and public spaces, the rationale being that a knowledge of such patterns might be useful in imbuing urban design with "timeless" sensibilities. Their methodologies were naïve and unreliable, and their logic was based on a simplistic kind of environmental determinism (built-form stimulus→social and cultural response). Nevertheless, their results were unquestioned and their work has been influential, largely because it lent an analytic dimension to a growing concern for the qualitative aspects of urban landscapes.[89]

A rather different reaction came from the neorationalist movement, led by the Italian scholar-practitioner Aldo Rossi. His book *The Architecture of the City*, published in 1966, sought to identify

109. Perth, Scotland. High street, an example of the kind of pathway that Kevin Lynch saw as a key element of the legibility of the built environment.

110. Bellinzona, Switzerland. The Castelgrande, a prominent landmark that is pivotal to people's mental maps of the town.

111. Todi, Italy. Like many hill towns, Todi has a clearly demarcated edge condition.

various "types" of architecture appropriate to economic and geographic context as an alternative to the totalising models of Modernist architecture. Neorationalists saw the built environment as a "theatre of memory" and hoped to identify "the fundamental types of habitat: the street, the arcade, the square, the yard, the quarter, the colonnade, the avenue, the centre, the nucleus, the crown, the radius, the knot […] So that the city can be walked through. So that it becomes a text again."[90] During the 1970s these ideas were pursued by the Movement for the Reconstruction of the European City, with Léon Krier as its chief exponent. Krier was an advocate of urban design based on identifiable, functionally integrated quarters and of architecture with the proportions, morphology, and craftsmanship of the pre-industrial era, with set-piece ensembles of buildings. He was influenced by Tönnies's sociology and the conviction that small towns provide the preconditions for *Gemeinschaft*, the most intense form of community.[91]

In 1964, the Museum of Modern Art in New York put on an exhibition entitled Architecture Without Architects, which greatly stimulated an interest in vernacular architecture.[92] In France, the impulse to regenerate traditional urban qualities resulted in "Provincial Urbanism," aimed at creating "the traces, the arrangements of streets and plazas, the types of housing (and especially individual houses with yards), the perspectives, the source of architectural composition which made our cities so pleasing, particularly our provincial cities before being submerged, first by the growth of suburban tract developments, then by the brutal push of the 'grand ensembles' with their density and severe geometry."[93] Several developments in this vein gained international attention. One was Port Grimaud, designed and developed by François Spoerry near Saint Tropez in 1973 to resemble a fishermen's village. In Italy, the inaugural international architectural exhibition of the Venice Biennale in 1980 took the theme of "The Presence of the Past: The End of Prohibition," seeking to recast urban design theory by "reawakening the imaginary." In the United States, the advocacy of "contextualism," as advocated by architectural theorist Colin Rowe, placed special emphasis on drawing upon all of inherited elements of the built environment, stressing the importance of the street, the axis, and the role of building mass as a definer of urban space.[94]

One way or another, history and geography were re-entering the discourse on urban design, and by the 1990s Vincent Scully, America's most venerable architectural historian, was able to assert that "[T]he most important movement in architecture today is the revival of vernacular and classical traditions and their reintegration into the mainstream of modern architecture in its fundamental aspect: the structure of communities, the building of towns."[95] The movement initially found expression in what proponents called Traditional Neighbourhood Development (TND), an attempt to codify tract development in such a way as to create the look and feel of small-town, pre-World War II settings in which pedestrian movement and social interaction are privileged over automobile use. American architects Andres Duany and Elizabeth Plater-Zyberk are generally regarded as the progenitors of TND in which a "traditional" small-town neighbourhood flavour is pursued through prescriptive design codes. The typical result is housing that mimics pre-World War II American housing styles. In a similarly motivated attempt to provide guidelines for a new typology of suburban development, San Francisco-based architect Peter Calthorpe developed the concept of the "Pedestrian Pocket." Harking back to the days of streetcar suburbs, Calthorpe's idea was for higher-density suburbs to be situated within walking distance of public transportation hubs. Thus, pedestrian pockets would become part of a regional scheme of "Transit-Oriented Development," or TOD.

Together, these ideas gave rise in the 1990s to a "New Urbanism," founded on the assertion that liveability can be propagated through the codification of design principles based on precedents and typologies derived from observations of patterns exhibited in traditional communities (Figs. 112–114). The canon was established by Duany and Plater-Zyberk, whose firm, DPZ, drew up a "Lexicon of New Urbanism" and shared it with the Congress for the New Urbanism, the movement's coordinating network. The tenets and rhetoric of New Urbanism are a derivative melange of ideas and impulses that go back to intellectuals' utopias of the nineteenth century and that include elements of:

- The City Beautiful movement (which was based on a rather authoritarian and regressive aspiration of creating moral and social order through the arrangement and symbolism of the built environment);
- John Nolen's insistence of urban design as a way to recover classical civic ideals;
- Patrick Geddes's idea of a "natural region";
- Clarence Perry's "neighbourhood unit" idea;
- Raymond Unwin and Barry Parker's assertion of traditional and vernacular design;
- The precedents of the garden suburbs of the late nineteenth century and the master suburbs of 1920s;
- The British Townscape movement;
- Christopher Alexander's notion of pattern language;
- Kevin Lynch's concept of legibility; and
- The prescriptions and inclinations of neorationalism, Provincial Urbanism, and contextualism.[96]

The physical configuration of streets is key to New Urbanism, as is the role of building mass as a definer of urban space, the need for clear patterns among elements of built form and public spaces, and the importance of having identifiable, functionally integrated quarters.[97] The belief is that civic architecture, pedestrian-oriented streets, and a traditional vocabulary of urban design (with a morphology that includes boulevards, perimeter blocks, plazas, and monuments) can act as catalysts of sociability and community. This is to be achieved, according to the Congress for the New Urbanism, through a sort of painting-by-numbers for urban designers: detailed prescriptive codes and conventions, embedded in a series of regulatory documents – a Regulating Plan, Urban Regulations, Architectural Regulations, Street Types, and Landscape Regulations – provide the template for New Urbanist developments.

New Urbanism has enlivened interest in urban design and brought fresh ideas to what had become routinised and bureaucratised issues of land use and planning. It has also reinforced sense of place, liveability, sustainability, and quality of life as important policy issues, and helped to resurrect the idea of a definable public interest. Nevertheless, and in spite of its strong commercial appeal to developers of new subdivisions, New Urbanism has come in for a great deal of criticism, especially by social scientists. New Urbanism's fondness for neotraditional design has been characterised as a form of cultural reductiveness that results in inauthentic settings – jejune and meretricious. Its practitioners and advocates are portrayed as an architectural derriere garde, trading on antique truisms that have been naïvely combined across time and space to form a New Age urbanism that is part conventional wisdom and part fuzzy poetic, resonant but meaningless. The distinctively hagiographic and shamelessly self-referential literature propagated by the Congress for the New Urbanism has not helped.[98]

Critics have also seen neotraditional urban designs as being inherently socially regressive. Sociologist Richard Sennett, for example, describes them as "[…] exercises in withdrawal from a complex world, deploying self-consciously 'traditional' architecture that bespeaks a mythic communal coherence and shared identity in the past." He

describes their designers as "artists of claustrophobia" and concludes that "place making based on exclusion, sameness, and nostalgia is socially poisonous and psychologically useless."[99] The principal underlying weakness of New Urbanism, however, is the conceit of environmental determinism and the privileging of spatial form over social process. In the prescriptive reasoning of New Urbanism, design codes become behaviour codes. "Good" (i.e., New Urbanist) design equals community, civility, and sense of place; "bad" design equals placelessness, ennui, and deviant behaviour. This, of course, is a chimera. Place is socially constructed and the relationships between people and their environments are complex, reflexive, and recursive.

The lesson for small towns is that while urban design can contribute to liveability and sustainability, it cannot determine either one. "True urbanism," observes Seattle-based architect, city planner, and urban designer Mark Hinshaw (seemingly unaware of the Making Cities Liveable movement's use of the term, but offering it in the same spirit), is "not the product of a singular vision" but, rather, emerges "from the collective decisions of many

114. Celebration, Florida, USA. Planned according to New Urbanist principles, the town has a grid plan for more than 8,000 residential units and a town centre that includes apartments above stores, a school, a branch college campus, and a hotel as well as office space. Architectural conformity in Celebration is ensured by a seventy-page pattern book of house designs, while the town's many "traditions" have been imagineered by the Disney Corporation, the town's developer.

organisations, associations, and government bodies." True urbanist communities, he argues, "are constantly evolving, infilling, and re-developing, with a broad mixture of architectural styles and sensibilities […] They have a gritty urbanity that values variety over uniformity."[100] The focus of urban design should be "on the diversity and activity which help to create successful urban places, and, in particular, on how well the physical milieu supports the functions and activities taking place there. […] With this concept comes the notion of urban design as the design and management of the 'public realm' – defined as the public face of buildings, the spaces between frontages, the activities taking place in and between these spaces, and the managing of these activities, all of which are affected by the uses of the buildings themselves."[101]

113. Seaside, Florida, USA. Established as a resort town on Florida's Gulf coast in 1982, Seaside quickly became an icon of New Urbanism. Laid out with a central square, a grid street plan modified with radial-concentric boulevards recalling City Beautiful and Garden City principles; an urban code controlling the interdependency between road width, landscaping, lot size, and housing type; and an architectural code drawing on Southern vernacular houses in pastel colours, Seaside was very photogenic.

114. Poundbury, England. Built on land owned by the Duchy of Cornwall on the outskirts of Dorchester, Poundbury has been designed based on new urbanist principles, with neotraditional building styles. Common areas are maintained by a management company to which all residents belong.

Kirchsteigfeld, Germany

Kirchsteigfeld is an entirely new development, explicitly modeled on the traditional morphology of small towns of central Europe. Located on the edge of Potsdam, just 36 kilometres from Berlin, Kirchsteigfeld has a population of around 7,500 on a compact site. Built in the 1990s adjacent to modernist apartment blocks dating from East Germany's socialist era, Kirchsteigfeld has been developed from a master plan established by the architectural firm of Rob Krier and Christoph Kohl.[102] Their plan ensured architectural variety by assigning different architects to the design of adjacent buildings. Most of the 2,300 housing units are social housing, supported by public subsidies. They are framed in medium-rise, high-density structures that are organised around courtyards with communal gardens, echoing in a larger and more spacious format the nineteenth-century tenement buildings of the region. The street network is punctuated by a pond and a linear water feature, its edges carefully landscaped and furnished with scalloped benches.

The generous landscaping of the town recalls garden city projects of the early twentieth century, such as Germany's Margarethenhöhe, and in fact the town's most distinctive features are its open spaces. Each section of the town has its own uniquely configured open space. The most striking of these is the teardrop-shaped park (bafflingly named Horseshoe Square) in the north part of the town. Surrounded by apartment buildings, surfaced with gravel, and planted with formal rows of trees, it is reminiscent of the Place Dauphine in Paris. Paired with a rondelle, a small space at the centre of a circular arrangement of six-story apartment buildings, the two spaces form an exclamation point in plan view. At street level, the tightly enclosed arena of the circular space gives way through a narrow opening to the more expansive vista of the central axis. More important functionally is the central market square, which has a landmark church and a grouping of retailing and commercial services and public institutions, including a community centre, a branch library, a high school, an elementary school, and two day nurseries.

Barely fifteen years old, to some observers the town "still feels like a set piece, a stage set in which it is not yet obvious that the quality of community will match the thoughtful design

115. Kirchsteigfeld town centre.

of most of its constituent pieces. Some of the beautifully landscaped communal areas seem to have been designed more for display than use."[103] Preliminary responses from residents, however, indicate otherwise. There is widespread recognition of the importance of the public squares and the way they frame urban spaces and lend identity and a sense of place. Residents "all cherish the attractive views the landscaped interiors offer from inside their apartments, and second, everybody recognises the possibilities for communal gatherings which these places offer."[104] The semi-public interior spaces of the blocks are used by children to move between houses, and the play areas in these spaces – safe and easy to supervise even from within the apartments – are highly valued by parents. Meanwhile, the central market square is universally identified by residents as a focal point for meeting neighbours and as important for the community as a whole, since it is the location of nearly all special events. Residents perceive both its location (especially in relation to nearby shops and public services) and its size as important.

116. Kirchsteigfeld. Most of the town consists of three- to five-story apartment buildings with colourful façades. Communal gardens inside each block provide green spaces, with access to parking tucked discreetly to the side.

117. Horseshoe Square. Each section of Kirchsteigfeld has its own public open space, each designed in a different shape and size, intended to foster the development of a very small-scale sense of place and identity.

118. Kirchsteigfeld. The town echoes earlier high-density urban patterns, with a well-defined network of relatively narrow streets with lively façades and generous courtyards. This photograph shows the landscaped central axis, with the adjacent rondelle and Horseshoe Park surrounded by mid-rise courtyard buildings.

Street Life: Content, Movement, and Conviviality

Urban design, then, is not simply about form and morphology. It is about content, context, and the capacity to foster conviviality, rhythm, and movement. As we noted in Chapter 1, successful places have plenty of opportunities for informal, casual meetings; friendly third places; street markets; a variety of comfortable places to sit, wait, and people-watch; and, above all, a sense of identity, belonging, authenticity, and vitality. Architectural theorist Nan Ellin has expressed this in terms of what she calls "Integral Urbanism." The key attributes of integral urbanism, she suggests, are *hybridity, connectivity, porosity, authenticity,* and *vulnerability*. Hybridity and connectivity depend on juxtaposition, simultaneity, and the combination and linking of urban functions, connecting people and activities at key points of intensity and along thresholds between districts. Porosity depends on the visual and physical integration of the historic and the contemporary, of nature and the built environment, and of the social, cultural, and physical dimensions of a town. Authenticity depends on both large-scale and small-scale interventions that are responsive to community needs and tastes and that are rooted in local climate, topography, history, and culture. Vulnerability depends on a willingness on the part of urban planners and designers to relinquish control, to let things happen, and to allow for serendipity. These qualities place a premium on process rather than outcome, and on the symbiotic relationships between people and places. The goal of integral urbanism is to ensure places that are "in flow," where their physical attributes and people's experiences of them are inseparable and reliant upon one another. "Encountering a place that is not in flow," observes Ellin, "the French typically remark that it lacks soul (*Il n'a pas d'âme*). Americans tend to say that it lacks character. Places that are in flow are characterized by the French as *animé* (animated, spirited, or soulful) and by Americans as lively."[105]

From this perspective, many small towns have the advantage of a legacy of built-in qualities that derive from their origins as market towns and central places in pre-industrial, premodern conditions, with buildings at a human scale and streets and squares evolved in response to people moving about on foot and needing to stay outdoors for a good deal of the time. Crucial to small town sustainability, therefore, is that urban design first does no harm to a town's inherited characteristics and advantages. Second, urban design should seek to enhance, strengthen and protect these characteristics – preferably in the spirit of integral urbanism.

Content: Townscapes

The existing urban fabric constitutes an ensemble of structures and spaces that present a series of townscapes, viewed from different vantage points in and around the town. As geographer Edward Relph observes, "[…] [T]ownscapes are simultaneously the contexts of temporal experiences and subject to temporality. They are the settings for diurnal, weekly, and seasonal patterns of human activity, the backdrops and reference points for recollections and expectations. They are an essential component of the geography of memory. And in a manner broadly similar to that of human life, albeit at many different and overlapping tempos, landscapes have rhythms of creation, change, and decay."[106] Townscapes must be understood and appreciated in the context of a town's economic, social, and cultural functions, past and present. An understanding of the town's role in relation to its surrounding cultural landscape is also important.

A first step toward urban design from the perspective of small town sustainability is to identify the key elements of townscapes. This can be undertaken formally and methodically in the form of a townscape audit that describes the physical and environmental characteristics of a town, identifies the elements that help define the town's character, and pinpoints developments that diminish or erode the quality of the place (Fig. 119). The audit can then form the basis for developing a set of guiding principles for developers and identifying priority areas for improvement and regeneration.[107] Nevertheless, townscapes will always require an aesthetic sensibility on the part of the observer. The work of town planners Gordon Cullen and Edmund Bacon provides some key insights regarding those aspects of urban form that generally elicit positive responses. Cullen, for example, describes the way

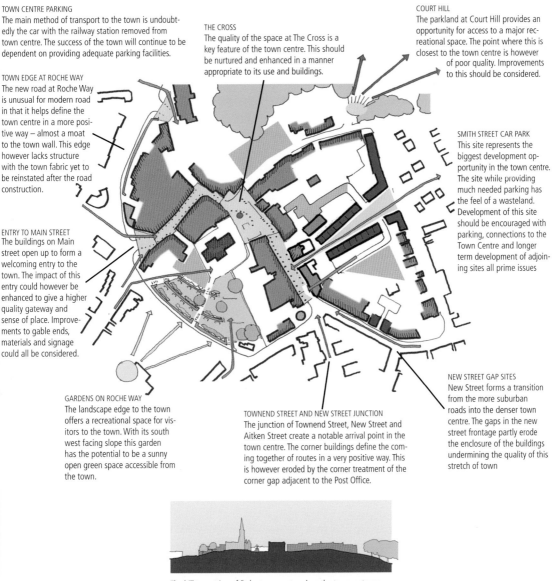

TOWN CENTRE PARKING
The main method of transport to the town is undoubtedly the car with the railway station removed from town centre. The success of the town will continue to be dependent on providing adequate parking facilities.

THE CROSS
The quality of the space at The Cross is a key feature of the town centre. This should be nurtured and enhanced in a manner appropriate to its use and buildings.

COURT HILL
The parkland at Court Hill provides an opportunity for access to a major recreational space. The point where this is closest to the town centre is however of poor quality. Improvements to this should be considered.

TOWN EDGE AT ROCHE WAY
The new road at Roche Way is unusual for modern road in that it helps define the town centre in a more positive way – almost a moat to the town wall. This edge however lacks structure with the town fabric yet to be reinstated after the road construction.

SMITH STREET CAR PARK
This site represents the biggest development opportunity in the town centre. The site while providing much needed parking has the feel of a wasteland. Development of this site should be encouraged with parking, connections to the Town Centre and longer term development of adjoining sites all prime issues

ENTRY TO MAIN STREET
The buildings on Main street open up to form a welcoming entry to the town. The impact of this entry could however be enhanced to give a higher quality gateway and sense of place. Improvements to gable ends, materials and signage could all be considered.

GARDENS ON ROCHE WAY
The landscape edge to the town offers a recreational space for visitors to the town. With its south west facing slope this garden has the potential to be a sunny open green space accessible from the town.

TOWNEND STREET AND NEW STREET JUNCTION
The junction of Townend Street, New Street and Aitken Street create a notable arrival point in the town centre. The corner buildings define the coming together of routes in a very positive way. This is however eroded by the corner treatment of the corner gap adjacent to the Post Office.

NEW STREET GAP SITES
New Street forms a transition from the more suburban roads into the denser town centre. The gaps in the new street frontage partly erode the enclosure of the buildings undermining the quality of this stretch of town

The hilltop setting of Dalry town centre gives the town a strong sense of place

119. Dalry townscape audit. North Ayrshire Council commissioned a townscape study that examined the existing character, qualities and activities in Dalry. This included an examination of the building fabric, materials, land use and history. Key areas of the town centre were identified as making a significant impact on the activity and townscape qualities of the town centre. By addressing these key points, the town hopes to identify priorities for major improvements.

After ARP Lorimer Architects for North Ayrshire Council.

in which "closed vistas," "narrows," "projection and recession," and "deflection" lend vitality and visual pleasure. Closed vistas occur when buildings or monuments are visible at the end of a street, providing a punctuating point of reference. Narrows occur when buildings are crowded together, with a low ratio of street width to building height, so that there is a strong sense of enclosure and an una-voidable nearness of detail (Fig. 120). Deflection occurs when line-of-sight to key structures is oblique rather than at right angles. Projection and recession occurs when irregular setbacks and street configurations provide an intricacy of detail that catches the eye.[108] Bacon emphasises the aesthetics of skylines, the way that buildings meet the ground, the way that key points on buildings and monu-ments make for pleasing compositions, the prosce-nium effect of the juxtaposition of different-sized structures, and the sense of depth and perspective, ascent and descent, and convexity and concavity in the spatial arrangement of built form.[109]

These insights tally with Gestalt psychology, which stresses the importance of being able to mentally group the various elements in a visual field into a synoptic construct with visual coherence. In this context, sociologist Peter Smith argues that there are four fundamental dimensions to people's capac-ity for aesthetic appreciation. The first is the ability to sense pattern amid complex visual elements. The second is the capacity to appreciate visual rhythms: groupings of elements that lend emphasis, accent, interval, and direction. Third is the ability to recognise "balance" in the mixture of shapes, textures, and colours within a visual field. Finally there is sensitivity to harmony in shapes, propor-tions, and perspective.[110] In terms of urban design, the attributes of built form that lend themselves best to these innate capacities include orientation, closure, continuity, similarity, and proximity.[111]

In the context of small town sustainability, these insights can inform policy and practice with regard to both conservation and change. Any approach to urban design must also be attentive to ques-tions of scale. In small towns, three of the most important scales involve the big-picture scale of the town's setting in the landscape, the meso-scale of the town's principal public spaces, and the small-scale detailing of public infrastructure.

120. Hersbruck, Germany. *Prager Straße*, the town's ancient routeway to the east and an example of Cullen's "narrows" condition.

Setting and Landscape

As we noted in Chapter 4, the relationship between the town and the surrounding countryside is an important part of the identity and sense of place in small towns. It follows that a town's visibility in the landscape and its contribution to the cultural landscape are key areas to address in planning for sustainability. They should condition the scope and nature of expansion, especially with reference to the height, massing, and scale of future development.

Topography and landscape help frame the town and are an important part of its identity. But it is not just that the surrounding countryside can usually be seen from many parts of the town; the converse is also often true – the approaches to the town present glimpses of the townscape or even a view of the town's skyline. Clearly, much depends on topography. The townscapes and skylines of hill towns are visible from afar, and from almost every direction, offering figure-ground, massing, and profile as well as skyline. The profiles of towns on the flat, open plains of the Netherlands, the American Midwest, and the Po Valley in Italy also offer iconic silhouettes. On the other hand, towns nestled in valleys present themselves suddenly at their approaches, their overall morphology hidden unless viewed from hillsides above.

Much also depends on the direction of approach, as illustrated by planner Stephen Owen's diagrams of Ludlow, England (Figs. 121–123). These diagrams show that the relationships between the components of Ludlow's profile change as the observer moves along routes through the approaches to the town:
"In the northern part of the arc, and particularly from viewpoints on lower-lying land close to the town, the profile has a rather narrow base, the castle dominates the skyline, and the figure-ground is not clear. Then, as the observer moves southwards and eastwards through the arc and up the slope, the profile broadens and deepens, with the castle and St Laurence church sharing dominance of the skyline, and a clear figure-ground emerges between the town and the Clee Hills in the background, particularly from more distant viewpoints. Finally, towards the easternmost part of the arc – as a combined result of increased distance, the shape of land and the presence of vegetation – the castle disappears from the skyline, which is dominated by the tower of St Laurence's church. The gridiron plan of the mediaeval town on the gentler south-facing slope now constitutes the body of the profile from more elevated viewpoints, with Mill Street and Broad Street cutting gashes into the profile, and the figure-ground dissolving."[112]

121. Ludlow, England. These diagrams illustrate the way that a town's visible structures change as people move through the surrounding landscape. After Owen, S. "Classic English Hill Towns: Ways of Looking at the External Appearance of Settlements." *Journal of Urban Design*, Vol. 12. No. 1, 2007, p. 111.

122. Ludlow, England.
After Owen, S. "Classic English Hill Towns," *op. cit.*

123. Ludlow, England.
After Owen, S. "Classic English Hill Towns," *op. cit.*

Public Spaces

The public spaces of a town – streets, alleyways, squares, market places, parks, and open spaces – are key to integral urbanism and place making. The spaces around and between buildings not only cater to the movement of vehicles and people but also function as meeting places and are the focus of a variety of social and commercial activities. One of the greatest legacies of European urbanisation is the traditional market place, town square, or piazza. Surrounded by buildings, with small entrances and exits leading in and out, these spaces provide a sense of inclusion and enclosure, a common shared space that lends focus and identity to a town. Most are lined with a mixture of shops and cafés, complemented by important civic and religious structures that are part of the contiguous urban fabric of the square.

The classic square, as in Vigevano, Italy (population 63,700), is self-contained and completely enclosed, interrupted only by the streets leading into it (Figs. 125–127). The plan of the square is based on regular geometric forms and the façades of the surrounding buildings are based on a rhythm of repeating elements. Another common format is the "dominated square," as in the Piazza del Popolo in Todi, Italy (population 17,399), where the space and surrounding structures are focused on a key building – in this case, the Duomo (Figs. 124, 129). "Nuclear" squares, as in Chichester, England (population 25,000), are dominated by a single central structure (in this case a market cross); conversely, "grouped" squares, linked by short streets (as in Perugia, Italy; population 162,000) or by a dominant building (as in Hersbruck, Germany; population 12,500), allow for functional differentiation as well as aesthetic coherence (Figs. 128, 130–132).[113]

Public open space is another important legacy of European urbanisation. Most medieval towns had an area of open space on which the townspeople had rights of grazing and collecting fuel, and which they used for recreation. Some also had archery butts where the men of the town held target practice. Many of these spaces survive as public open spaces, converted into parks or recreation grounds. Some towns also have more formal pleasure gardens and arboretums, added in the eighteenth or nineteenth century to provide promenades and landscaped settings for socialisation and entertainment. These are often settings for monuments and statuary that are specific to the town, *aides memoire* to civic identity and sense of place.

124. Todi, Italy. The Piazza del Popolo.

125. Vigevano, Italy.
Widely considered to be one of the finest piazzas in Italy, the Piazza Ducale is a product of early Renaissance town planning, designed by Bramante for Ludovico Maria Sforza in 1492–93 as a noble forecourt to the Castello Sforzesco. Unified by the arcades that completely surround the square, the piazza now provides an important social space for the citizens of the town.

126. Vigevano, Italy.
Piazza Ducale.

127. Vigevano, Italy.
Piazza Ducale.

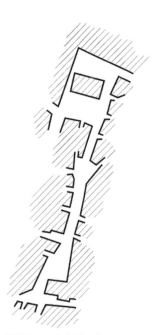

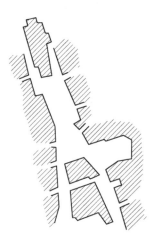

129. Todi, Italy. Piazza del Popolo and the Piazza Garibaldi.

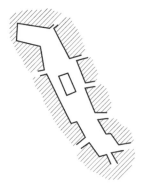

130. Hersbruck, Germany. *Oberer* and *Unterer Markt.*

128. Perugia, Italy. The Piazza IV Novembre, Piazza della Repubblica and Piazza Italia are all linked by the broad pedestrian space of the Corso Vannucci.

131. Hersbruck, Germany. *Oberer Markt.*

132. Perugia, Italy. Corso Vannucci.

133. Bellinzona, Switzerland. A contemporary piazza in a redeveloped fragment of the medieval core of the town.

134. Perth, Scotland. Public art can be an important aspect of detail in urban design, and at its best can be conducive to a town's identity and sense of place. This example, by William Soutar, located on the town's pedestrianised High Street, has the additional quality of interactivity, serving as a meeting place and attracting adults to lean on it.

135. Modena, Italy. Arcades provide shade and shelter, and a transitional zone that is conducive to lingering social interaction. Arched walkways are a common urban design element in towns that are located in Southern regions.

136. Hersbruck, Germany. *Prager Straße*, originally part of an important trade route, the "Golden Road" (*Goldene Straße*) between Nuremberg and Prague, a key east-west trade route that saw Oriental goods and spices brought into northern Europe while linen, wine, and other goods travelled in the other direction. The Golden Road is commemorated in Hersbruck's *Prager Straße* by brass strips and stone plaques, set into the cobblestones, recognising Nuremberg, Prague, and the commodities that were traded along the route between them.

Detail

Detail is what holds the eye, and attention to detail helps to humanise urban settings and enhance liveability. As sociologist Jan Gehl observed in his pioneering book on urban design, "[I]t is not enough merely to create spaces that enable people to come and go. Favourable conditions for moving about in and lingering in the spaces must also exist [...] In this context the quality of the individual segments of the outdoor environment plays a crucial part. Design of individual spaces and of the details, down to the smallest component, are determining factors."[114]

The use of colour on buildings, for example, not only enlivens townscapes but also helps to determine the relative sharpness of the figure-ground distinction, especially in towns where background landscapes or dominant building materials are pale or dull. Flowers and landscaping can also make a significant difference, as can sculpture and public art. The quality and organisation of street furniture such as benches, planters, railings, and fountains can contribute to identity and liveability, or, if cluttered and poorly designed, can detract from them. At night, "amenity" lighting (in contrast to street lighting for wayfinding, which can easily cause light pollution) can enhance townscapes through accenting or floodlighting key buildings and features, providing colour and vitality as well as enhanced security.

Floorscapes are also important (Figs. 136, 139, 140). Visually, they can provide a sense of scale and unify spaces by linking and relating centre and edges, bringing order to what otherwise may be a disparate group of buildings. Patterns and textures can break down the scale of large, hard surfaces into more manageable human proportions. Symbolically, floorscape materials can reinforce identity and heritage. Functionally, floorscape patterns can subtly signal invitations to move along or to dwell, while porous floorscape materials can contribute to environmental sustainability by allowing polluted rainwater to filter back into the aquifer.

137. Street furniture. Stanchions provide an aesthetically pleasing means of demarcating a safe pedestrian area while preventing illegal parking (Abbiategrasso, Italy).

138. Colour. Bold colours add to a sense of vibrancy, as in this street in Überlingen, Germany.

139. Floorscape. Traditional cobbled paving in the Piazza Collegiata, Bellinzona, Switzerland, adapted to provide recessed utility outlets for use on market days.

140. Bellinzona, Switzerland. Piazza Collegiata.

Life Between Buildings

While the physical content and composition of townscapes is important to liveability in terms of aesthetics, character, identity, and sense of place (as well as the ability of a town to function efficiently), it is the capacity of the built environment to sustain animation, conviviality, and sociability in public spaces that is perhaps the most important contribution to liveability and sustainability (Figs. 141–143). As Jan Gehl put it, "Life between buildings is both more relevant and more interesting to look at in the long run than are any combination of coloured concrete and staggered building forms."[115] It is the social experience that is key to liveability. "Compared with experiencing buildings and other inanimate objects, being among other people, who speak and move about, offers a wealth of stimulation."[116] Gehl's point is that urban design influences how many people use a town's public spaces, how long individual activities last, and which kinds of activities can flourish. In this context, he makes a distinction between necessary activities (such as shopping or going to work), optional activities (such as taking a stroll or stopping for a coffee at a sidewalk café), and social activities (such as chance encounters, gossiping, bantering, storytelling, joking, flirtation, and serious conversation).

Better quality public spaces offer more options for social activities. People are attracted to other people. Small towns have the great advantage that people who may work and live in different buildings or neighbourhoods use many of the same public spaces and often meet through the rhythms of their daily and weekly activities. Familiarity, intersubjectivity, and sociability tend to be reinforced. Positive affect is generated and social capital is developed. People's sense of civil society is intensified and the probability of their participation in local affairs and local democracy is increased.

Squares and market places are the loci of these activities in small towns, followed closely by pedestrianised streets and small parks. Because people are attracted to other people, stationary activities – standing around talking, sitting and people-watching or reading a newspaper, napping, sunbathing, sitting at a sidewalk café – are the ones that bring life to the streets. In most settings, there is an "edge effect" to these activities – people preferring to stay along the sides of streets and squares or in

141. Chiavenna, Italy. Chance encounters are an important aspect of social life in small towns.

142. Mendrisio, Switzerland.

143. Ludlow, England.

the transitional zones between one space and the next, allowing them to linger and observe while remaining relatively inconspicuous (Fig. 144).

Yet public spaces are also spaces of circulation and movement, and there is also a need for balance between vehicle and pedestrian movement, and between optional movement and necessary circulation. Vehicle movements have a significant impact on the built environment and affect the quality of life for residents. In terms of circulation, the legacy of narrow, winding streets in many small towns presents a major challenge. On the other hand, walking distance to many of the amenities available in small towns is, by definition, relatively short. This places a premium on urban design that facilitates and enhances pedestrian and, where topography allows it, bicycle accessibility. In an increasingly fast-paced world, unhurried walking or cycling along safe and interesting routes is becoming a key dimension of liveability. Walking allows people to engage in a kind of mobile contemplation, a slow but thorough immersion in the rhythms of everyday life. Repetitive walking or bicycling along the same routes has the additional benefit of routine encounters with acquaintances and familiar faces, a precondition for familiarity, intersubjectivity, and sociability.

Pedestrian experience also enhances the aesthetic dimension of the built environment, the serial encounters and unfolding sequencing of street scenes delivering the kind of anticipation and fulfilment that so enthused Gordon Cullen and Edmund Bacon in their writing on townscapes. Last, and not least, is the importance of pedestrian activity in terms of people's physical health. A good example in the context of progressive urban design is the mobility programme for children aged 6–10 in Enns, Austria (population 10,816), a Cittaslow town. To counter the "fast world" tendency for young children to be dropped off and picked up at school by parents – even when they live only short distances away – a partnership between local schools, the Austrian Ministry of Environmental Issues, and Climate Alliance Austria has developed a series of "parent stop" drop-off areas for cars. From each of these stops there is a subsequent 10-minute escorted walk to school along varied routes. The short walk not only provides exercise for the children and gets them used to the idea of walking but also gives them time for social interaction before arriving at school.

144. Edge effect. People's predilection for sitting and watching other people tends to mean that the edges of public spaces are filled first.

145. Bellinzona, Switzerland. Saturday market.

6

Sustainable Economies

Maintaining and developing a sustainable economy is critically important for the viability and live-ability of small towns. Small town economies need to generate and retain quality jobs for local residents and they should nurture locally owned businesses. Such sustainable economic development efforts go beyond maximising profits and involve social, environmental, and cultural considerations. Economic developers in small towns need to take the so-called triple bottom line into account when designing strategies and policies to develop the local economy. The triple bottom line embraces the goals of improving the life of people and protecting the planet while also making profits. The Centre for Community Enterprise – a Canadian group that has worked for 30 years to strengthen local economies – notes that sustainable and community-based economic development "is the process by which people build organisations and partnerships that interconnect profitable business with other interests and values – like quality jobs, marketable skills, good health, affordable housing, equal opportunity, and ecological responsibility. Businesses become an integral part of a far greater agenda – a local movement to build (or

rebuild) a community that is creative, inclusive, and sustainable in the near and distant future."[117]

Sustainable community or small town economic development stands in contrast to most traditional efforts to build local economies, which embrace the idea of growing the number of jobs and firms located in a community regardless of how much these jobs pay and what kind of businesses they are. Sustainable strategies, on the other hand, focus on the quality and holistic impact of economic activities. This nontraditional approach promotes the development of human capital and skills, initiates long-term structural change, avoids expensive tax breaks to corporations, builds community assets, focuses on the environmental benefits, and tries to avoid ecological degradation. It emphasises the economic and social importance of locally owned businesses such as book stores, specialty shops, cafés, and restaurants that serve the community as "third places." Planning for sustainable small town economic development should be participatory and inclusive, and it should seek to build "alternative economic spaces" that can be more resilient to changes resulting from globalisation and deindustrialisation.

Economic Challenges

Small towns face many economic challenges that make adopting sustainable economic development strategies difficult but increasingly important. In the United States, many small towns lack economic diversity and they typically derive their livelihood from one or two industries. Residents have been employed for generations in resource-based sectors such as mining, forestry, and agriculture or manufacturing industries such as textiles or furniture making. These types of small towns are the "old economy places in slow decline"[118] because firms – primarily those in low-value-added sectors – have been closing plants and relocating jobs overseas. According to the U.S. Department of Agriculture, the United States lost more than 800,000 textile and apparel jobs over the past decade. This economic decline especially impacted small towns which are now struggling with high poverty rates, drug abuse, deterioration of the urban fabric, insufficient access to health care, and a general feeling of hopelessness and despair. Rural America, where most small towns are located, has a poverty rate of about 14.2 percent and more than 11 percent of rural households are considered food insecure, a measure that describes access to sufficient food for a healthy lifestyle.[119] At the other end of the spectrum, small towns in the United States that are close to urban areas or are amenity-rich experience enormous growth challenges: suburban residential development is spoiling their character, chain stores moving to the edge of town force local businesses on Main Street to close (Figs. 146 and 147), and their unfettered growth may mean loss of identity and heritage.

While small towns in the United States have experienced these types of problems for more than two decades, towns in Japan have only recently started to go down a similar path. As the Japanese economy has expanded in the last five years, urban centres such as Tokyo have been thriving at the expense of peripheral areas. American-style economic liberalisation has been used to stimulate the Japanese economy and sectors such as insurance, banking, and grocery retail have been deregulated. As a result, large retailers – many of them domestically owned – began to set up chain stores at the edge of small towns, threatening the livelihood of locally owned businesses. Increasingly, Japan's small towns are turning into ghost towns; they are losing the younger population to the thriving urban centres and they are becoming more politically divided.[120] Similar developments are taking place in Europe where the phenomenon is known as "shrinking cities."

The economic decline of small towns is a real challenge across the world. The New Economics Foundation has found that in the United Kingdom, more than 1,000 communities lost their banks and 50 specialist stores closed per week between 1997 and 2009.[121] The same studies indicate that more than 5,000 post offices closed between 1999 and 2009 and about 8,600 independent grocery stores closed during a five-year period. The loss of locally owned businesses and services means that money

146. Petersburg, Virginia, USA. Once an important town in the development of the Commonwealth of Virginia and during the Civil War, Petersburg has become a shrinking city due to extensive suburbanisation and economic decline. Petersburg has experienced a population decline of 18 percent since it peaked at 41,055 in 1980.

spent at national chain businesses does not stay in the community (Fig. 148); it is channelled back to the corporate headquarters. The community becomes dependent on corporate decisionmakers who do not have any local ties and often only worry about making profits. In contrast, small local retailers and shops keep profits in the community. These locally owned businesses often hire local residents and their owners are civically engaged. The challenge for small towns is to foster a locally rooted economy. Adopting a community-oriented economic development practice, however, depends on the ability of policymakers to think outside the box and to reorient their traditional strategies. This constitutes a paradigm shift for economic developers.

147. Petersburg, Virginia, USA. Many retail buildings at the centre of town are abandoned and vacant. To turn around the economy, Petersburg's economic developers are focusing on supporting local businesses, tourism, and urban revitalisation, with a farmers' market as an important anchor.

Chasing Smokestacks or Developing Community?

Traditional approaches to local economic development have primarily focused on quantitative growth instead of qualitative improvements to local economies and to a community's quality of life. Many economic developers engage in place promotion and marketing with the goal of attracting new businesses from the outside. Such practice is often referred to as "smokestack chasing." These mainstream approaches assume that exogenous factors stimulate economic growth and that it is important to lower the costs of production so that businesses locate in an area. Planners and economic developers often work hand-in-hand with corporations and offer tax breaks, cheap land and buildings, subsidies and assistance in hiring workers, etc. Many towns and cities feel compelled to pursue such corporate-centred economic development strategies because they need to enhance their municipality's economic standing in an increasingly competitive and global environment.

Political scientists have drawn attention to this dependence in the so-called City Limits theory and have examined development struggles engaging business interests and public officials in theories of urban regimes or growth machines.[122] The City Limits theory especially applies to the United States, where the urban system is characterised by a decentralised political and fiscal structure. This structure in turn creates a strong local autonomy that allows local governments to compete with each other for mobile residents and businesses that seek the best tax-to-service ratio. In this rational choice model, it is presumed that economic development policy oriented toward growth keeps and attracts residents and businesses. Thus, policymakers favour strategies that induce growth rather than policies that focus on redistribution, structural change, and development. Such a growth orientation is further aggravated by the political alliances that business interests form with local policymakers. These alliances are described by Urban Regime theory, which argues that "the relationship between popular control of government and private control of the means of production, distribution, and exchange is a fundamental dichotomy in society that tends to play out in favour of business interests."[123] As a result, alternative – more equitable, democratic, and sustainable – approaches are not put forward because of the perceived dependence on growth and a lack of representation from groups other than business interests.

148. Mendrisio, Switzerland. This designer-store outlet mall attracts shoppers from a region that extends as far away as Milan, some 60 kilometres to the south. While it employs a few dozen people and brings tax revenue to the town, it has created a "shadow effect" on apparel retailing in the region, making it difficult for smaller and independent stores in Mendrisio and neighbouring towns to survive.

The Danger of Becoming a "Would-be City"

Corporate-centred or mainstream approaches to urban development have distinct characteristics. They typically involve large-scale projects – sometimes referred to as mega projects – such as stadiums, entertainment centres, and large-scale office complexes at the expense of more community-based development. Small towns often adopt similar strategies because they would like to imitate successful big-city development. Geographers Bell and Jayne argue, however, that such big-city policies will lead to the development of "would-be cities" that have lost their unique characteristics stemming from their smallness (Figs. 149 and 150).[124]

Corporate-centred strategies are motivated by a perception of global competition among cities for private investments. Often these projects are fairly homogenous and similar in nature and are illustrated by nondescript office parks or suburban fast-food and franchise shopping places that create a geography of what sociologist George Ritzer calls "islands of McDonaldization."[125] These projects are "cathedrals of consumption" and contribute to the erosion of local economies. Their roots, deeply grounded in the culture of consumerism, go back to the mid-1950s when the United States experienced significant economic growth and prosperity. Economic development practices aimed at creating such developments adhere to the single imperative of economic progress; they do not benefit marginalised groups and they heighten inequalities.

Scholars and activists have challenged the deterministic view of corporate-centred urban development programs. David Imbroscio, a political scientist, presents six elements of an alternative economic development regime.[126] These include strategies to increase human capital and community economic stability; to provide for proper accounting of development costs and benefits through public balance sheets; the development of asset specificity and economic localism; and lastly the development of alternative institutions. Combined, these strategies would decrease the dependence of public officials on outside resources and corporate interests because each would increase the endogenous economic capacity of a community.

149. Metzingen, Germany. Metzingen and other towns of the Swabian Alb were once thriving because of textile mills. In recent years, Metzingen has developed as an outlet city. More than 70 fashion labels such as Joop! and Escada operate an outlet there. It is also the headquarters location of Hugo Boss, a high-end fashion design company.

150. Danville, Virginia, USA. The Institute for Advanced Learning and Research is the result of a strategic attempt to bring high-tech economic development to Danville, a town of 45,000 in Southside Virginia, a region that has experienced severe economic dislocation as a result of the decline of the tobacco and textile industries. But with little else in the town, the Institute is unlikely to result in significant economic growth.

Community Economic Development

Even though the corporate-centred approach to economic development is still very dominant, a new practice has emerged over the past couple of decades. In the United States, the movement is called Community Economic Development (CED) and it addresses normative goals of equity and democratic representation of grassroots efforts in economic development. CED is focused on smaller-scale areas such as neighbourhoods and it attempts to benefit groups that have traditionally been left out of the mainstream economic system (homeless, minority, immigrants, etc.). Programmes may have different areas of emphasis, such as the community, the economy, or on development (see Table 6.1).

Depending on the emphasis, the community with its social ties and interactions is at the centre as illustrated in the "Ced" approach. Alternatively, in the development-oriented approach, the goal is to bring about structural change ("ceD" approach). The aim of community economic development is to produce socially useful and sustainable

development. As such, the movement differs from traditional economic development, where the focus is often "just on growth" and not on "just growth." The main advocates of CED are nonprofit groups, advocacy organisations, neighbourhood councils, community banks, and other community-based organisations. CED seeks to benefit local residents and create beneficial linkages or synergies between the economy and society. It seeks to avoid negative environmental externalities and it reinforces stable, independent community structures.

Table 6.1: Community Economic Development

	cEd (Economy)	**ceD** (Development)	**Ced** (Community)
Concept of Economy	Monetary transactions	Monetary and non-monetary transactions	Production and distribution based on market and non-market principles
Concept of Community	Locality	Home	Mutual commitment
Primary Goal	Growth of jobs, income	Stability and sustainability	Sharing and caring
Primary Strategy	Increase monetary inflows	Increase local control through structural change	Integrate social and economic development
Examples	"Would-be cities"	Community ownership	Cittaslow

Source: After Boothroyd, P., & Davis, C., "Community economic development: Three approaches." *Journal of Planning Education and Research*, 12, 1993, pp. 230–240.

Alternative Economic Spaces

Community economic development is a movement that holds a lot of promise for the future of small towns. If combined with sustainable development, it seeks to build "alternative economic spaces" that challenge the conventional capitalist paradigm. Alternative economic spaces restore the community, increase its self-reliance, and provide services and products to groups neglected by the mainstream economy. Building such alternatives is important because exogenous forces such as global trade, urban sprawl, and the competition for jobs among localities have undermined the economic capacities of small towns. Strategies to build alternative economic spaces aim to create economic circuits and cycles that are separate from the mainstream economy. It is assumed that such disconnectedness will increase self-reliance and shelter a community from external economic shocks. Within this framework, the practice of building alternative economic spaces is mostly targeted at a small geographic scale such as the local community or neighbourhood. The assumption is that within a limited geographic scope there exists a better sense of connection to the locality among its citizens. It is hoped that citizens frequent local shops and that their purchases benefit local owners (Fig. 151). The financial gains resulting from these local expenditures will stay in the community and will be reinvested.

The practice of building alternative economic spaces is echoed by environmental activist Bill McKibben who writes about the "deep economy." His concept of deep economy has its roots in deep ecology, a phrase coined by the Norwegian philosopher Arne Næss in 1973. Deep ecology describes the integration of human beings and the environment and ascribes greater value to the nonhuman aspects of the ecosystem. It is considered deep because the philosophy claims to be more thoughtful about the role of human beings in the ecosystem than other environmental movements, which often consider the environment as separate or even subordinate to the human sphere. In his 2007 book *Deep Economy: The Wealth of Communities and the Durable Future*, McKibben pleads for large-scale restructuring of local economies with a greater focus on development rather than growth. Contrasting the mainstream economy, he states, "[B]uilding a local economy will mean [...] ceasing to worship markets as infallible and consciously setting limits on their scope. We will need to downplay efficiency and pay attention to other goals. We will have to make the biggest changes to our daily habits in generations – and the biggest change, as well, to our worldview, our sense of what constitutes progress."[127] McKibben demands structural changes that involve a shift away from an orientation of growth – bigger, richer, larger, and more efficient – to an orientation that takes quality of life, meaningfulness, and happiness into account. Such a development approach recognises that being richer does not make a person happier. In fact, research in psychology has shown the opposite – that life satisfaction derives from nonmaterialistic factors such as health, family life, friendship, and social connections.

buy local. eat local. be local.
Downtown Blacksburg
Downtown Merchants of Blacksburg   Blacksburg Farmers Market

151. Blacksburg, Virginia, USA. Buy local campaigns have mushroomed in the United States. This campaign is supported by the Downtown Merchants of Blacksburg and the Blacksburg Farmers Market. Both organisations try to educate consumers to shop in locally owned stores and at the market in the town centre rather than in globally operating suburban retail chains.

Finding a Niche

The lesson for small towns is that economic development needs to create an environment in which residents can fulfil their economic and financial needs. But more importantly it needs to build an economic system that also provides residents with a sense of place and ownership. Ultimately this will lead to higher levels of civic engagement and social capital. Such a reorientation contributes to the creation of alternative economic spaces because goals and practices will go beyond the economic imperative.

This is recognised by the asset-building approach to community and economic development. The approach was developed by sociologists John Kretzmann and John McKnight in the early 1990s. Assets of a community are the "gifts, skills and capacities" of individuals, groups, associations, and institutions.[128] A focus on assets diverts the traditional attention on needs of a community. Typically these needs have been associated with negative stereotypes, such as the community that is crime-ridden and poor and needs to be assisted by outsiders. In contrast, the asset-based approach empowers communities because it recognises community resources as capacities for structural change and empowerment. Typically, planners – in cooperation with the community – engage in the process of asset mapping to analyse a community's capacities (Fig. 152). Economic assets are identified by community members who map various capacities such as work experiences, skills, entrepreneurial capacities, cultural and creative assets, consumer behaviour, untapped demand and supply potentials, as well as niche markets. Small towns may

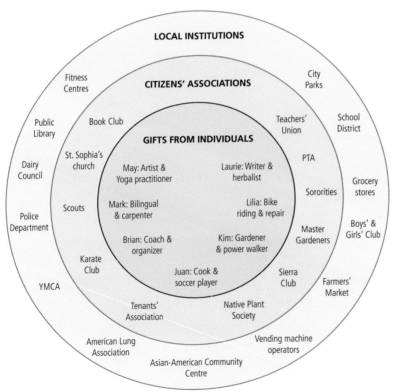

152. Asset Mapping. The asset building approach is an important component of sustainable community and economic development. Communities can visually map their unique strengths and create diagrams like this one developed by the California-based Center for Collaborative Planning. At the centre of the circles are the individual's gifts such as occupational skills or proficiencies. The second circle lists existing civic institutions such as local clubs and associations. The third circle illustrates local institutions such as public agencies, schools, and retail establishments. Maps like this can illustrate the wealth of assets and create a better sense of community.

want to consider the asset-building approach to economic development because it allows them to focus on their endogenous competencies.

Finally, small towns should find their "Unique Selling Points" (USPs) and trade on their distinctiveness to attract investments from outside, but to also enhance and build on their heritage, identity, and culture.[129] The danger, however, is that selling a town's uniqueness may be close to the commodification of small town assets. Also, small towns may fall into the trap of trying to imitate their larger counterparts. Bell and Jayne state, "[C]aught between the bigness of the global metropolis dominating global flows of capital, culture and people, and the openness of the rural, small cities are faced with a problem of definition and redefinition, caught between bulking up and staying small."[130] The task is to find the right balance between leveraging and trading on the unique assets and preserving and sheltering them from change and turning them into tradable commodities.

Tapping into a Wider Network

Creating alternative economic spaces in small towns is not easy and several challenges need to be considered. The biggest obstacle for small towns is their limited economic capacity. Small town economies – especially those that are depressed and have experienced significant economic decline – might not have the necessary consumer demand to build self-reliant alternative economies. This in turn makes the expansion of the local economy difficult if not impossible.

Successful and sustainable small town economies, such as those in the Cittaslow movement, thrive because of their connections to outside markets. Tourists visit these towns and spend money (Figs. 153–155). The small town economies specialise into certain products – often niche products – that may be exported and in turn help local shops compete at a larger geographic scale. Ironically, these links to the outside economy (i.e., the global economy) are critically important for the maintenance of small town economic capacities. To avoid the creation of so-called ghetto economies, small towns need to "tap into wider, non-local network and markets."[131] This, however, does not mean that small town economies should imitate global fads and lose their identities. Rather, the homogenisation that results from globalisation may even allow small town economies to be distinct and to draw economic success from being different. To strike this balance, small towns need to adopt sustainable economic development strategies that foster local entrepreneurship, nourish place economies, and develop social and human capital.

153. Todi, Italy. The intimacy and historic legacy of many small towns attracts tourists and day visitors that are important in helping to sustain businesses.

154. Hvar, Croatia.

155. Vence, France.

Small Business Development

Business development is at the heart of a small town economic development strategy because small and medium-sized businesses located in a small town can benefit from public policy in more ways than their large counterparts. Activities should encourage new business start-ups, sustain and expand existing businesses, and increase innovation and entrepreneurship within the community. Small businesses and entrepreneurs are critical to small town success (Figs. 156–160). In the United States, fully 99 percent of businesses are small, each employing on average about ten people. The 23 million small busnesses in America account for 54 percent of all U.S. sales and provide 55 percent of all jobs. These small businesses have been critical to the country's overall economic success and the number of self-employed individuals has increased.

The importance of small businesses to the European economy is similar: More than 99 percent of all enterprises in Europe are small to medium-sized enterprises (SMEs, defined as firms with up to 50 employees). Ninety percent of SMEs employ fewer than ten people and the average company has just five workers. These microenterprises account for more than half of all jobs in Europe.[132] Small businesses range from craft enterprises such as butchers, carpenters, and bakers to firms offering information technology or personal services. Because of their small size and limited resources, these businesses face many problems. They are challenged with finding the necessary financial resources, skilled staff, overcoming bureaucratic hurdles, and accessing markets. It is because of these challenges that economic developers need to pay attention to these types of businesses.

Economic Gardening

There are many exciting approaches to creating and sustaining small businesses in small towns. Small town leaders and economic developers across the world are realising that giving out costly incentives and tax breaks does not get them anywhere and that they have to reorient their practice toward nurturing locally owned and operated firms. In the United States, several small towns and states have adopted the "economic gardening" approach to business development. Economic gardening focuses on developing businesses from within the community rather than trying to attract them from the outside. Towns such as Littleton, Colorado have ceased to spend public resources on business attraction strategies. Instead, Littleton's economic developers focus on creating the right infrastructure and entrepreneurial environment and providing firms with critical market information. The economic gardening approach seems to be a promising new practice and the network of towns that are adopting this approach is growing rapidly.

156. Unterkrumbach, Germany. Herwig Danzer is the founder of a local cabinetmaker's workshop called *Die Möbelmacher*. His business is located in Unterkrumbach, a small town near Hersbruck. His workshop uses wood from the region, the so-called Frankalb, to create custom-made furniture and kitchen cabinetry. The business is dedicated to the ideas of sustainability and employs about 17 workers. Herwig Danzer was also instrumental in the application of Hersbruck as the first German Cittaslow member.

157. Sokndal, Norway. Sokndal is a very small town – its population is just 3,286 – in a relatively remote region. In such settings, small general stores represent an important social resource as well as being vital to the town's economic well-being.

158. Hersbruck, Germany. This small shop is a shoe repair establishment in Hersbruck. Small businesses like these are often located in the town centre. They are typically owned by local families and benefit from local patronage. These shops add to the vitality of small towns.

159. Sokndal, Norway. As in many small towns, small business often serve dual purposes, as in this café and hardware store.

160. Seppenrade, Germany. This local bakery has been family-owned for five generations. The business has expanded into a second location in the nearby town Lüdinghausen, a Cittaslow member since 2007. The bakery makes and sells a traditional dark break called Pumpernickel. To make this type of bread, family Holtermann uses traditional recipes that are typical for the region which is called Münsterland. The bakery does not use any industrially available premixed ingredients to make its bread and only uses traditional, slow baking methods.

Littleton, Colorado, USA

Littleton is a small town about 16 kilometres south of downtown Denver, Colorado. Even though today Littleton is considered a suburban small town, it had its humble beginnings as a farming and railroad town in the late nineteenth century. Located along Highway 85, Littleton is home to about 41,000 residents; in 2007 *Money Magazine* rated the town among the 100 best places to live. Littleton's origins go back to the gold rush in the late nineteenth century, when nearby Denver City grew because of an influx of gold-seekers, merchants, and farmers. Richard Sullivan Little arrived from the East Coast to help engineer and construct a water system to provide the region's fledgling farmers with the ability to irrigate the dry land at the foot of the Rocky Mountains. Little claimed land and ultimately settled with his wife on the site that later became Littleton. The town was founded in 1872 when the Littles subdivided their property in the village of Littleton. At the same time, the railroad expanded in Colorado and, as a result, Littleton began to grow very rapidly. In 1890 the town was incorporated following a vote by its 245 residents.

Since then, Littleton has flourished as a county seat and location for agriculture and manufacturing. In the twentieth century, the town benefited from a growing aerospace and electronics industry that had expanded into Western states such as Colorado and Arizona. Littleton's close proximity to Denver and the growth of the military-industrial complex put the small town into an advantageous economic position. This, however, did not last too long: During the late 1980s the state of Colorado experienced a major economic recession. In Littleton, the aerospace manufacturer Martin Marietta, the town's largest employer, laid off several thousand employees. As a result, city leaders and economic developers began to reorient their economic development policies and developed an approach now known as "economic gardening."

161. Littleton town centre.

Economic gardening is an economic development strategy that focuses on growing the economy from the "inside-out" by supporting entrepreneurs and small businesses. Littleton began to follow this strategy in 1989. Rather than investing time and public resources in trying to recruit businesses from the outside ("outside-in" economic development), the town identifies and fosters small businesses and entrepreneurial ventures with promising growth opportunities. Economic developers provide the right infrastructure and community assets – not just bricks and mortar infrastructure but also including soft assets such as education and cultural amenities. The economic developers in Littleton also play matchmaker: They improve the interaction and exchange among business owners and other community groups such as trade associations, academic institutions, etc. Besides infrastructure and connectivity, policymakers make sure that small firms have access to information and competitive intelligence on customers, competitors, and target markets. The provision of information is especially critical to small firms that often do not have the resources to gain important insights that are critical to their growth.

What is Littleton's experience with shifting its economic development strategies from smokestack

Table 6.2: Change in Wage-and-Salary Employment, 1990–2005 (percent)

	Littleton, Colorado	Denver Metro	Colorado	United States
1990–2005	135.3	64.2	47.2	21.4
2000–2005	35.0	-2.6	1.2	1.5

Source: Small Business Administration (2006), p. 174. The Small Business Economy: 2006.
Retrieved April 22, 2007, from http://www.sba.gov/advo/research/sb_econ2006.pdf

162. Littleton, Colorado, USA. Littleton is a small town on the edge of Denver, the largest metropolitan region in the state of Colorado. Once a thriving railroad town, Littleton benefits from Denver's spillover effects. Local economic developers invented a new approach to economic development called economic gardening.

chasing to economic gardening? Giving up the smokestack chasing policies and solely investing public resources into economic gardening has paid off for the small town. The number of jobs in Littleton has doubled from about 15,000 to 35,000 since the beginning of the programme (Table 6.2). Some of these gains may be related to rapid growth and suburbanisation of the Denver metropolitan region, the resulting spillovers, and to the growth of knowledge-based industries in this part of the country.

The entrepreneurial inside-out strategy, however, has gained credibility, especially among the local businesses. At times when politicians wanted to cut the funding for the economic gardening programme, business leaders testified in favour of it. Littleton's new strategy also bolstered the existing small town entrepreneurial spirit and culture, something that is critical to the survival and success of small communities.

Economic gardening approaches are proliferating throughout the United States and the movement is growing. Economic gardeners across the country regularly meet at annual conferences and are virtually connected through e-mail lists. They share insights into their practice and network. The approach is especially applicable to small towns because of their lack of resources

to engage in the high-stakes games of corporate subsidies. Also, small towns such as Littleton are home to entrepreneurial individuals who may just need a little support from the public sector in order to start their own businesses.

163. Littleton, Colorado. *JaJa Bistro* is a wine bar and bistro. Littleton's economic gardening program assisted the owner, who is originally from France, in setting up not only the bistro but also another shop called *Ambiance Provence* which carries cloths and glassware from France. The economic gardening program helped with business development services such as marketing to Francophiles and creating websites. The photo shows the grand opening with city council members and other downtown merchants.

164. Matakana, New Zealand. The co-operative retail movement, which started in Britain in the mid-nineteenth century, has spread around the world and in many small communities remains an important community non-profit enterprise.

Community Ownership

Another promising practice in small town economic development is the movement toward establishing community-owned businesses. The idea is to create small businesses through community ownership. Local ownership keeps control and revenues in the town and creates loyalty among residents who consume at community-owned stores, for example. There are many examples of community-owned stores in small towns that are too small or too isolated to attract and retain national retail stores (Fig. 164).

Several towns in the United States have developed an innovative model that keeps retail services in the community but also makes the business more community-based. In a small town about 160 kilometres northeast of Yellowstone National Park, local residents decided to keep their downtown economically vital by opening a community-owned clothing store. The catalyst for the development was the opening of a Wal-Mart Supercenter about 32 kilometres away. Powell Mercantile (Fig. 165) opened in 2002 and functions like a small-town department store. The store was financed through community stock that was sold to residents at $500 a share. There is a cap at 20 shares per person. Selling shares to community members ensures

their sense of ownership and loyalty because the more shareholders there are the more shoppers the store will have. It also allows for the revenues to stay within the community: In 2007, McKibben reported that investors received a 7 percent return on their $500 shares. Powell Mercantile has served as an anchor and catalyst for downtown redevelopment. As a result of the store's continued presence, several other stores have

165. Powell, Wyoming, USA. This community-owned store replaced a chain store that shut down. Powell's 5,370 residents would have needed to drive a long way to the next store and engaged residents decided to be pro-active. *Powell Merc* sits along Main Street and is part of a vibrant town centre.

opened on Main Street. Similar community-owned stores have opened in small towns in Nevada and Montana. Community-based management allows for greater control over the businesses and operations such as buying, making it a more tailored approach to the community's needs.

Alternative Financing

Small and locally owned businesses only survive if they have the right financing in place. Several innovative programmes that offer start-up loans and financial resources allow communities to support entrepreneurs. The Northern California Loan Fund, for example, provides small loans to emerging enterprises in disadvantaged and rural communities. The fund is part of the growing community of Community Development Financial Institutions (CDFIs). According to the CDFI Coalition, which is based in the Washington D.C. region, there are more than 1,000 CDFI organisations in the United States. These institutions provide credit to communities and groups that usually have a hard time receiving financial assistance from mainstream institutions.

Such community-based finance institutions especially make a difference in rural and small town communities. For example, Craft3 (formerly Enterprise Cascadia) brings financial resources to natural resource-dependent communities in the Pacific Northwest area of the United States. Craft3 follows the triple bottom line and pays attention to economic, social, and environmental concerns in struggling communities. The group seeks to support "the emergence of new business, civic, and conservation strategies that deliver both community prosperity and healthy ecosystems."[133] According to the organisation, the bank has invested $20 million in 200 businesses and social and civic groups that work toward economic security and ecological health. Its founding group, ShoreBank Corporation, brings a lot of experience to investing in struggling communities because the bank has been instrumental in the rebuilding of Chicago's South Side, one of that city's most impoverished neighbourhoods.

One project that Craft3 calls a "triple bottom line deal" is the Shoalwater Bay Wellness Center (Fig. 166). The Center is located in the Shoalwater Reservation in Tokeland, which is home to Washington State's third smallest and most remote tribe. Before the Center was built, tribal members had to drive 80 miles one-way to get medical care at another reservation. The Center is now located in the middle of the community and offers medical, dental, drug and alcohol counselling, and mental health services. The facility is designed such that water run-off from its roof and parking lot is captured and channelled into bioswales that are planted with native plants. The bank invested $1.57 million in the Center. Loans like these achieve several outcomes, such as the creation of jobs (30 in the case of the Center), water diverted from waste streams (340,000 gallons per year), support to minority entrepreneurs, assistance to low-income families (600 families), and keeping local land tenure (which is worth more than $251 million).

166. Tokeland, Washington, USA. The Shoalwater Bay Wellness Center opened in 2005 and provides critical medical services to the third-smallest and one of the most remote tribes in Washington State. Before the centre opened, tribal members and small town residents had to drive more than 80 miles one way to the nearest clinic. In 1992 the tribe also declared a health emergency because of the high infant mortality. The centre was built using sustainable architectural techniques and it created about 30 jobs.

Place Economies

Small towns must foster their place economies. In other words, small towns need to be aware of the ways in which their locations are shaped by business activities. Local ownership of land and buildings, for example, is critical to sustainable small town economic development. Such ownership shields business owners from unexpected financial problems such as dramatic increases in rents that may result from development and gentrification. Economic developers in small towns must pay attention to the health and vitality of their downtown districts and commercial streets and corridors (Fig. 167). Because small towns typically have close ties with the agricultural hinterland, small locally owned farms are important for the economic health of the region. Several programmes in the United States that address the health and vitality of place economies may offer other regions in the world some interesting lessons.

One such programme, the Main Street programme, focuses on creating viable downtown economies through historic preservation, urban design, and business development. The National Trust for Historic Preservation, a nonprofit membership association in the United States, operates the National Trust Main Street Center. Since the 1970s the Center has offered technical assistance and research to small towns interested in maintaining and developing their main streets. The Center combines historic preservation with business development and provides certification to towns interested in becoming a Main Street community. The programme has been important to the successful redevelopment of small downtowns. Small towns and their downtown areas can only succeed if they offer a unique environment for residents, tourists, and shoppers. Such a unique environment is created through the provision of small retail specialty stores that can compete with national chains located on the suburban outskirts. Heritage, historic preservation, culture, a unique setting, and distinctive architecture can also facilitate the use and vitality of downtown. Small towns need to enhance the differentiation of their cores.[134] To accomplish this kind of place making, physical redevelopment efforts must be complemented by the kind of entrepreneurial and business development strategies described earlier.

Small towns need to create place economies not only in their urban cores but also through linkages with their agricultural hinterlands. Community supported agriculture (CSA) and other types of programmes aimed at linking producers and consumers of agricultural products are examples how small towns can revive traditional links to their agricultural hinterlands. In the United States, the CSA movement has mushroomed in recent years. The idea behind the movement is that individuals support a small farm through the up-front acquisition of shares. A participant might, for example, pay 500 dollars to a CSA farmer at the beginning of the planting season. In return, all through the growing season the participant receives (usually on a weekly basis) a specified amount of whatever farm products are at hand. The goal is to connect the consumer through his or her shares with the farmer who produces the goods. The support allows the farmer to obtain working capital before the season begins. The consumer in turn will be more connected to food production because the weekly deliveries have their own rhythms and seasons. CSA farms are relatively new businesses – on average only about five years old. They also tend to be run by younger farmers with an average age of 43.7 years. Supporting farms through CSA links the hinterland with the small town and also encourages younger generations to take on farming as an occupation. Furthermore, CSA shares give farmers working capital and help with financing their operations.

Sustainable small town economies need to create viable, locally owned businesses and places that offer business owners the opportunity to link to the consumer. Through local ownership and vital place economies, small towns can develop resiliency to the pressures of globalisation, industrial decline, and restructuring. Describing the local market in Oaxaca, Mexico, marketing scholar Dennis Rondinelli highlighted the central role of small town economies:

"The market in Oaxaca provides outlets for agricultural produce, livestock, nonagricultural goods like fibers and firewood, and artisanal products such as pottery, baskets, mats, and household and agricultural implements. An impressive array of people find employment directly or indirectly through market activities – carpenters, stonecutters, healers and curers, butchers, blacksmiths,

167. Staunton, Virginia, USA. Main Street redevelopment has been an important planning issue for small towns in the United States. Supported by the National Trust Main Street Center, towns like Staunton in Virginia have managed to keep their centres vital. The programme focuses on façade improvement, street beautification, but also marketing and business development.

small-parts sellers, marriage arrangers, mechanics, and vendors of seeds and equipment. The market offers opportunities for farmers to sell their goods and for a large number of intermediaries to engage in trade. Oaxaca supports traders who buy and resell goods in the market, traders who travel to small rural markets to collect goods for resale in Oaxaca, and traders who buy goods in the market and resell them door-to-door in the city. Rural visitors have the opportunity to shop in stores along the periphery of the market and to call on doctors, dentists, lawyers, and lenders. Wholesalers collect small quantities of local products from the Oaxaca market and sell them in bulk to retailers in larger cities and bring small lots of goods back to Oaxaca. The employment network of the market is thus extended to include field buyers, agents, truckers, and small-load haulers."[135]

Rondinelli's description of the importance of the public market in Oaxaca echoes Jane Jacobs' notion of the economy of cities. Small towns and cities are "primary economic organs" and the principal source of rural and agricultural work.[136] The excerpt also illustrates how small towns are embedded in larger urban systems. Small town economies need to exploit linkages to outside markets and avoid being locked into their own economic systems. A balance must be struck between preserving local character and identity and the influences resulting from connections to the global economy.

168. Chiavenna, Italy. Convivial atmosphere on the *Piazza Pestalozzi*.

7

Conviviality, Hospitality, and Local Products

The vitality of small towns depends on the social relationships that residents form and on how welcoming a place is to newcomers and outsiders. Social ties are an important foundation for collective action and democracy in small communities. They are fostered through convivial and hospitable practices and rituals. Such rituals ensure the continuation of the history and heritage of a place and build social capacity in a community. As a result, a community is able to differentiate itself and define its position in the global urban system. Small towns are in a unique position to foster social ties: Their scale allows people to engage in more dense interactions, becoming networked and connected while still retaining the heterogeneity and diversity necessary to keep ideas and networks fresh. The density of interactions may, however, become oppressive and there is a danger that the strength of social networks and ties may negatively impact the community. Yet unlike their neighbours – large metropolises and rural villages or hamlets – small towns are large enough to balance the positive and negative aspects of social relationships.

Conviviality and hospitality are expressed through rituals and everyday practices (Figs. 169–171). The most visible of these practices involves the pleasures derived from eating a meal in the company of others. The ingredients, the preparation, and the serving of food are highly contextual. To be sustainable, the production and consumption of food needs to be connected to the specific local context of a town. Thus, efforts to foster social relationships through conviviality and hospitality need to be sensitive to the essential connections that exist between production and consumption of food and other local products. In doing so, small towns will not only further their democratic capacities but also enhance their local economy.

Conviviality

The concept of conviviality describes the ways in which groups of people interact and is often associated with happy notions of social relationships such as feasting and drinking in good company, friendliness, merrymaking, and companionship. Small towns offer a variety of convivial places. In the public sphere it is the pub on the street corner; the courtyard where neighbours gather to share stories of the day; the town square where teenagers hang out after school; or the street café where people enjoy each other's company over a good cup of coffee. Conviviality can also be expressed in the private sphere. For example, the dining table in a private home around which family members gather for a meal is a convivial place. Such convivial places bring people together and connect them with each other. They can build social relationships that in turn encourage community initiatives and create social capacity at the community level.

In his 1958 book *Personal Knowledge: Towards a Post-Critical Philosophy*, philosopher Michael Polanyi highlights the concept of conviviality as a critical form of tacit knowledge. He refers to the emotional aspects of conviviality and the ability to transfer knowledge about a community's existence, heritage, and culture through convivial practices. To him, conviviality addresses the need of individuals to forge emotional connections to each other to overcome the hostility of individualism. Polanyi describes how conversations are the tools of conviviality: "[T]he exchange of greetings and of conventional remarks is an articulation of companionship, and every articulate address of one person to another makes some contribution to their conviviality, in the sense of their reaching out to each other and sharing each other's lives."[137]

Creating companionship and sharing requires places that facilitate such activities. It also requires time and dedication to the practice of sharing. Polanyi refers to the importance of conviviality in preserving group identity and affirmation. Compassion and companionship may encourage people's identification with a community and in turn may foster their willingness to participate in community events. This "sharing in joint activities," as Polanyi describes it, is expressed in rituals and common practices. Examples of such rituals are town festivals, sport events, homecomings, and seasonal events such as the annual harvest festival. Polanyi notes that "[B]y fully participating in a ritual, the members of a group affirm the community of their existence, and at the same time identify the life of their group with that of antecedent groups, from whom the ritual has descended to them."[138]

Affirmation of a community's existence ensures its continuation. This is especially important in the context of growing and declining small towns. Small towns struggling to retain citizens – especially young people – because they do not offer job opportunities or are lacking in other ways are losing potentially vital members of their community who might otherwise be primary actors in convivial rituals and practices. They lose vital memory because people who grew up around long-standing traditions are leaving. At the opposite end of the spectrum are towns that are growing too fast and are threatened with losing their memory and identity because newcomers might not be familiar with or might not be willing to share in the rituals and practices of conviviality.

Others have defined conviviality from the perspective of the individual and the constraints imposed on them by modern society. The Austrian philosopher Ivan Illich, for example, defines conviviality "to be individual freedom realized in personal interdependence and, as such, an intrinsic ethical value."[139] A critic of modernity and institutionalised specialist knowledge, Illich describes the need to allow individuals the opportunity to create new meanings. In doing so, Illich claims, society can reclaim traditional and practical knowledge of its citizens and free them from expert knowledge and the constraints of the modern society. Illich describes the characteristics of a convivial society and says that it "would be the result of social arrangements that guarantee for each member the most ample and free access to the tools of the community and limit this freedom only in favour of another member's equal freedom."[140]

Threats to Conviviality

Whatever definition we apply to conviviality, the concept describes the ways in which people get together and share each other's lives through social interaction. Conviviality and the building of social relationships take time. The fast-paced modern world, however, is threatening our ability to take time to get together, connect with others, and share in rituals such as eating a meal. In 2007, the *Washington Post* reported that the number of food products labelled "On the Go" had increased from 134 in 2001 to around 500.[141] Food companies cite consumers' desire for convenience. Yoghurt becomes Go-Gurt and candy bars are cut in half so that one can easily eat them in spurts while doing something else. These conveniently packaged snacks allow the consumption of food while writing e-mails, driving, or going from one meeting to another. So-called beverage sticks offer individually packaged cappuccino drinks, and more than 100 different types of these quick drinks have been introduced since 2006. Foods labelled "on the go" transform our eating habits both from a social and a health standpoint. Research has shown that people drastically underestimate the calorie intake, most likely because one does not count food consumed in a hurry between meals. Meanwhile, the family meal, which has a significant impact on a person's nutritional diet and fulfils an important positive social function, has declined in frequency over the last decades.[142] Small towns and communities are aware of these patterns. In 2002, Ridgewood, a town of 25,000 people in New Jersey, scheduled its first "family night." That night, schools did not assign homework and sports teams avoided scheduling practice. The effort is aimed at making time for unscheduled rituals such as the family dinner, playing games, and talking to each other.

The rise of food "on the go" is part of a trend of increasing popularity of fast food, which undermines efforts to strengthen small town conviviality. In Germany, for example, almost 90 percent of the population visits a fast-food restaurant at least occasionally and a full 60 percent eat fast food once a month. More alarming are the trends among young people: One-quarter of the 14- to 30-year-olds visit a fast-food place once a week. Most popular are McDonald's, Burger King, and snack bars. A full 26 percent reported that they also like to go

169. Cremona, Italy.

170. Waldkirch, Germany. Weekly farmers markets function as third places. People meet and talk with each other.

171. Citta di Castello, Italy.

172. On the Go. Fast food restaurants and convenience shops cater to a fast lifestyle. IKEA's restaurants are a popular place to have a quick meal.

to the IKEA restaurant (Fig. 172), illustrating how popular the furniture store has become as a place to spend time not only with shopping but also with eating food. Even though every fourth fast-food enthusiast in Germany has a bad conscience after eating fast food, the average consumer still spends about 22 euros per month at these fast-food restaurants.[143] These trends threaten communities in two ways. Fast-food consumption takes away the emphasis on taking time and sharing during meal times. Fast food is also part of the larger agro-industrial complex and divorces the consumer from the production of food. That is why threats to conviviality – especially as they are related to food – also threaten the local economic system.

Diversity is Necessary for Conviviality

The need to create conviviality and companionship exists among all kinds of demographic groups, young and old. Moreover, the ability to facilitate connections across demographic and ethnic groups is one of the defining features of urbanism and small town vitality. Jane Jacobs, for example, noted that cities thrive because they are diverse and heterogeneous, which in turn facilitates the sharing of ideas and innovation.[144] She argued that cities need to facilitate these kinds of interaction through mixed uses, as opposed to separate and segregated uses. Where the ability of people to mix is threatened, interaction is diminished. In contrast, planners need to make sure that everyone has the rights to use and interact in public spaces because such spaces provide for the experience of difference. Being confronted with the "other" will foster a shared understanding and will ultimately contribute to a community's civic capacity.

The rights to public spaces are threatened especially for groups that are seen as unfit or antisocial: teenagers, the homeless, etc. This is most clearly expressed in efforts to discourage teenagers from hanging out in public places (Figs. 173 and 174). In the United Kingdom, for example, some businesses now use a noise-making device that deters teenagers from hanging out in front of supermarkets or shopping malls. The device, called the Mosquito, can only be heard by young people under the age of 25 because it emits a high-frequency ultrasonic tone that older people cannot hear. Similar efforts use classical music or uncool music (Barry Manilow's recordings are a favourite) to deter youth. A supermarket in the small town of Barry in South Wales was one of the first to use the Mosquito device and has successfully deterred a group of teenagers from hanging around outside the store. Today an estimated 3,500 Mosquito devices are in use in the United Kingdom. The BBC reports that it is now also used by public institutions such as the Wyvern Theatre in Wiltshire in an attempt to stop youngsters from gathering around Theatre Square. In the meantime, critics have raised concerns about the anti-teenager devices and are calling for a ban. The Buzz Off campaign, led by the Children's Commissioner for England, aims to draw attention to the increasingly negative ways society deals with young people and their perceived antisocial behaviour.[145] If free

from crime, hanging out in a square or in front of businesses may be considered a convivial practice by youth and facilitates bonding and connections.

These examples raise the questions of for whom spaces of conviviality are created and how convivial practices impact different groups. Conviviality is an important concept that needs to be considered in community-building processes in small towns because it creates the type of relationships that are needed to build the capacity to take collective action. Ideally, this kind of community capacity is created across the broad spectrum of residents, including different age and ethnic groups.

173. Chichester, England. Widespread concern about anti-social behaviour among youths has prompted some towns to introduce special controls in key public spaces.

174. Anti-social behaviour. In parts of northern Europe, binge drinking among young adults has become a chronic problem, not only in city centres but in some small towns.

The Role of Community and Social Capital

Convivial practices and rituals build social capital and community cohesion, and small towns are in a unique position to facilitate social networking processes (Figs. 175 and 176). The concept of community and community-building in the context of urbanism, however, has been discussed in the past in terms of polar opposites. Urban and social theorists have noted the differences between traditional rural societies and metropolitan communities. On one hand, the city is depicted as an alienating space that isolates individuals from each other because they are around strangers always rushing past each other without connecting. On the other hand, writers note the density of social relationships in traditional rural or less urban settings that facilitate social interaction, reciprocity, and solidarity. On the urban-rural continuum, small towns are placed somewhere between urban alienation and rural social stability. These towns are small enough to foster dense social interactions but they are large enough to eschew isolation and lock-in resulting from a lack of diversity and exchange. The Cittaslow movement, for example, sets a size limit and certifies cities with no larger a population than 50,000. By limiting the size and focusing on small towns, the movement recognises that social interactions, convivial practices, and the implementation of the movement's criteria on a city-wide basis might be jeopardized if the city is too large.

Gemeinschaft and *Gesellschaft*

Theories about urban alienation were developed during a time when Europe was rapidly urbanising due to industrialisation. Writing in the late nineteenth century, European urban theorists considered the virtues of cities for social relationships. They typically compared and contrasted rural life with that in large and growing metropolises without any regard for smaller-sized urban places. Ferdinand Tönnies, a sociologist and co-founder, in 1909, of the German Society for Sociology, distinguished between *Gemeinschaft* and *Gesellschaft* to describe rural life that is characterized by intimate, communal ties and the more public, anonymous, and transitory life in cities.[146] *Gemeinschaft* is loosely translated as "community"

and *Gesellschaft* means "society." Describing Tönnies's ideas, sociologist William Flanagan writes that "[T]he rural village was compatible with the feeling of unity; it was stable, and small scale, and the web of relationships within it were seasoned with age. But the city introduced division of social class, created tensions between the interest of capital and labour, was characterised by hostility, and had no natural need or place for family."[147]

Several decades after Tönnies wrote about *Gemeinschaft* and *Gesellschaft*, Louis Wirth, who grew up in a small town in Germany and emigrated to the United States to study and teach sociology in Chicago, wrote about life in the metropolis in his 1938 essay "Urbanism as a Way of Life." Wirth critiqued life in the city and described how it undermined primary relationships between people. Both Tönnies and Wirth may be considered anti-urban because they painted a bleak picture of the future of social relationships in cities. Granted, cities were growing at a very rapid pace at the time of their writing and, as a result, public health and the widening division between the rich and the poor had become contentious issues. Thus, the romantic notion that rural hamlets and towns were richer in social relationships and therefore provided higher quality of life may have been the result of such dismal urban conditions. The sociologists writing at the time did not focus on small towns. Their attention was on the rapidly growing cities that benefited from industrialisation. As mentioned earlier, small towns – especially those in Europe – were often left out and did not struggle with the messy social order such as unfolded in Britain's Manchester, Birmingham, or London.

In his essay, Wirth identified three qualities of the type of urbanism that he associated with the growing metropolises: size, density, and heterogeneity.[148] The size of a city, he argued, determines the strength and quality of social relationships. The larger the city, the more shallow and transient are social interactions and the more people rely on so-called secondary relationships (as opposed to primary relationships such as family ties). While shallow relationships may have negative impact on the ways in which individuals relate to each other,

175. Mantua, Italy. In good weather, the cafés around town plazas are a popular hangout.

176. Community and conviviality. In the towns of south-central Europe, streets and piazzas are characterized by a special rhythm. From 10 to about noon the streets bustle with shoppers. Everything is quiet during lunch time and the city awakes around four or five in the afternoon when people start to take a stroll, eat and drink in the local restaurants and cafes. Top: Mantua, Italy; bottom: Bellinzona, Switzerland.

they also allow for freedom from peer control and social pressure. Too often we think of small towns as the quaint, nostalgic places that we all would like to live in. But their smallness may also take a toll on the individual if social control is too strong. The second quality Wirth describes is density – the amalgamation of many different people and the resulting competition, processes of specialisation, and division of labour. Heterogeneity is the third quality of urbanism and Wirth described the ways in which city residents interact with many different types of people with varying interests and preferences. In contrast to Jane Jacobs, however, who described heterogeneity and diversity as necessary elements in urban progress and economic innovation, Wirth assumes that individuals could become alienated by the heterogeneity of the city.

Yet, Community Still Exists

The view that the city alienates individuals from themselves and from each other gave rise to the idea that community disappears as cities begin to grow. This school of thought has been described as "community lost."[149] A wealth of studies, however, have shown that community and cohesion still exist within cities and that the social ties are very strong, especially among certain ethnic or neighbourhood groups. Writing in the 1940s, sociologist William Foote Whyte examined a neighbourhood in Boston in his book *Street Corner Society* and found that even though the community may have looked

disorderly to the outside observer, it showed a strong sense of belonging and cohesion. In the 1960s, Herbert Gans wrote his book *The Urban Villager*, which described the ways in which a Boston community (the West End) defended itself against threats from the outside. Community studies like these have shown that kinship and social ties still exist even within large cities; this field became known as the "community saved" school of thought. Nowadays, people live their lives in multiple spaces and not only in specific neighbourhoods or within specific socioeconomic groups and communities. Someone might work downtown and cultivate a network of friends and colleagues there, but live in an outlying suburb and belong to another community in that place. This third type of community is often referred to as the "community liberated" and the school of thought describes the social ties a person may have that are free of any spatial constraints.

177. Todi, Italy. Cities are not only characterized by their built environment but also by social and demographic aspects. What makes cities unique is their heterogeneity and the ability to interact and meet different kinds of people. Multiple generations need to feel welcome in their city. They need to have space for social interactions and conviviality. These senior citizens gathered on a bench and enjoyed some quality time.

Small Town Social Capital

Small towns fit neither the stereotype of urban alienation nor the stereotype of romantic notions of rural traditional life. Small towns typically have a traditional sense of community and exude cohesion. This, however, can easily be undermined if the main employer in the town is losing jobs and people are forced to move or if the town is experiencing unprecedented economic growth and in-migration. Small towns also need to be aware that social cohesion may negatively impact development because, as communities form bonds and become more cohesive, they do not allow outside perspectives and newcomers to join them. Fresh ideas and outside influence, however, are vitally important for towns to survive.

Many small towns are now focusing on community building and the creation of social capital. The most prominent scholar of social capital, Robert Putnam, defined social capital as the "connections among individuals – social networks and the norms of reciprocity and trustworthiness that arise from them."[150] Like human capital (skills) or financial capital (money), social capital represents a resource from which individuals and communities can draw. At the community level, social capital facilitates collective action, and the more a community has of it, the better it can weather changes and become resilient. Personal relationships – fostered through convivial practices and rituals – form a social web of relationships from which small town residents can draw. This web consists of two different types of relationships: bridging and bonding social capital.[151] Bonding social capital connects individuals to likeminded others (knitting groups, teenager cliques, book clubs, etc.), whereas bridging social capital (connections across social groups or even between communities) allows individuals to connect to people across the socioeconomic spectrum. The latter concept is related to the idea of the "strength of weak ties" developed by sociologist Mark Granovetter. He conceptualizes weak ties between individuals as instrumental connections that often help individuals to advance. Related to communities, small towns need to develop bridging capital through connections to other towns. These networks will facilitate information exchange. Bridging networks bring in new ideas and keep small towns fresh. At the same time, communities need to develop bonding networks because they facilitate community cohesion and allow identity formation and affirmation.

Small town communities need to develop the right balance between bonding and bridging social capital. In communities where both types of capital are low, inequalities cannot be solved and the communities lack the capacity for change. If bonding capital is high and bridging capital is low, communities may resist change and experience "lock-in." Such communities may also experience infighting because the different groups might not trust each other. If bridging capital is high and bonding capital low, communities are in danger of losing control over their own destinies because externally located power influences a community's existence. This may be the case in small towns where industry is dominated by externally controlled companies. The ideal situation, as rural sociologists Cornelia Butler Flora and Jan Flora describe, is the community that has both high bridging and high bonding social capital.[152] In these communities healthy social relationships develop and networks to the outside ensure the introduction of new ideas and resources. Flora and Flora suggest that small towns and rural communities strive to increase bonding and bridging capital to develop what they call the "entrepreneurial social infrastructure."[153]

Hersbruck, Germany

Hersbruck became the first German Cittaslow in May, 2001. The town is located about 30 kilometres east of Nuremberg and has about 12,500 residents.[154] Hersbruck was founded as a small hamlet sometime between the eighth and ninth centuries. The town has traditionally served as a central place along the medieval trading route between Prague and Nuremberg. Hersbruck is a town that exhibits a high degree of bonding and bridging social capital and its entrepreneurial social infrastructure is put to work on very innovative small town programmes such as the preservation of traditional pasturelands, a farm-restaurant programme, and cooking classes for kids.

Hersbruck's local environmental groups have formed strong coalitions (bridging networks) with farmers, city government, and small businesses to protect traditional pastureland and orchards. This protection is linked with regional and community economic development to create income opportunities for local residents. The city-owned pastures (*Hutanger*) were traditionally used by herdsmen who were employed and paid by city government and who would take cattle owned by local residents out for grazing. Typically the pastures were located just in between the city's border and the agricultural fields and provided open space for the adjacent urban areas. The pastoral landscape became emblematic of the community and served multiple purposes: Tall standing oak trees and various fruit trees (apples, cherries, etc.) provided not only shade for the cattle and wildlife habitat, but also fruit that would be auctioned off to the locals during harvest season. The trees and brush would provide habitat for birds, insects, and other wildlife. Hersbruck's pastures were used until the late 1960s and early 1970s. By that time, however, the industrialisation of food production as well as more efficient uses of barns for keeping the cattle inside all year put an end to the tradition of taking the cattle to communal pasturelands. The *Hutanger* was subsequently neglected and orphaned. Some pastures would even be turned into trash dumps or housing and industrial subdivisions. Consequently, not only open space was lost but also the knowledge about the traditional uses of the land, one-of-a-kind heritage fruit trees, and, most critically, the connections between protecting and using

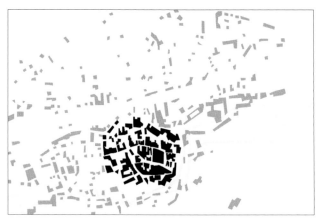

178. Hersbruck town centre.

179. Hersbruck.

180. Hersbruck. Typical for Bavarian towns like Hersbruck is the location of the city hall at the end of the central market square. Densely built houses line the square and today they house shops and apartments. The *Oberer Markt* in Hersbruck is the heart of the town.

the land for cattle and fruits that in turn provided economic opportunities for the local population.

A local environmental group that called attention to the blight of these pasturelands in the early 1980s is now an important partner in the town's Cittaslow coalition. The group's strategy of working to revive and protect the pastures is intimately connected with the goal of enhancing and strengthening the local economy. For example, they formed a network of local farmers who now sell their products directly from the farm (*Bauerngemeinschaft landwirtschaftlicher Direktvermarkter*). In 1998 the group conducted the first regional fair of local products (similar to Slow Food's *Salone del Gusto*). Since then, such a fair is held every year in a different village in the vicinity of the town and it showcases what local entrepreneurs and business owners have to offer.

Another programme involves the protection of heritage apple trees. The goal is to produce and market organic apple juice by using the fruit trees in the local orchards and pasturelands. A third initiative aimed at linking the cultural landscape with community economic development is a project that promotes the use of local produce in traditional region-specific dishes in restaurants. Twenty-nine farmers and 17 restaurants have formed a group of suppliers and gastronomic producers. The farmers supply the restaurants with their seasonal products and the restaurants offer special menus that also identify the producers by name and location for the benefit of the consumer. The programme is known as *Heimat auf'm Teller*. Parallel to this project are efforts to educate children about food and taste. Over a two-year period, children are involved in a local cooking school where they learn how to prepare and serve food. Through this approach, Hersbruck ensures that the next generation of its citizens is knowledgeable about local traditions and the connections food provides with the locality and territory. The programme seems to be effective since some of the participating children have apparently wrinkled their noses at home when frozen pizza was served for lunch.

A fourth project that connects the environment with the local economy derives from a group that formed to discuss and implement better uses of local woods. This group promotes the use of local

181. Hersbruck. Peter Bauer is the chef at Cafe Bauer, a hotel and restaurant in the town. His restaurant participates in the *Heimat auf'm Teller* initiative which links local farms to restaurants. The hotel was remodelled extensively to accommodate guests with allergies. For the furniture, Peter Bauer contracted with Herwig Danzer's Möbelmacher shop. By working with local businesses and farms, Cafe Bauer integrates into the local economy.

wood species for alternative energy production (in the form of woodchip heating systems), house building, and furniture. One of the restaurant and hotel owners in the town has contracted with the local furniture maker to equip the hotel rooms with furniture made from locally available woods.

Collectively, these examples illustrate how efforts to connect agents of change in a small town can also improve the local economy. In addition, by being part of the international Cittaslow network, Hersbruck is able to create bridging networks and draw on best practices and examples in other small towns around the world. Hersbruck's Cittaslow efforts show how cities can connect the three Es of sustainability in a way that pays attention to local histories and cultures and connects environmental protection with community economic development. The projects, moreover, demonstrate how a town can build local distinctiveness through the revival and protection of local traditions in a forward-looking way.

Hospitality

The concept of hospitality is closely related to that of conviviality. Small towns need to be hospitable to their own residents, but also to outsiders. They must extend a generous and cordial welcome and provide a pleasant environment to guests and residents alike. Tourism is often associated with hospitality and small towns have employed strategies to increase the number of visitors. Sustainable tourism strategies incorporate the geographic and cultural aspects of small towns. In the state of Virginia in the United States, for example, several small towns have joined forces and established "The Crooked Road: Virginia's Heritage Music Trail." The three cities and ten towns along the 250-mile trail highlight their musical heritage and hope to attract visitors to the Appalachian region (Fig. 182). In Europe, farms in rural areas or small towns have started to rent out rooms to tourists. The idea is known as *Agroturismo* (Fig. 183) or farm tourism and promises to improve the local economy by giving the farmers additional income. Tourism development, however, can be a double-edged sword. On one hand, tourism might promise new development for small towns, but on the other it may also increase the share of lower-paid service jobs. In addition, if small towns become too popular because of the tourist attraction strategies, they may experience negative spillover effects (as was the case in Orvieto, Italy).

Even with these negative aspects in mind, tourism can contribute to small town sustainability. Small mountain towns in the Alpine areas of Austria, Switzerland, France, and Italy face tremendous pressures to transform themselves and increasingly they are using the concepts of hospitality, tourism, and authenticity. These small towns experience depopulation, a decline in traditional agricultural practices, aging, difficult access from the outside, a lack of planning ideas and strategies, and, as a result of these trends, a loss of local heritage and culture. Even though some of the small towns, as documented by the European network AlpCity, have managed to grow specialised small and medium-sized businesses (especially related to traditional craftsmanship) and are realising a renewed interest of their young people to stay, they are still struggling to shape their future.

One interesting programme has emerged in Italy, specifically in the region of Friuli Venezia Giulia, which encompasses the Alpine area of Carnia and the lower-lying regions around Udine and Trieste. The project is called *Albergo Diffuso* and the idea is to turn the village as a whole into a "hotel" by developing affordable and authentic accommodations for tourists. A centralised reception at the centre of the town streamlines accommodation requests and also lowers the associated overhead costs. Houses used as *Alberghi* are renovated and restored to the local architectural standards and

182. Virginia Music Trail.
The Crooked Road, Virginia's Heritage Music Trail, winds through the mountains of Southwest Virginia. The music trail is intended to support economic development by promoting Heritage Tourism and Blue Ridge and Appalachian culture.

a pine tree symbol signals the different levels of accommodation. Guests can stroll in the village and shop for locally made crafts and eat at local restaurants. The Assembly of European Regions (AER), the political organisation of the Regions in Europe, praised the concept as a model that values sustainability and authenticity and respects local traditions and culture. AER notes that the "authenticity of the location is at the heart of the whole project. Tourists can get a real feeling of genuine places, where the memory of the old times lives on in the tales of local villagers."[155] The idea started in 1978 in Carnia in response to an earthquake that destroyed much of the region two years earlier. Italy now has more than 90 *Albergo Diffuso* structures and the AER is promoting the model in other European countries.

The lure of these once-forgotten mountain villages and small towns is great, especially to foreigners. In the mid-1990s a Swedish-Italian preservationist discovered the small town of Santo Stefano di Sessanio in the Abruzzi region of Italy. He acquired the town's Palazzo delle Logge and surrounding structures and invested more than $5.1 million in their renovation. The palazzo is now an *Albergo Diffuso* and its goals appeal to those interested in the "territory's archaeological heritage."[156] The place seems to incorporate – and advertise – all the right ingredients: authenticity, local culture, food, and traditions. On its website, the *Albergo Diffuso* markets itself to global cities, locating itself with reference to Berlin, London, Paris, and Madrid.

Local Products

Efforts to foster conviviality and hospitality are easier if they are centred around certain rituals and practices. Often these involve food and the habits of eating and sharing a meal. Food is also an essential component of a small town economy; if we are to develop sustainable place economies, planners need to pay attention to the way food is produced and, equally important, how it is consumed. Localising food systems is increasingly part of broader efforts to localise the economy. A focus on products that use local resources allows small town economic developers to engage producers and consumers. Often these efforts have positive side effects. The cultural landscape is maintained because the fields are used to grow produce; small business owners realise a market for their goods; towns can maintain and enhance their local distinctiveness and authenticity; and food is put at the centre of everyday social and convivial practices.

Authenticity is a central aspect of local distinctiveness. According to planner Sue Clifford and environmentalist Angela King, authenticity is about the "real and the genuine" that "hold a strength of meaning."[157] Illustrating authenticity, they note the example of Wensleydale cheese, a handcrafted cheese from the United Kingdom's North Yorkshire region:

183. Orcia Valley, near Siena, Italy. An agroturismo development.

184. Chiavenna, Italy. Slow Food's Ark of Taste is a means to protect almost extinct food items such as the Violino ham in Chiavenna. This ham is very typical of the region. It is made of goat meat and aged in caves of the area that are formed by the unique Alpine geology. The ham became almost extinct as fewer and fewer butchers knew how to make it.

"Why is it important to makers and gourmets that this cheese continues to be made in this valley and not the next? Amongst the reasons to do with the need for jobs, comes also an understanding that cows of this place, eating grass in this valley, with expertise built here over generations combine to create a food which is particular, authentic, and good. Its making brings dignity and pride to the place, since the people who make it are experts, the people who grow the grass to feed the cows are implicated in this. The relationships breed culture and identity that has meaning for the people who live and work here and for those who chance upon it or make it their destination. The landscape that is created and sustained by this activity is one in which mixed grass, wild flowers, and barns have a real role and sustain a landscape plotted and pieced with interrelationships."[158]

Conviviality and local products go hand-in-hand. The popularity of farmers markets in the United States, for example, is not only an expression of the new-found value in sourcing local products; these markets also serve as convivial places. In contrast to many European markets, U.S. farmers' markets have become festivals with live music, cooking shows, communal tables, and tastings of artisanal products.

Consumers as Co-producers

Writing about the necessity for good, clean, and fair food, Slow Food founder Carlo Petrini notes that the consumer has to become a co-producer. He argues that "*consuming* is the final act of the production process"[159] and that we need to be aware about where food comes from, how it is produced, who produces it, how it is processed, and how it is prepared. Food, as he argues, is "far more than a simple product to be consumed: it is happiness, identity, culture, pleasure, conviviality, nutrition, local economy, survival."[160] By being informed and educated, the consumer is able to make different choices.

Research in the United States has shown that there is a great interest among consumers in purchasing local products. A recent study of consumers and farmers in Nebraska, for example, illustrates that consumers were willing to pay more for local food because they valued its taste and quality.[161] Farmers, in contrast, had low interest in producing for the local market and were mainly interested in selling to the large-scale food industry. This consumer-producer mismatch points to an important role small town planners can play: They can connect consumers with producers and educate both parties about available local products.

There are a handful of promising examples that illustrate how this can be done. As noted in Chapter 2, Slow Food signed an agreement in 2001 with Coop Italia, the largest supermarket chain in Italy. Coop Italia adopted 11 *presidia* products and included them in its stores. Most products experienced high levels of demand, which supported price increases. As a result, the number of producers also increased and Slow Food

185. Zurich, Switzerland. The Swiss supermarket chain Coop has offered Slow Food products since 2007. The offerings include more than 50 products. Coop also helped create five presidia in Switzerland that support food products such as a special rye bread from the Valais region.

These locally made and rooted products may strike a chord with consumers. The German sociologist Ulrich Beck writes that in the age of cultural, political, and economic globalisation, society needs to define new goals.[163] He argues that differentiation is rewarded and that there is a chance to "re-regionalise" local products. A product's biography is becoming more important as the global world takes away certain particularities. Local markets, Slow Food, connecting consumers with producers, Buy Local campaigns, etc. are expressions of this sentiment. The connection between conviviality, hospitality, and local products seems far-fetched but, if production and consumption are embedded in a local context and if space and time are reserved for social interaction around consumption, then the conceptual connection between these ideas is quite obvious.

successfully connected niche product producers to the mass-consumption market. The number of Cinta Cenese pig producers (suppliers of one of the *presidia* products), for example, increased from 9 to 130.[162] The Swiss supermarket chain Coop has implemented a similar programme (Fig. 185). In 1994, the regional development agency in the province of Bolzano in Northern Italy initiated an EU-funded project to reintroduce a traditional bread roll – the so-called *Vinschger Urpaarl* – that uses rye flour and is produced from a traditional recipe originally developed by the region's Benedictine monks. The project connected farmers with the mill and the mill with local bakers. Strict quality control ensured the integrity of the ingredients while the involvement of Slow Food encouraged sales. As a result, the traditional landscape of small-scale grain fields in the valleys of the region has been maintained and the prices the farmers, millers, and bakers are able to command are higher than for regular grain or flour. In the United States, similar group marketing efforts include the North Carolina project Handmade in America, which markets crafts and artistic products from the Appalachian mountain region; and Arkansas's DeltaMade, which features locally produced and (for the region) typical products. Such efforts are aimed at connecting producers with consumers.

186. Blacksburg, Virginia. The Lyric is a restored movie theatre in downtown.

8

Creativity and Culture

Some commentators have advocated the transformative potential of cultural activities for economic competitiveness. This more instrumental perspective is focused on attracting customers to cultural events, creating hip, bohemian neighbourhoods as spaces of consumption, or becoming a globally recognised creative hub. Such an instrumental perspective on art, culture, and creativity is rooted in the postindustrial society and the emergence of a knowledge-based "experience" economy. A fashionable view is that the economic competitiveness of cities and regions depends on their ability to attract certain kinds of knowledge workers: a "creative class" of scientists, engineers, writers, artists, architects, designers, and managers.[166] This creative class not only acts as the creators but also as the consumers of creativity, which takes on a commodified meaning because it is solely used to create economic benefits.

Creative expressions of small town culture and heritage can be considered an essential element of social sustainability. Art and culture have always been important to the vitality of towns and cities. Cultural heritage and traditions are woven into the social fabric of small towns and give meaning to their continued existence. Art, culture, and especially the notion of heritage play an important role in preserving and developing identity in small towns and rural areas. As early as the 1930s, studies in the United States described the vibrant role of creativity and art in the rural context.[164] More recently, researchers from the McKnight Foundation studying small towns in rural Minnesota found that arts and creativity can play a strong catalytic role in the social and, to some extent, the economic revitalisation of small towns. They highlight four findings regarding the role of arts in small towns and argue that art can:

1. Create important opportunities for engagement among citizens, visitors, neighbours, friends, and families;
2. Enhance the ways in which citizens collaborate and create community solutions through diverse leadership;
3. Help shape a community's identity; and
4. Contribute to the development of a new rural (small town) economy.[165]

Increasingly, cities around the world exploit art, culture, and creativity for instrumental purpose, and planners, architects, and policymakers often forget to pay attention to the intrinsic values of creative endeavours and their contribution to social sustainability. Small towns, however, must pay attention not just to the instrumental benefits of culture and creativity, but also to their immanent values and their social contribution. In fact, most small towns cannot realistically compete with large cities in the race to attract members of the creative class. Rather, being creative and using art and culture for development may mean something completely different to these small towns.

Community-based Art, Culture, and Creativity

The instrumental and intrinsic perspectives on the role of art, culture, and creativity differ in important ways. From the instrumental perspective, art and culture are seen to create place-based economic benefits, whereas the intrinsic perspective values creativity for its potential to introduce social change and shift prevalent thinking. Two theories are representative of each perspective. The so-called Creative Class theory recognises the monetary and economic benefits of creative expressions. In contrast, community-based theories about the role of arts in social transformation describe the ways in which creativity emerges from a community's artistic and cultural expressions. The latter are more applicable to small towns than the former.

Community-based theories suggest that the use of arts and culture for small town sustainability and regeneration should go beyond its instrumental benefits (i.e., economic competitiveness, creation of creative industries, etc.) and integrate the intrinsic characteristics of creativity. Creativity is not just about innovating or creating new things, products, processes, or consumer experiences. Rather, creative endeavours shift our thinking and change stereotypes. Through the arts and culture, residents and artists can imagine a different future for a community or a place, and they can introduce paradigm shifts once they are empowered through creativity. Arts and culture also value the past through the use of traditional skills and expertise or history and stories. Art, culture, and creativity also cross boundaries and blur lines between the known and the unknown, the past and the future. Community-based arts encourage creative expressions in communities through participatory practices that empower community members. These processes create social change. Instrumental benefits in the form of economic vitality and revitalisation might follow social transformation. They will, however, be more powerful if the activities pay respect to the communities' needs and desires and are embedded in social capacity-building processes.

187. Diss, England. In 2004 the town held a year-long festival to commemorate the life and work of John Skelton, who moved to Diss in 1504 as rector and poet laureate, having previously been tutor to the young Henry VIII.

188. Überlingen, Germany. This house is a vivid portrait of a long-standing cultural tradition in Überlingen: The sword dance that was performed during carnival. Nowadays the dance is performed during a festival in July. It was officially recorded in 1646 and was typically performed by vintners who were single.

In small towns, culture and creativity take on distinct meanings. Small towns have unique histories that shape a specific type of cultural heritage. Often this heritage is rooted in the agricultural history of the past and is creatively expressed through folk art and festivals more akin to the "rural way" of life than the cosmopolitan practices of global cities (Fig. 188). Traditional crafts such as lace making, embroidery, pottery, or furniture making are creative expressions of small town cultural heritage. Cultural heritage practices express creativity – defined as the creation and expression of ideas – and connect the past to the future: "[C]ultural heritage connects us to our histories, our collective memories, it anchors our sense of being and can provide a source of insight to help us to face the future."[167]

Community-based art can also contribute to place-making. In a 2007 publication about the role of creativity in neighbourhood development, Jeremy Nowak of The Reinvestment Fund pleads for an integrated perspective on the role of art in community development. He notes that "community-based arts and cultural activity has place-making value […] Artists are expert at uncovering, expressing and re-purposing the assets of a place – from buildings and public spaces to community stories. They are natural place-makers who assume – in the course of making a living – a range of civic and entrepreneurial roles that require both collaboration and self-reliance. And they are steeped in a creative

dialogue between the past and the future."[168] Artists can engage residents of a place in creative undertakings. Residents can themselves become artists and express their creativity. Community-based art in the form of theatre, music, visual arts, dance, poetry, or electronic media can establish cultural identity and create social transformation and change. Small-town residents interact with each other in cultural events and thereby build social capital. Organising a folk art festival or setting up a visual art exhibit not only attracts visitors to a town, it also allows residents to be exposed to creativity or even showcase their own art and, the process of organising these events, builds critical social connections and civic capacity (Figs. 190–192).

189. Diss, England. Customised signage can lend a sense of distinctiveness and identity.

190. Blacksburg, Virginia, USA. The annual Stepping Out street festival, held the first weekend in August each year, brings vitality to the campus town at a time when most students have left town for the summer.

191. Floyd, Virginia, USA. Flatfooting – a form of tap-dancing – and traditional music are part of the weekend activities at Mabry Mill, a restored grist mill on the Blue Ridge Parkway.

192. Bra, Italy. The bi-annual Cheese Festival attracts more than 150,000 people to the town.

Small Town Creativity and Revitalisation

There are many examples where community-based culture and creativity contribute to small town revitalisation. Paducah, a small town of 25,009 residents in Kentucky, revitalised a crime-ridden historic neighbourhood by offering relocation incentives to artists (Figs. 193 and 194). Lowertown is Paducah's oldest neighbourhood with historical homes built in the Italianate, Gothic Revival, Romanesque, Queen Anne, and Classical Revival architectural styles. In 1982 the area was placed on the National Register of Historic Places, but soon experienced significant decline. Families moved out to the suburbs and shopping malls opened on the outskirts, sucking the life of the former bustling, close-in neighbourhood. Lowertown was plagued by drugs and prostitution and many of the historic houses were run by slumlords. In 2000 the town started its Artist Relocation Program, which was designed to attract artists to the Lowertown neighbourhood by offering cultural and financial incentives that encourage artists to purchase buildings and set up their galleries and studios. A local bank works with artists and offers them fixed-rate mortgages. The programme was the brainchild of Mark Barone, a local artist and resident of the area. He and the city's planner, Tom Barnett, saw the potential of artists as change agents for the area. The area has dual zoning, which allows commercial and residential uses to mix. Artists can live upstairs and have studio or gallery space inside their residence.

So far the town has attracted more than 70 artists from across the United States and abroad. The programme is especially attractive to artists who cannot afford the high real estate prices in cities such as New York or Chicago. Nationally recognised, the programme has a high success rate because about 25 percent of the artists who visit Paducah end up staying. Paducah has benefited from the artists in two ways. The neighbourhood economy received a boost as Lowertown's success in attracting artists has influenced local real estate costs; local property values have tripled since 2000. But also, after a period of adjustment to having artists around, residents are discovering the creative sides of a neighbourhood that they once eschewed.

Artists are change agents and they are often early entrants into sketchy neighbourhoods or areas

193. Paducah, Kentucky, USA. The Artist Relocation Program started in 2000 and has since then attracted more than 70 artists. Paducah's Lowertown was set up as an arts district and dual zoning for commercial and residential use allows artists to live and work in the same building.

194. Paducah, Kentucky, USA. The Mentor House Gallery is located in the heart of Paducah's Lowertown district. The 5.5-metre-high giraffe was created by the artist George Bandarra. It adds a unique perspective to the building and the neighbourhood.

marked by decline. In Paducah, for example, artists were the ones who took the risk of moving into a run-down neighbourhood. They envisioned the future and reinvested in the area. They thereby stabilised the neighbourhood. Artists are also skilled at adaptive reuse of old buildings such as warehouses and, as Jeremy Nowak has argued, they value the opportunity to remake the space. Artists also provide entrepreneurial vigour to a neighbourhood or community, and through their business activities they contribute to local economic development.

Several small towns in Minnesota have experienced such stabilising forces. New York Mills, a town of less than 1,200 people about 3.5 hours northwest of the Twin Cities, benefited from the establishment of a regional cultural centre (Figs. 195 and 196). New York Mills was founded in 1884 by Finnish immigrants and it has traditionally been a rural farming community. Over the last two decades the town has seen out-migration and economic decline along its Main Street. In the late 1980s, the artist John Davis bought a dilapidated farmhouse and moved to town. He became New York Mill's change agent because he spearheaded the effort to create an artist's retreat. To convince local residents, he formed a board of directors representative of New York Mills's demographic make-up and was able to obtain a bank loan. He also convinced the City Council to provide $35,000 for the Regional Cultural Center that was to be housed in an abandoned building on Main Street. This financial commitment of New York Mills's residents to the centre is remarkable. In their review of artist's centres in Minnesota, geographers Markusen and Johnson note that "a comparable per capita investment from the Minneapolis City Council to a metropolitan art organisation would be $13 million."[169] The renovation of the building became a civic project involving major volunteer efforts on the part of local residents. The centre opened in 1992 and has since then become an important local and regional arts hub. Artists come and visit the town and enjoy the rural setting as their retreat. They also volunteer in the local community and contribute to civic capacity. Once a month, an Artist Forum facilitates networking among the artists in the region, and seasonal events, including an ice-house design competition, add vitality to the town. The City Council contributes $10,000 annually to the organisation, but this falls significantly short of the $133,000 required to operate the centre on an annual basis. As a result of the centre, the town has seen population growth, an increase in the number of local businesses, the establishment of a new school, and downtown revitalisation.

Even though most artists' facilities like the Regional Cultural Center struggle to obtain sufficient funds for their operation, they are invaluable. Cultural events provide artistic content and local residents are enriched through quality programming. Visitors who come to the town to partake in these offerings will also add economic value. These centres energise communities

195. New York Mills, Minnesota, USA. The New York Mills Regional Cultural Center has been an important social and cultural institution in this small Minnesotan town. As a non-profit institution, the centre offers a range of activities for the town's residents. It functions as a satellite centre of the Minneapolis Walker Arts Center and offers arts education to children such as ballet classes.

196. New York Mills, Minnesota, USA. The cultural centre has become an important community institution for all generations, young and old. The gallery space on the second floor of the building exhibits art throughout the year.

and facilitate civic pride – especially if historically significant buildings are rehabilitated. Artists visiting and working in small towns stimulate creative thinking among local residents.

Examples of how small towns have used art for revitalisation are too numerous to describe here (Figs. 197–199). In many small towns movie theatres that were once thriving cultural centres have been renovated (Fig. 186). They now serve as important anchors in downtown revitalisation efforts and such facilities have created new reasons for people to visit small towns. The small town of Jackson, Michigan, transformed a former prison into a live/work building for artists and is trying to connect resident artists with industry people in an incubator that will be integrated into the complex. Arts facilities and artists themselves can change places and they contribute to small town vitality. But these kinds of activities have to go beyond the notion of "just becoming hip and cool." Art and culture should engage citizens and empower them. The social benefits derived from this kind of community-based art transform small towns.

197. Bridport, England. The town's Art Centre has a 200-seat theatre, three exhibition spaces, a café and bar.

198. Perth, Scotland. A new 1,600-seat concert hall on the site of the former Horsecross Market, funded mostly from national lottery revenues as part of the United Kingdom's Millennium celebrations.

199. Überlingen, Germany. Public art in Überlingen. The fountain was designed and built by a local artist (Peter Lenk). The horseman is an ironic depiction of the famous writer Martin Walser, who calls Überlingen his home. Public art stimulates thinking and can be provocative.

Pogradec, Albania

Pogradec is a small town in the southeastern part of Albania. It is located on the shore of Lake Ohrid and serves as the main urban centre in the region. With about 30,000 residents, the town is small but its proximity to Macedonia and Greece makes it a cosmopolitan hub where different peoples merge and interact. Pogradec's historic roots go back to antiquity when the dominant community known as Illyrians settled in the region. Subsequently, the region was always subject to the vagaries of various empires, including Greeks, Romans, Venetians, Ottomans, and Italians. The Communist Party took over modern day Albania in 1944. Their dictatorial leader Enver Hoxha presided over a Stalinist state for four decades, isolating the country from its surrounding region and larger European cultural trends and geopolitical currents. Surrounded by hills and bordering on the lake, Pogradec is a popular tourist destination, and during the communist regime it served as the summer escape for government officials. Pogradec and Albania as a whole have gone through tremendous political and cultural changes. During the 1990s, liberalisation allowed travel abroad. Political competition, clan divisions and disputed elections led to widespread unrest and anarchy in the early 1990s. International peacekeeping forces intervened in the larger region in the mid 1990s in Bosnia and later in 1999 in Kosovo. Albania experienced firsthand spillover effects from these neighbouring civil war conflicts.

Small towns in Albania (and also in other former communist countries) struggle with gaining normality. Often the speed of introduction of the market economy overwhelms them and they fear losing their local identity. Countries in transition also experience enormous changes in their social systems. Charles Landry, an eminent scholar of the role of creativity and culture in urban development, notes that in countries like Albania "there was a culture of control rather than one of transparency and openness."[170] The Swiss Arts Council Pro Helvetia, mandated by the Swiss Agency for Development and Cooperation (SDC) at the Ministry of Foreign Affairs, established the Swiss Cultural Program (SCP) in South-Eastern Europe and Ukraine to assist transitioning countries through the promotion of art and culture. In 2004 the programme started its first project in Albania and began to work in two cities, Shkodra and Pogradec. The idea was to transform

200. Pogradec town centre.

201. Pogradec. A bookstore and a café were set up along the main street in Pogradec. The café, initiated by a female Creative City project volunteer, functions as a third place in the town not only for residents but also for tourists. The Creative City project in Pogradec succeeded with eliciting imaginative solutions and ideas to common urban problems such as the decline of the main street and the lack of cultural institutions.

202. Pogradec. Part of Naim Frasheri Street before renovation and beautification (2005).

these two towns into creative cities and to bring about social transformation and change through arts and culture. SCP invited Charles Landry to facilitate this – for Albania – completely new approach aimed at changing the prevailing culture from one of control to one of transparency and openness.

Pogradec's Creative City project is led by a team of citizens interested in initiating change and responding to problems such as social and urban decline. Building on local and natural assets such as Pogradec's flowers and beautiful lake setting, the team started a street beautification project and a flower festival. A local artist then began to paint the doors of his house and after a while other residents wanted to also have their doors painted. These voluntary efforts functioned as creative triggers and even led the local government to repair the main street and to beautify the area some more. A library/café opened and now functions as a third place, tourist information and literary centre. A local artist has renovated a traditional fountain that is now a meeting place for others. Another member of the local Creative City team staged a mono drama and started a regional theatre competition for young residents of Pogradec and the nearby town Struga in Macedonia. These small creative efforts have brought about visible changes in the townscape.

In Progradec, traditionally known for its literary heritage, a poetry festival has become a regional attraction and is now drawing visitors from surrounding areas. Local cultural practitioners, artists, and policymakers also revived the puppet theatre tradition, and national and international artists come to town to take part in Pogradec's puppet theatre festival each year. Pogradec plans to join the Cittaslow movement and emphasise local food and culture in its tourism development.

Pogradec's Creative City team will take on a coaching role for other cities in Albania as the Swiss organisation initiates a second round of Creative Cities projects. This time towns are asked to develop proposals at a regional scale and to coordinate their efforts with other jurisdictions. Asked about the success of the Creative Cities project in Pogradec, Charles Landry responds that "there will be more colour in Pogradec." The challenge, however, for cities like Pogradec is to address larger political and economic problems such as corruption, illegal buildings, weak governments, and greedy individualism as the prevailing mood. Creativity and culture expressed in public goods such as the flower and street beautification, the library as a third place, and cultural festivals signal a different modus of operandi and have the potential to create social transformation and change.

203. Pogradec. Part of Naim Frasheri Street after renovation (2007).

Creativity and Social Transformation

Community-based art not only contributes to physical transformation, but also to social transformation and civic renewal of small towns. Artistic and cultural expressions that are embedded in a community create civic engagement and discussions about important issues and challenges. In Australia, for example, where small towns are often referred to as country towns, researchers and government officials used art to facilitate community-based discussions about sustainability. In June, 2000, the Centre for Sustainable Regional Communities at La Trobe University hosted a conference to discuss the future of Australia's country towns. Similar to small towns in Europe and the United States, these country towns face severe challenges such as aging of their population, out-migration of young people, economic decline, and shrinkage. In addition, many country towns are isolated geographically. Researchers and policymakers recognised that country towns have to change from within and find ways to adapt to their challenges. They set out to build social capital and to assess small town sustainability through a set of indicators. University researchers from the Centre for Sustainable Regional Communities started such efforts for five small communities in the goldfields of Central Victoria. They selected the towns of Dunolly, Wedderburn, Carisbrook, Talbot, and Maldon, and planned to develop sustainability indicators, strategic community plans, and benchmarks.[171] They soon realised, however, that the community did not understand the tasks at hand and consequently it was difficult to stimulate much citizen involvement.

The researchers changed course and formed a partnership with the Cultural Development Network, a nonprofit organisation that links communities, artists, and local organisations across Victoria to promote participatory art and community sustainability. They renamed the project from TBL Community Audit to Small Towns: Big Picture, a more imaginative and evocative title. The partnership engaged eight artists to work alongside the researchers in the communities. The artists included a playwright, a website developer, a photographer, a print maker, a textile artist, a ceramicist, a film maker, and a community artist who acted as a coordinator. The playwright, for example, closely followed the development of a community cohesion index and used the focus groups researchers held to create a theatrical performance called Right Where We Are. Community members acted in the play and illustrated the different perspectives of the various community members. A local film maker created a documentary about the research project, which was later shown in Melbourne. A visual art exhibit included artwork created by residents. Using arts to draw residents to the project was successful and more than 1,500 community members became engaged in the project. The artwork created in the communities has travelled to far-flung places such as Melbourne and has contributed to a shared understanding among urbanites of what life in country towns is like. Furthermore, the Shire codified the role of art in community development and planning in an arts policy, which was passed by local policymakers. Small Towns: Big Picture is now linked with the region's Connecting Confident Communities programme, which is designed to build community cohesion among the region's small country towns.

In the case of the Australian country towns, creativity was used to elicit the intrinsic values of art and culture. Artists facilitated community discussion and interpretation and allowed residents to interpret their feelings, perspectives, and views about their towns in very different ways. This suggests an alternative understanding of culture and creativity than the Creative Class theory suggests: Creativity is used not for economic competitiveness, but for building social capital and civic capacity.

The Creative Class Debate

In recent years, creativity has become an urban planning buzzword. Planners and architects have rallied around the notion of a so-called creative class and its contribution to "creative cities."[172] According to commentator Richard Florida, the creative class includes architects, designers, artists, entertainers, scientists, as well as managers, sales people, lawyers, accountants, and bankers.[173] The argument is that the transition from an industrial to a postindustrial society profoundly influenced the makeup of urban labour markets and that today about 30 percent of the U.S. labour force (38 million people) create new ideas and knowledge. Similar research indicates that about 38 percent of the total workforce in eight European countries (about 26 million people) belong to the so-called creative class.[174] People in these creative occupations are highly mobile and choose cities that are tolerant, diverse, and open to creativity. Florida argues that it is not the jobs that attract the creative class. Rather, it is the milieu or the city's environment that this group finds appealing.

204. Saugatuck, Michigan, USA. Originally a lumber town, Saugatuck is now an art town and was labeled a Cool City by the state of Michigan.

Florida shows that this class is unevenly distributed across cities and regions, with a bias toward the large metropolises. San Francisco, Boston, and New York rank high while traditional blue-collar towns such as Maryland's Cumberland and Virginia's Danville rank low. Indeed, Florida seems to discount small towns. In an interview with the online magazine Salon, he notes, "The hopeless places are the Enid, Oklahomas, the Youngstown, Ohios, the small places with huge working-class backgrounds, or places that are service-class centers that aren't tourist destinations. They're all at the bottom of my lists. They're the places that are just being completely left behind. So size really is an advantage. If you're big, you can offer a lot of options and do a lot of things."[175]

Nevertheless, the notion of the creative city is seductive and many towns are trying to become hip and cool in order to attract members of the creative class. For example, the state of Michigan began to implement a creativity-based redevelopment agenda in 2003 when Governor Jennifer Granholm kicked off the Cool Cities initiative. Michigan is a state battered by industrial restructuring, a declining industrial base, high unemployment

rates, and countless towns that Florida would consider "hopeless places." Young people leave the state and many small towns are faced with the challenge to revitalise and avert shrinking. The Cool Cities initiative is geared toward urban renewal by focusing on physical redevelopment. Once a Michigan city receives the Cool City designation it is able to apply for state funding. The programme is primarily focused on a bricks and mortar strategy without much attention to the intrinsic benefits of art and culture. For example, the small community of Saugatuck (Fig. 204), located on the Kalamazoo River, was dedicated as a Cool City and received funding from the state for the renovation of an old pie factory. The empty factory was purchased by a local group of citizens and, when funding from the state came through, it transformed into a community-based arts facility. The centre has classrooms and exhibit space and is also home to a theatre and a film festival. Additional funding was used to build an eco-friendly sculpture garden.

Creative Class theories have been widely criticised. First, it should be borne in mind that the original notion of the creative class was developed in relation to large metropolitan areas. Its application to the context of small towns is therefore question-able, given that large metropolitan areas benefit from agglomeration economies and deep labour markets, and are therefore natural creative class hubs. Even within metropolitan settings, however, the theory is problematic. The geographer Jamie Peck, for example, notes that a focus on attracting the creative class allows policymakers to follow a neoliberal agenda by diverting their attention away from more difficult policies that address redistribu-tion issues and urban problems such as poverty or homelessness.[176] Some criticise the theory's heavy focus on people and have argued that the industrial structure and the resulting nature and availability of jobs are more important than the creative milieu in determining whether a city ranks high on the creative class index.[177] Others have probed the definitions of creativity and creative occupations. Economic geographer Ann Markusen, for example, suggests that nurses are as creative as scientists or artists and notes that a nurse's job demands the creative skill of dealing with people on a daily basis and that this type of creativity should not be discounted. Others argue that Florida's defini-tion of the creative class is too broad, suggesting that it should not include managers, sales people, lawyers, accountants, bankers, and such. Excluding these occupations, of course, weakens the case for the economic impact of the creative class. Definitions based on arts-centric occupations account for only between 5 and 7 percent of the workforce in Europe and North America.

This critique highlights the often difficult and contentious debate about what constitutes creativ-ity. In particular, the question arises as to whether the type of human capital that is prevalent in small towns (farmers, nurses, teachers, etc.) can also be considered creative. After all, the word creativity is often defined with "being able to create," and the creation of ideas, art, culture, and products in small towns may be more closely associated with manual work and labour than high-powered sci-ence and ideas. Are small town occupations such as farmer, shop owner, teacher, and nurse considered uncreative in the context of Florida's Creative Class theory? What about the farmer who has to find novel ways of growing crops in the face of climate change? What about the nurse who paints folk

art in her spare time? And what about the local butcher who plays the trumpet in the local music club? Small town creativity is a much larger concept than the Creative Class theories would imply. Applied to the small town context, conceptions of creativity need to take different dimensions and definitions into account – specifically, notions of traditions, heritage, high and low cultures, as well as community-based arts play an important role.

Creative Class and Globalisation

While the ideas of the creative class originally emerged in the North American context, they have also been applied in Europe, Asia, Australia, and New Zealand. Common to their application is the primary focus on large metropolitan regions or cosmopolitan cities. The European Commission, for example, started to study the role of creative industries in 2006 and adopted the first European strategy for culture in 2007.[178] The focus on cultural and creative industries follows a well-established tradition of selecting a European City of Culture annually since the mid-1980s. The selected cities are usually larger cities such as Linz (Austria) and Vilnius (Lithuania), which were selected for 2009. In 2007, the European Commission adopted a new cultural policy (A European Agenda for Culture in a Globalising World) to intensify the efforts regarding the role of culture in develop-ing social cohesion, diversity, as well as eco-nomic development. Although peripheral and rural development are seen to benefit from a focus on cultural heritage, the more prominent goal of the agenda seems to be economic competitiveness.

Small towns have been left out of the European creative class discussions. It is the larger, hip, and often up-and-coming metropolitan places such as Dublin or Tallinn (Estonia) that are talked about. The emphasis on large regions plays into the current discussion about the competitiveness of European metropolitan regions. These European metropolitan regions are urban agglomerations that are embedded in the larger network of regions. The goals are to further connect the network of cities through, for example, high-speed rail connections (the rail connection between Paris and Stuttgart only takes 3.5 hours one-way) and to transform these cities into European and global engines of economic development. Even in countries that have traditionally thought of themselves as having geographies dominated by rural villages and small towns, discussions centre around this concept of metropolitan regions, and critical questions arise about the fate of areas outside of these regions, the so-called periphery. Peripheral regions such as the Alpine regions with small mountain towns are hampered by a demographic exodus and the attenuation of traditional social structures. In Switzerland, for example, urban planners and architects have suggested that the structurally weak areas in the "alpine waste land" (Fig. 205) be left behind in favour of developing the economically strong metropolitan regions.[179]

Is There a Creative Class in Small Towns?

The question of whether the Creative Class theory could be applied to the rural or small town context in the United States was taken up by researchers at the U.S. Department of Agriculture in 2007.[180] They have found that only 11 percent of the nonmetropolitan counties in the United States ranked as creative class counties in 2000. These rural creative class locations have certain characteristics that attract people. They are rich in natural amenities (mountains, lakes, etc.) or host higher education institutions such as the land grant universities, which, in the United States, are traditionally located in rural areas. As a result, creative class small towns are often those that are recreational hotspots (Aspen, Colorado, or Bend, Oregon) or they are college towns attractive to students and possibly other types of entrepreneurs and businesses (Blacksburg, Virginia, or Ithaca, New York). Sometimes these small towns may have developed from historical accidents such as what occurred in Fairfield, Iowa. In 1974 the Maharishi International University was established there and part of its curriculum is teaching transcendental meditation. The presence of the university and the town's adoption of an economic gardening strategy (outlined in Chapter 6) have attracted and created a creative class environment. The researchers also note that in the rural and small town context, the "presence of the creative class may itself create amenities. For instance, a place that has attracted artists and designers may appeal to people who like artistic communities."[181] The study, however, seems to be a flawed application of the Creative Class theory to the small town context because the researchers apply a similar occupational definition of the creative class with only minor acknowledgment of the different labour market or demographic context of small towns. Studying the role of culture and creativity in a small town or rural context would require a different conception of what constitutes their economic and social contributions.

205. Aquila, Switzerland. Aquila is a town of about 500 residents and it is located in a valley about 40 kilometres north of Bellinzona. The area is part of the so-called "alpine wasteland." In 2006 Switzerland began to implement a new type of regional development policy, the so-called Neue Regionalpolitik. The policy aims to foster collaboration of small towns in rural regions, sometimes through annexations or mergers with other towns.

The High Cost of Art

Many cities, regardless of their size, desire to build or expand arts and cultural facilities such as museums, symphonies, casinos, convention centres, or sports arenas. These facilities are typically larger than the artists' centres or cultural districts that places such as Paducah or New York Mills built. These are large-scale facilities with expensive price tags for the taxpayers because they are typically not economically viable. Although not a small town, the small city of Roanoke, for example, built a 75,000-square-foot art museum whose annual operating budget is estimated at $3.5 million. Roanoke's Art Museum of Western Virginia (Fig. 206) cost $66 million and, with its novel architecture reminiscent of Frank Gehry's (the facility was designed by Los Angeles architect Randall Stout), it represents an attempt by this former railroad town to use a large-scale arts facility for economic revitalisation.[182] Mid-size cities like Roanoke are vying for the "Bilbao effect," often without acknowledging the difficult cost-benefit relationship of such a consumption-based development strategies. As Ann Markusen argues, only a few of the large and highly specialised cities such as Las Vegas or Orlando benefit economically from such facilities because they manage to attract a disproportionate share of businesses, visitors, and tourists. Most cities, however, only experience modest benefits from cultural tourism. This stands in contrast to the often overly optimistic consultant reports that try to persuade policymakers of the economic potential of such facilities. Typically, large-scale cultural facilities operate at a financial loss because costs associated with debt service and on-going operation are high and lagging revenues do not justify public investments. Such "mega-projects" fit the instrumental perspective of the role of arts and culture and turn small towns into "would-be cities."

In contrast to large metropolitan regions, small towns may be better positioned to take advantage of culture and creativity as tools for urban regeneration when they are implemented with greater attention to the community's needs and when they are spatially dispersed. Small towns benefit from their smallness and will be able to rally and engage various community members and groups. As in Paducah or New York Mills, where citizens and artists join forces to create art and culture, small town residents can bring about change through culture. Markusen notes that "smaller towns find it easier to join forces with potential partners to develop a vibrant cultural life and economy."[183] She argues for cultural activities that are spatially dispersed in many different neighbourhoods rather than one

206. Roanoke, Virginia, USA. The Taubman Museum of Art – a $66 million building – is a good example of a cultural facility designed not only to provide exhibit space for an art collection but also to signal the town's aspiration to be "on the map."

single facility or one single area that is labelled as a cultural district. By integrating culture and art into the entire fabric of small towns, residents – and not just visitors – can experience cultural activities.

The Danger of Commodification

Efforts to use art, culture, and creativity to revitalise small towns touch on the subject of commodification of space. If creativity is solely used in instrumental terms, then small towns merely become commodities for those who can afford a life in an idyllic small town that has retained and enhanced its local identity through the work of artists and bohemians. The rural or small town idyll becomes commodified because its traditional functions – agricultural work, resource-based economy, connection with nature, etc. – serve as ideal images or backdrops to the modern lifestyle. Geographer Edward Relph was one of the first to talk about this development when he refers to it as the imagineering of landscapes.[184] He cites the example of a small mining town in British Columbia that decided to adopt a Bavarian theme to market itself to tourists. Culture in this case is the adoption of an illusion (Bavarian *Lederhosen* in the Canadian province) to an existing place that has a very different heritage and legacy (working class tradition in a mill town). Sociologist Sharon Zukin, in *Landscapes of Power: From Detroit to Disney World*, highlights the trend to transform urban landscapes into spaces of consumption driven by the challenges of de-industrialisation and the rise of a postindustrial economy.

Arts and culture in the small town context are in danger of creating what geographer David Harvey calls "degenerate utopias" – harmonious spaces, set aside from the "real" world. Such spaces incorporate arts and creativity as spectacles and invoke a sanitized identity. Small town planners and architects must walk a tightrope between the commodification of art and the real and genuine application of creativity as a change agent in community revitalisation and development.

207. Harpers Ferry, West Virginia, USA.
Situated within a National Historical Park at the scenic confluence of the Potomac and Shenandoah Rivers and with a celebrated history because of an abolitionist uprising in 1859, Harpers Ferry – with a population of just over 300 – receives over a million visitors a year.

208. Lewes, England.

9

Equity: Housing, Work, and Social Well-being

Quality of life and social well-being are often characterized as preoccupations of the affluent middle classes – issues that do not address the needs of the poor and that therefore gloss over the question of socio-economic inequality. In the literature on sustainability, however, equity is firmly established as one of the three Es, a key element in relation to both economic and environmental sustainability. Structural economic change, new technologies, and changing patterns of retail distribution have impacted the economy of many small towns and, as a result, some have high levels of unemployment, above-average levels of poverty, and above-average numbers of disadvantaged and service-dependent households. The growth of large supermarkets and out-of-town superstores, together with the increased mobility of shoppers, the growth of Internet shopping, and the proliferation of planning, policy, and tax incentives that have favoured large-scale businesses have led to the closure of independent retail outlets and the withdrawal of private businesses such as cinemas and bank branches. In the United Kingdom, for example, the number of local banks, post offices, pubs, and independent grocers and corner shops has fallen by a total of more than 65,000 units since 2000.

Over the same period, independent fresh food specialists (including bakers, butchers, fishmongers, and greengrocers) have seen their sales drop precipitously as supermarkets have expanded their market share. Not all of these losses accrued to small towns but the impact in small towns has been disproportionate, resulting in the trend toward "ghost towns."[185] Meanwhile, neoliberal policies and increasing economic rationalism have meant that many central and local government services have been privatised and schools, hospitals, and public transportation have experienced significant cutbacks in funding. The loss of shops and services has not only impacted employment and incomes, but also adversely affected the vitality, conviviality, and social cohesion of towns. In towns with high levels of poverty and unemployment, it is difficult to generate support for environmental sustainability.

Downward spirals of cumulative economic causation (Fig. 209) are therefore paralleled and reinforced by downward spirals of cumulative sociocultural causation. Economic decline and disinvestment result in job losses, out-migration, diminished demand for local goods and services, an attenuated local tax base, a deteriorating infrastructure, and an increasingly unattractive environment for new economic investment. Low incomes, restricted economic opportunities, and the absence of social or cultural amenities contribute to feelings of despondency and isolation, while socio-economic inequality contributes to tensions and resentment. Low community morale and weakened social cohesion contribute to a sense of fatalism and discourage leadership and innovation, while restricted municipal services leave disadvantaged and vulnerable households and individuals with little support. As a result, sustainability becomes an impossibility.

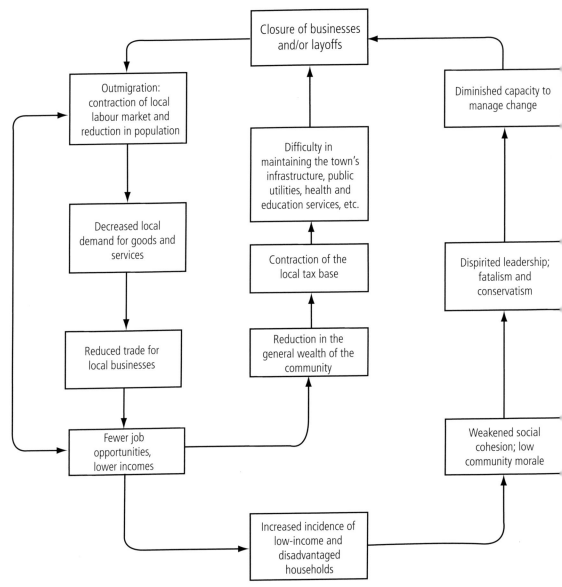

209. Cumulative causation. The closure of local businesses often leads to a self-reinforcing, downward spiral of economic and socio-cultural decline.

Equity and Social Well-being

The question of equity hinges to a large extent on ethical and political judgments. Those on the right end of the political spectrum tend to believe in an "economic justice" of free-market competition in which differences in ability and merit result in more productive people and localities receiving greater rewards, so that social well-being will naturally be higher in highly productive places and regions. Those on the left end tend to believe in a "social justice" based on the broad principle of equality of outcome. In between are those who accept a certain amount of inequality of outcome as the price of economic efficiency. Geographer David Harvey has suggested that equitable distributions need not involve equality of outcome but should reflect the criteria of need, contribution to the common good, and merit, while ensuring that the prospects of the least fortunate places are maximized.[186]

At the broadest level there has been a long-standing consensus in most Western countries that equality of individual opportunity and equality of access to collective resources are fundamental rights, along with the idea that there should be certain minimum thresholds of living in terms of income, housing, education, and health care. This consensus has been eroded since the 1980s by the shift toward a neoliberal political economy in which progressive notions of the public interest and civil society have been eclipsed by a grassroots resistance to taxation, resulting in cutbacks and closures to schools, hospitals, clinics, post offices, and bus services; a reduction in investment in physical infrastructure and public utilities; and cutbacks in redistributive welfare programmes. Nevertheless, it is clear that equity is key to sustainability.

In addition to a resilient economy with diverse employment opportunities, the availability of suitable and affordable housing to buy and to rent is essential for maintaining the social diversity of small towns, to enable people to retain support networks of families and friends, and to support the growth and viability of local services. Underpinning these, in a sustainable community, is the ability for local people to exercise control and influence over the decisions that affect their lives. In this chapter, we focus on these key issues, looking at examples of innovative approaches to affordable housing, education, and health care before going on to review the attributes of successful institutional infrastructures.

Affordable Housing

The shortage of good-quality, affordable housing is one of the most pressing problems facing small towns, threatening their long-term vitality and viability (Figs. 210–212). Without an adequate supply of affordable housing, some households are denied the opportunity to live or remain in towns, thus creating serious imbalances in the demographic composition of communities. In addition, many of the people facing affordability problems are key to economic development, and help to maintain a healthy labour market profile in terms of their age, skills, and needs. All too often, however, the relatively small scale of housing markets in small towns means that both government policies and the market strategies of big building companies fail to address adequately the key issue of affordable housing. In the United Kingdom, for example, it is government policy to give priority housing, including a set proportion of affordable housing, to "key workers." Yet the tightly defined criteria for what constitutes key workers (those working in the police, health care, and education) take no account of the needs of particular local economies. Meanwhile, the higher per-unit cost of delivering small developments in small towns has sometimes meant that housing schemes simply come too far down the priority list for government agencies to fund or for private companies to build speculatively. In particular, the pressure on government agencies to maximise the number of units they deliver for their set budget works against small towns and in favour of big cities. Ideally, of course, the focus should be on enabling small housing developments, responsive to local needs, with high-quality design that is in keeping with the fabric and character of the town and its region.

The complex nature of the housing problem in small towns is strikingly illustrated by the situation in eastern England. The region has the highest proportion of market towns in Britain (over 17 percent) as well as the highest proportion of people living in rural and coastal towns. Housing pressure in the region arises from an increasing population, lengthening patterns of commuting around London, Norwich and Cambridge, and the demand for second homes, especially in coastal areas. House prices have risen considerably in recent years and it has become increasingly difficult to find affordable housing. The central government's Regional Housing Strategy 2003–2006 estimated that 7,000 affordable homes are needed each year to meet existing, known demand, whereas just over 3,000 homes are actually being provided. Meanwhile, the government's Sustainable Communities Plan, launched in February, 2003, set out a framework for large-scale housing development in four growth areas, three of which lie partly or mainly within the east of England: Milton Keynes, the Thames Gateway, and the London-Stansted-Cambridge corridor. This will have a major impact on the small towns of the region. The focus of the Sustainable Communities Plan is on providing housing much faster within the designated areas while providing more intermediate-cost housing for middle-income households such as key workers.

One of the small towns in the region with an acute problem of housing affordability is Newmarket (population 16,947). The problem was identified as part of the Countryside Agency's "Healthcheck" and Newmarket has now become one of Natural England's network of Beacon Towns – places in which partnerships among local government, business, and community groups are intended to help inform the work of other town partnerships and the development of national policy (see Chapter 2).

Newmarket is a typical English market town, providing a centre for services and employment for surrounding rural settlements. Its profile of housing needs reflects that of many market towns and, as the centre of the horseracing industry in England, it also generates a high level of demand for housing from young and single people who are particularly disadvantaged with regard to access to the housing market. In addition, there is above-average demand for housing – both to buy and to rent – from the district's large population of U.S. Air Force (USAF) personnel and their families based at RAF Mildenhall and RAF Lakenheath. Demand is also influenced by Newmarket's close proximity to the

210. Şeica Mică, Romania. Şeica Mică is a small town of about 1,800 residents in Romania. The town is undergoing tremendous social transformation processes that are visible in the physical infrastructure. Founded in the 14th century, Şeica Mică's main population was a German-speaking minority. After the fall of the iron curtain, the town experienced outmigration. Some migrants are now coming back and are renovating houses (such as the two houses to the left).

211. Bridport, England. In small towns that are reasonably prosperous and attractive to retirees and second home owners, the limited size of the housing stock often leads to problems of affordability for indigenous households.

212. Diss, England. Sheltered housing for elderly households.

Cambridge growth area as well as long-distance commuters to London. The result of this demand has been a dramatic increase in house prices in Newmarket and the 20 villages that surround it. Local residents in the lower- and middle-income brackets find it increasingly difficult to afford to stay in their own communities. The situation has been exacerbated by a reduction in the available social rented housing stock through the government's "Right to Buy" scheme. Another problem is that the amount of land that is available for new housing within Newmarket is extremely limited, which means that development costs are high. Part of the problem stems from the terms of Newmarket's Town Charter, which protects land that is connected with the racing industry. About 1,940 hectares (4,800 acres) in and around Newmarket are owned by Jockey Club Estates, which includes stud farms, training establishments, farms tenancies, and some 90 residential and commercial properties.

When Newmarket carried out its Healthcheck in 2003, affordable housing became the dominant issue. As a result, the Newmarket Community Partnership was formed and its activities have become the focus of Newmarket's role as a Beacon Town.[187] The Partnership has established three task groups to tackle the issues of housing needs, site identification, and participative design in relation to the provision of affordable housing. The Partnership now works with social housing developers, local government agencies, and the horseracing industry, developing a local definition for key workers in and around the town; identifying potential sites and empty buildings for affordable housing development; evolving a participative design and development process that involves the use of modern methods of construction wherever possible; and working with local employers to develop an affordable housing scheme to accommodate key employees. The Partnership also has an interest in green design and in promoting the vernacular design of the region, influenced especially by the legacy of horseracing and the many listed stable yards within the town.

213. Waldkirch, Germany. A new neighbourhood called "Am Stadtrain" was developed in Waldkirch. House owners used so-called building groups – coalitions of home owners who decided to design and build their houses together – to share costs such as design, construction, and infrastructure.

214. Waldkirch, Germany. The houses in Waldkirch's new quarter are affordable.

215. Waldkirch, Germany. Small town planning needs to address the needs of different generations and sustainability objectives should focus on social equity.

Education and Health Care in Small Towns

Education and health care are critical components of social sustainability in small towns, and they are typically considered as public goods. The provision of these services often suffers from under- and disinvestment as a result of population decline or political unwillingness to support peripheral or declining communities. Economic and social prosperity, however, depend on an educated and healthy population. Economist and regional scientist Andrew Isserman and his colleagues have studied prosperity in rural areas in the United States. In contrast to most economists who look at quantitative measures such as the growth of jobs or income, Isserman defines prosperity in qualitative terms.[188] He examines rural counties in terms of quality of housing, jobs, poverty, and education. Rural areas — defined as those areas with no urban centre of more than 10,000 or more residents or where 90 percent of the population live in rural areas — that are prospering are those that make sure that kids graduate from high school, where educational attainment in general is high, where the unemployment and poverty rates are low, and where residents have access to affordable and good quality housing. The implications of Isserman's research are that small towns and rural areas do not need to be victims of their smallness or remoteness. Rather, if they make the right investments and develop unique programmes to keep education and health levels up as well as unemployment and poverty down, they can prosper.

Health care is an important social issue in the small town context. Many remotely located small towns experience a serious shortage of critical health services such as doctors, hospitals, or pharmacies. In Minnesota, for example, the number of independent pharmacists has dropped by 20 percent between 2002 and 2008.[189] Meanwhile, the number of deaths from drug overdoses — mostly from misuse of prescription drugs — is a major problem in areas dominated by rural and small towns. In rural areas and small towns that experience job loss and economic decline, the leading cause of death is drug overdose. In addition, healthy food choices are often scarce if small towns do not leverage their agricultural assets through community supported agriculture (CSA) or farmers' markets.

Similar to health care, educational services in small towns are suffering from a variety of problems. In the United States, rural and small school districts are chronically underfunded. Population decline leads to a loss of a viable tax base and a shortage of public dollars that can be invested in educational facilities. In addition, many U.S. state governments place the burden of education funding on local communities. In Minnesota, for example, 83 percent of rural school districts depend on operating levies to fund education.[190] Such levies (e.g., increases in property tax) can easily fail next time they are on the ballot. In addition to declining population and a general unwillingness to fund public goods, many communities are not able to raise enough funds for critical investments in education. In the case of Minnesota — a state typically known for a higher level of public support for education compared to others — school superintendents report that the quality of education has dropped in recent years and that this trend will continue unless a different funding system is designed.

Some communities and small towns across the world are addressing these issues and are finding innovative solutions. Each year, America's Promise Alliance — a nonprofit organisation that aligns a diversity of educational and social organisations — identifies the 100 best communities for young people.[191] Small towns such as Orofino in Idaho (population 3,139) or Lamoni in Iowa (population 2,320) work toward improving educational and social opportunities for youth. Many of these towns have created alliances and networks among local groups to facilitate the integration of various social and cultural services. Some have created youth commissions that advise mayors, mentoring programmes, drug prevention programmes, early childhood education programmes, or programmes that allow high school dropouts to continue their educational pursuits.

Municipalities in Germany are becoming increasingly aware of the importance of family friendliness of the urban environment. The availability of a diverse range of educational facilities and child care options has become an important quality-of-life concern. In Germany, these considerations are in the context of demographic changes such as the aging of population and the decline in birth rates as well as the increasing rate of female labour force participation. The availability and the quality of child care is an important area in which small towns are developing ways to address societal needs.

216. Waldkirch, Germany. The so-called Red House (*Rote Haus*) in Waldkirch functions as a multi-generation community centre. It houses a community kitchen, the offices of social workers, and several communal rooms. It works as an anchor in the neighbourhood and added to the social stability of the community.

217. Waldkirch, Germany. The church, St. Margarethen was built between 1732–1734 in the baroque style.

Waldkirch, Germany

Waldkirch, a town of about 20,000 residents, is located in a picturesque valley in Germany's Black Forest region. The town is in close proximity to Switzerland and France and a train connects residents with the nearby larger city of Freiburg, Germany's model city for environmental sustainability. Waldkirch joined the Cittaslow movement in 2002 as the second German member town. Its historical roots go back to the year 926 C.E. when it was officially mentioned for the first time. The region is known for its gemstone grindery industry and for its craft tradition of building musical organs, which started around the year 1799. What makes the town special is an unusually high degree of civic and social activities as well as public and private efforts to facilitate equitable community planning. There are 217 local clubs of various kinds, and a range of model projects focus on the role of social sustainability and civic engagement.

Waldkirch provides a good example of how a city can propagate social sustainability and underpin its economy with considerations for the socio-economic well-being of its community members. One early project in Waldkirch was the revitalisation of a house that formerly was a flop house surrounded by an auto junk yard in a neglected and rundown neighbourhood. Waldkirch's city government spent about 900,000 euros for the renovation of the house, which is now known as the Red House because of its bright red façade. Today, the structure functions as a community meeting place, houses the office of a neighbourhood social worker and a communal kitchen that serves meals to the neighbourhood. Since the fall of 2003, a weekly farmers' market provides fresh fruit and vegetables, bread, and fair trade products. Since the Red House opened, neighbourhood crime and vandalism have gone down and neighbourhood residents of all ages and ethnic groups have built stronger social networks.

To connect the social efforts with economic opportunities for the residents, Waldkirch initiated an employment programme that provides job opportunities for residents who have been long-term unemployed. The kitchen in the Red House, for example, employs neighbourhood residents and many workers graduate to paid employment in the region's restaurants. Other opportunities

218. Waldkirch town centre.

219. Waldkirch. The market square is a central meeting point. It is automobile-free and hosts the weekly farmers market. The renovation of the fountain was funded through citizens.

220. Waldkirch. Lange Straße, one of the main shopping streets.

for employment are at a second-hand shop and in various service-oriented business activities (e.g., lawn care, window cleaning, courier services, home remodelling, moving services, etc.). Another employment programme aims at those who are close to retirement and allows them to split their jobs with unemployed people, leaving the job holder to get involved ahead of retirement in social and cultural activities in Waldkirch.

Through providing a neighbourhood with a physical space around which to build social networks and by giving unemployed residents the opportunity to work, Waldkirch's planners connect their concerns for equity with economic goals. In 2004, the town was recognised with a federal award for being a model "Social City" and in 2007 the German minister for Family, Seniors, Women and Youth awarded the house the designation of a so-called multiple generation house (*Mehrgenerationenhaus*). As a result, Waldkirch will receive 40,000 euros per year to operate the house as a meeting place for young and old people.

Waldkirch is also implementing a nationwide initiative aimed at family friendliness. The project creates local grassroots alliances that work toward creating a more family-friendly city. The goals of the project are to create an urban environment in which families feel welcomed and where there is a better work-life balance. One key element is an adequate supply of child care and education facilities. In Germany, every municipality has to guarantee and finance child care for local families, and Waldkirch is proactively planning the availability of facilities through its Room for Kids programme. One achievement was the recent opening of an all-day school, which are still rare in German communities. The small town also offers a variety of pedagogical approaches such as a Montessori school, a Waldorf school, and a forest kindergarten.

Family-friendliness and concerns for equity and social sustainability extend into the ways Waldkirch approaches physical planning and land use. The town's planners used so-called building groups (*Baugruppen*) to develop a new neighbourhood. Building groups are formed among those who wish to build a house but may not have the means to realise homeownership. The groups work together through planning and realisation of the project.

The outcomes include a dense social network and integration among neighbours, cost savings for the builders because of shared services such as architects and craftsmen, participation early on in the building process, and individuality and customisation of building and area design. Building groups are used increasingly frequently in neighbourhood revitalisation and urban regeneration in Germany. In other countries, such as the United States and those in Scandinavia, such socially oriented physical development is often called co-housing.

Waldkirch emphasises the protection and creation of social sustainability in diverse areas of urban life. For example, a strong sense of place in Waldkirch's city centre is maintained by the tradition of conducting the main farmers' market on the prominent central square. Twice a week the market attracts local residents as well as visitors from outside. Because the local square is car-free, vendors and visitors use the square without being disturbed by traffic. Market visitors typically take time to sample produce and to interact with friends and acquaintances. Such "habitual movement around significant places"[192] produces increased identification and a strong sense of place, and this in turn produces social sustainability. Social sustainability maintains a sense of belonging, and ownership and identity with the urban environment – a goal that is central to the Cittaslow movement.

Waldkirch's efforts in sustaining local identity extend into neighbourhoods whose sense of place is threatened because they are losing vital functions such as small local shops, post offices, or bank branches. Waldkirch is one of several pilot communities for a state-sponsored project that aims at rebuilding a sense of local community and social networks. This project, roughly translated as "quality of life through proximity" (*Lebensqualität durch Nähe*), aims at building local awareness of the connection between quality of life and the availability of services and products that are locally produced and sold. Waldkirch will build projects and programmes around three key elements of the project – building social networks and a sense of place; developing a lifestyle as well as food production and consumption that is sensitive to the locality; and locating and securing local jobs.

Antisocial Behaviour

In surveys of liveability in small towns, concerns about antisocial behaviour typically run a close second to concerns about employment and facilities for young people. Antisocial behaviour is often interpreted as an aspect of social malaise that is rooted – in part, at least – in feelings of disadvantage, inequality, and deprivation. Yet antisocial behaviour is, like liveability, difficult to define because it is influenced by the context of regional cultural values and mores. In Britain, where antisocial behaviour in large urban areas has become a major topic of concern, research has identified three broad categories of antisocial behaviour.[193] The first involves malicious behaviour directed against specific individuals or groups, such as intimidation or threats by neighbours, vandalism, and serious verbal abuse. The second centres on obstructive behaviours that prevent people using public spaces: intimidating behaviour by groups of youths, drug abuse in public places, and street drinking or drunkenness, for example. The third is environmental antisocial behaviour that, either deliberately or through carelessness, degrades the local environment. This includes graffiti, abandoned vehicles, setting fire to rubbish, noise nuisance, dog-fouling, and littering and fly-tipping (illegal dumping).

All three categories can affect life in small towns, though it is restrictions on the use of public space and antisocial environmental behaviours that are of most concern in relation to community cohesion, conviviality, liveability, and sustainability. There are, of course, policies and strategies that can combat antisocial behaviour. Recall, for example, the Mosquito device (described in Chapter 7) deployed against groups of youths who hang out in public spaces. Other strategies include neighbourhood watch organisations, the deployment of CCTV technology, and, of course, increased funding for community policing. Nevertheless, the most effective way of precluding antisocial behaviour in the long run is through community engagement and the propagation of settings that contribute positively to the three Es of sustainability – economy, environment, and equity.

The Institutional Infrastructure: Partnerships, Community Capacity, and Community Engagement

The nature of socio-economic disadvantage in small towns can make it difficult to identify people in need and, therefore, difficult to deliver the appropriate services and support and to develop appropriate strategies for eliminating antisocial behaviour and improving liveability and social well-being. This is often exacerbated by institutional structures, policy frameworks, and planning strategies that tend to favour large concentrations of indigent and needy populations. As a result, the prospects for sustainability in many towns can be significantly restricted. On the other hand, the voluntary and community service sector in small towns is often strong – perhaps of necessity, as a result of the absence of statutory service provision – and able to meet some of the needs of disadvantaged households. What is critical with regard to both institutional and voluntary efforts in small towns is the existence of partnerships that span the public, private, and voluntary sectors. Partnerships can help to identify local needs; coordinate the complexities of funding applications; collate information sources and good practices; build community engagement and consensus; and develop the capacity to manage change strategically. Successful partnerships can overcome entrenched conservative views and cynicism or fatalism about the sustainability of a town, and can avoid the "consultation fatigue" that is often characteristic of bureaucratic planning processes. They can also enhance the visibility of a town's efforts, which is undoubtedly important in attracting external support and funding.

The Beacon Towns programme in England has emphasised the importance of establishing partnerships. Healthchecks of network members typically reveal the need for stronger and more representative partnerships, whatever the programmatic focus of the town. Thirsk, North Yorkshire (population 9,099), for example, formed a partnership specifically to try to address the issue of antisocial behaviour, including crime and the fear of crime. "Safety Thirsk" comprises representatives from various community, public, and private organisations, including local authorities, the police, the Hambleton Community Safety Partnership, Thirsk School, Thirsk Clock (a youth centre), the Army, the Thirsk Business Association, and local housing associations.[194]

In another Beacon Town, Faringdon, Oxfordshire (population 6,187), an initial steering group carefully developed a formal partnership structure after taking professional consultancy advice about options for the group's constitution and structure. The result is a highly developed nonprofit partnership structure, the Faringdon Area Project, with trustees, formal membership, and a forum. Faringdon's healthcheck identified a number of obstacles that were preventing businesses from starting up or expanding, including a shortage of business space, no business support or advice networks, and no broadband access to the Internet. The Faringdon Area Partnership has provided "brand identity" that has encompassed these needs, and has begun to develop a range of support mechanisms for local businesses focused on an "Enterprise Gateway" that has been set up by the UK government's regional development agency, SEEDA. The Gateway provides business advice and support for the infrastructure for new and existing businesses to develop and flourish. As part of this work, it is helping various business support groups that have emerged in Faringdon, including a group to support local food businesses and one to bring broadband Internet access into the area.[195]

Good partnerships have vision, strategic know-how, and the right structures in place. The interrelationships between individuals and partners, and between contributory working groups, must be clearly defined, properly understood, and respected. Public-sector agencies attempting to do things alone can achieve only limited success, given that they are essentially outsiders. No matter how well-developed their policies, programmes, or research instruments, the key to effective change relies on community motivation and action. The key to fostering the necessary creative, energetic, and collaborative action is deep and sustained engagement of the community with the issues at stake and the goals to be achieved. By adding their professional expertise to that of local voluntary groups while engaging local private-sector business interests in strategic alliances, everyone gets the best of all possible worlds. Public agencies are liberated to give the expertise, funding, and other support for which they were created. Voluntary organisations find themselves with a strategic framework and greater opportunities for funding, and local businesses can strengthen their ability to compete with external competition. Programmatic activities aside, partnerships (and networks of partnerships such as Action for Market Towns, AlpCity, Cittaslow, and *Lebensqualität durch Nähe*) build community capacity and social well-being by engaging a broader section of the community. Their everyday activities and interactions, projects, and events improve trust and reciprocity among people, encourage cooperation and collaboration, and help to build energised, responsive, vibrant, and engaged communities.[196]

208. Gaochun, China. Old Town.

10

Small Town Development in Emerging Countries

Small towns have the potential to play a crucial role in balancing spatial development patterns in emerging countries such as China, South Korea, and India. These emerging market economies are characterised by rapid urbanisation processes that are constantly fueled by rural–urban migration. Millions of people move from rural areas and small towns to the largest cities in search of a brighter future and greater economic security. As a result, such countries face serious imbalances in their urban systems. Social and economic disparities among rapidly growing cities, emptying rural regions, and stagnating small towns are widening dramatically. Rural regions and small towns face significant challenges, with declining economies and obsolescent infrastructures making it difficult to maintain diverse populations.

Yet it has been urbanisation and the rapid growth of large cities that has been fueling the economic ascendance of emerging market economies. In 2011, for the first time, China's city dwellers started to outnumber its rural residents. Of China's more than 1.35 billion people, 51.3 percent lived in urban areas at the end of 2011. Fifty years ago, only 20 percent of China's population lived in cities. Projections suggest that by 2015 the urban population in

China will be between 680 and 700 million people, a staggering number that is 2.5 times larger than in the United States and 1.6 times larger than in India. By 2025, China is projected to have more than 200 cities with populations of more than 1 million, and within the next 20 years a full 75 percent of its population is expected to live in cities.

South Korea shows a similar pattern: The urban population stood at 28 percent in 1960. By 2010, a full 83 percent lived in cities and most of the growth is concentrated in the seven largest metropolitan areas, including Seoul and Busan. Urban development experts project that by 2050 South Korea will be more than 90 percent urbanised. India's urban population has also charted new grounds: Provisional data from the 2011 census show that, for the first time since India's 1947 independence, the absolute increase in population is greater in urban areas than in rural areas. The level of urbanisation increased in India from almost 28 percent in 2001 to 31 percent in 2011, and the portion of rural population declined from 72 percent to 69 percent.

Urban growth in these countries primarily takes place in megacities, often at the expense of small towns and rural villages. Nevertheless, villages and small towns play an important role in stabilizing the rural hinterlands of these nations and they account for a significant share of the population. Accurate data on how many people live in small towns in countries such as India or China are hard to obtain because many small towns are still classified as rural and would not count as urban according to definitions of urban centres commonly used in Europe and North America.[197] Insights into the distribution of population according to the size of settlement, however, show that a significant share of the population in emerging economies in Asia, Africa, and Latin America live in urban centres with fewer than 50,000 inhabitants and in centres with between 50,000 and 199,999 inhabitants. For example, 6 percent of India's 1.2 billion people live in small towns of no more than 50,000 residents. Almost 15 percent of Malaysia's population are small town residents. In Mexico, almost 10 percent live in small towns and in Costa Rica about 45 percent of the population lives in small towns.

Small Towns in China

Small towns in China play a prominent and significant role, particularly in facilitating urbanisation. Chinese small towns (*xiaochengzhen*) can be classified as two types.[198] The first are the officially recognised towns, the so-called *jianzhizhen*. Such officially recognised towns must comply with certain population and employment thresholds. They serve as centres for the political, economic, and cultural life for rural areas. The second type are the rural towns, the so-called *nongcunjizhen*, which serve as market towns for the rural countryside.

As in Europe and North America, the role of small towns as centres for the exchange of goods and for the provision of social and cultural services has been important. Historically, they connected the rural hinterlands to a network of larger towns and cities. Since the Ming and Qing dynasties (1368–1911), small towns have been important administrative centres and have prospered economically.

In many cases, these small towns were located strategically and their massive walls, gates, and towers protected their inhabitants. Strong hierarchical administrative relationships allowed these small cities to control the rural countryside.

During the Mao period (1949–1976), however, small towns began to stagnate and eventually declined due to the collectivisation of the economy and the state's monopoly of production and distribution systems. The elimination of the free-market system in Communist China rendered small towns obsolete as commercial centres for the exchange of goods and services. Small towns, however, continued to play a role during the Communist era as headquarters of the people's communes, thereby further reducing their historic role as economic centres. During the 1950s, 1960s, and 1970s, small towns experienced further decline as Communist politics (including the Great Leap Forward and the Cultural Revolution) undermined and destroyed their economic and cultural roles.

209. Hongcun, Ahui Province, China. Together with Xidi, Hongcun has been listed as a UNESCO World Heritage Site since 2000. The architecture dates back to the Ming and Qing dynasties and the village is reminiscent of those in traditional Chinese paintings.

Since 1978, when China started to adopt its Open Door policy under the leadership of Deng Xiaoping, national policies have changed in favour of small town development. Several reforms facilitated the urbanisation of small towns during this period. First, the collapse of the commune system in rural China led to the establishment of the "household responsibility system," which allowed farmers to farm individually rather than for a collective. As a result, rural productivity increased and a large amount of surplus farm labour became available. At the same time, the central government supported the establishment of so-called township and village enterprises (TVEs), which were able to absorb this surplus labour. TVEs are market-oriented enterprises that are located in and run by towns and villages. They thrived until the late 1980s, but many were dismantled and privatised in the mid to late 1990s. Nevertheless, TVEs played an important role in urbanising Chinese small towns. Under the slogan "Leaving the land but not the villages, entering the factories but not cities," Chinese policies regarding TVEs and rural–urban migration lured millions of farmers into small towns across the country. Small towns grew not only as sites of industrial production but also as locations where farmers started new lives. The government also allowed the number of designated towns to increase from 2,874 in 1980 to 9,088 in 1989.[199]

During the 1990s, the state began to deliberately use small towns to tackle rural development. Policies encouraged TVEs to locate close to each

210. Gaochun, Jiangsu Province, China. Goachun is known for its well-preserved old town along Laojie Street. Goachun is also the largest city in the county and is home to the first Chinese Cittaslow town.

211. Gaochun, Jiangsu Province, China. Modernisation and development in China often go along with large-scale destruction of existing housing stock.

212. Urban system in China. China's urban system features a specific hierarchy of places. Small villages and designated and undesignated towns are distributed across the territory and have traditionally served as central places for the commerce of goods. With rapid urbanisation, large metropolitan regions have grown beyond the administrative boundaries and are now encompassing many lower-level jurisdictions. As a result, a centre-periphery pattern is evolving.
Source: after Kamal-Chaoui, L., et al., *Urban trends and policy in China*. OECD Regional Development Working Papers. Paris: OECD, 2009, p. 21.

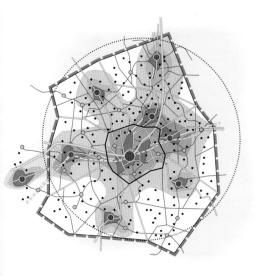

● **Major city** (generally > 1 million inh. true urban)

◉ **Medium-sized city** (500,000 - 1 million inh. true urban)

○ **Small city** - designated or undesignated town (100,000 - 500,000 inh. true urban)

● **Village**

▨ **Suburban zone** - high density (>750 inh/km^2); high secondary and tertiary sector activity (GDP-S> 50%); high levels of output by non-traditional enterprises

▨ **Peri-urban zone** - medium density (>500 inh/km^2); medium secondary and tertiary sector activity (GDP-S> 40%); high levels of output by non-traditional enterprises

other in nearby towns, and enterprises in large cities were encouraged to outsource production to small towns. The central government began to realise that small town development would help alleviate rural problems. In 2004, six ministries published a list of Beacon Towns in the country. Currently, 1,887 towns in all provinces are listed and can receive funding from the central government. A total of 350 billion RMB (about US$51 billion) is currently available for the development of Beacon Towns.

Nevertheless, policies such as those in support of Beacon Towns need to be considered in a broader context. China's economy has been driven by special economic zones located primarily in the largest coastal cities. As a result, foreign direct investment has flowed into these cities along with rural migrant workers, who, in spite of strategic planning policies favouring small towns, bypassed smaller settlements. Migrants were able to obtain higher earnings in large coastal cities than in the traditional TVEs or in farming. As a result, the role of small towns as stabilising forces along the rural–urban continuum was undermined. Policies that emphasised small town-based urbanisation during this time thus had limited

success, simply because the gravitational economic pull of the largest cities was just too powerful.

In recent years, China has accepted the inevitability of these big-city attractions and has shifted its strategic planning policies to emphasise the development of metropolitan regions. In these regions, small towns play a different – but still crucial – role as suburban housing and employment centres, integrated into a larger metropolitan context. For example, Shanghai's strategic development plan for the metropolitan region proposes nine new town centres that are set up to achieve a more polycentric development pattern. At the same time, rural areas are supposed to develop under a "new countryside initiative" which aims to improve infrastructure and public services and increase income in rural areas.[200] In short, China is transforming from a traditional agricultural society into a modern industrial and urban society, and small towns are facing serious issues related to social and economic restructuring processes.

213. Dashan village, Jiangsu Province, China. Dashan village is part of China's first Cittaslow region called Yaxi. The village is home to about 532 people, some of whom have returned from larger cities because they are seeing more opportunities now that the village has become attractive for tourists.

Challenges and Problems of Chinese Small Towns

Small towns in China are facing numerous challenges that threaten their sustainability in multiple ways. Historically, the process of industrialisation has led to serious environmental problems. Many of the TVEs that were set up in small towns were engaged in highly polluting industries such as pesticide and fertiliser production. There is a lack of adequate access to safe drinking water, and the effects of environmental degradation on rural and small town livelihoods are dramatic. It is estimated that more than 450 places in China have been labeled as "cancer villages" and in early 2013 the government began to acknowledge their existence. The problem was openly acknowledged in the current Five-Year Plan with the inclusion of the goal of environmental management of chemicals.

Rapid urbanisation processes and pressures to modernise also influence the built form and sense of place of Chinese small towns. New housing developments are built to uniform styles and do not take local customs and lifestyles into account. While modernisation is welcomed and much needed in many rural and small town areas (particularly with regard to dilapidated housing stock and decaying infrastructure), middle-class housing projects are often promoted by private developers and local government officials.

Sometimes these developments take on bizarre forms: Several small towns near Shanghai have been planned and built according to European precedents. Thames Town, for example, imitates British towns such as Lyme Regis and Bath, and includes exact copies of existing pubs and bars. Nearby is Anting New Town, which was planned by the German architects Albert Speer and Partner and was built using Bauhaus-style modern architecture. Even though it is home to a cluster of automobile companies, including some from Germany, the town has not fulfilled its promises and falls short of the goal to house about 28,000 residents. In the southern province, Guangdong is a small town that is an exact copy of the picturesque Austrian town of Hallstatt, near Salzburg. Its central plaza has the same proportions as the original town in Austria, complete with a copy of the town fountain, and is bordered by the same style of houses. Generally, however, as Chinese megacities are growing, their traditional architecture and housing styles are torn down and replaced by faceless new housing blocks. There seems to be a yearning among the Chinese urban population for tradition and history, yet architects and planners seldom take account of vernacular architectural styles, customs, and traditions.

Small towns in China are also facing a number of economic challenges. Many small towns prospered during the 1980s due to the success of TVEs. Today, however, many small towns are dependent on only a few large businesses which originated as TVEs. Often these firms have great power over local affairs. One example illustrates this: The town of Xinghuacun in the Shanxi province is home to one of China's most important alcohol manufacturers, the Fenjiu Brewery.[201] Fenjiu Brewery was set up as a state enterprise in 1949 and, after rapid growth in the 1980s, the enterprise was privatised as a corporation with more than a dozen subordinate companies. Its annual rice wine production is more than 4,800 gallons and the brewery employs more than 8,000 workers. Due to its size and market power, Fenjiu Brewery has great influence in the small town. The brewery consumes a great deal of water and, as a result, the water table has fallen and household water supplies are diminished. Due to the privatisation of water facilities in the province, and as a result of decreasing water availability, water prices have increased rapidly. The brewery also exerts great influence over new development projects, including one that draws in tourists.

Because of economic challenges such as this, many small towns in China are deeply in debt. To improve their budgets, small town governments are understandably keen to make a profit and many have been willing to sell land-use rights to developers in order to raise funds. Thus, valuable farmland is often transformed into urban settlements or used for large-scale infrastructure or tourist projects. In addition, local governments often do not have the power to steer their own developments because higher-level authorities such as county or provincial governments ultimately determine the development plans and projects.

Yaxi, China

Yaxi (桠溪) is the first certified Cittaslow ("slow city") in China, and the region became part of the movement in 2010. Yaxi is not a single town but a collection of six small villages (total population 22,000) in the rural part of Gaochun County. Gaochun is located about 90 minutes south of Nanjing in Jiangsu Province. The landscape around the villages is characterised by lush fields of tea, pears, grapes, and other crops. In spring, the fields surrounding the settlements bloom with yellow rapeseed flowers and attract many visitors to the annual Festival of Golden Flowers, which was started in 2008.

With its fertile landscape, Yaxi seems like an oasis within the bleak surrounding area. Many hills in the region were overexploited in the 1980s and the region's agricultural land is used for the extensive monoculture of fruits and vegetables. A chemical plant has polluted many of the streams and lakes in the county. As a consequence, Gaochun has declared 70 percent of its territory as "no-industry development zones" and Yaxi is included in this designation. This shift toward a slower lifestyle is remarkable if one considers the fact that Jiangsu Province receives the highest amount of foreign direct investment in China and is therefore one of the fastest-growing and most prosperous regions in the country.

Yaxi has experienced many of the problems familiar to other rural areas and small towns in China. Agricultural land near Yaxi has been lost to urban and industrial development, and young people have left the countryside for a more promising future in the fast-growing cities of the region. Meanwhile, the housing stock in Yaxi's villages has been in decline and the economic prospects of the remaining residents have not been bright.

After Yaxi was certified as a Cittaslow town in 2011, the county started to construct a 48-km-long scenic road linking all six villages. The villages have also experienced a makeover: New houses were constructed and their architecture incorporates gabled roofs and whitewashed walls adorned with delicate paintings. Dashan is also home to a new county-financed community centre that is set in an historic structure. This much-needed

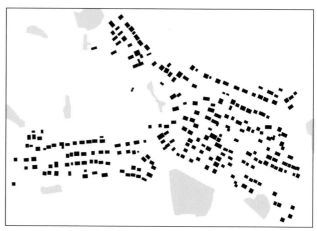

214. Dashan village, part of Yaxi Cittaslow.

215. Yaxi. Yaxi is China's first Cittaslow region. Six villages are within the designated boundary and some are set beside ponds.

216. Yaxi. The surrounding region is characterised by agricultural lands and small villages.

modernisation sometimes seems to clash with traditional ways of life. In Dashan village, for example, the new houses are set around the ponds that are still used for washing clothes.

As a result of these developments, Yaxi has attracted returning migrants. One local resident who worked as a migrant worker in the construction industry in a nearby large city has returned and set up an agro-tourism business that includes a hotel and restaurant. Young college graduates are also returning to their rural home to work in tourism and they may be part of a beginning phenomenon of counter-urbanisation (*ni chengshihua*), representing the new urban youth (*xin zhiquing*) in rural areas. The owner of a small gallery is selling local crafts, including shoes that are handstitched by local residents. Finally, farmers are able to supplement their income by operating small restaurants that serve simple yet delicious Chinese country food. These developments indicate a great potential for Yaxi to develop in a way that is sustainable and fitting to local cultures and traditions.

County officials have great interest in seeing Yaxi succeed and grow as a Cittaslow town. Ironically, there are also many expectations from the increasing number of tourists who come to visit China's first "slow city." They arrive in the area expecting to see a city, not a collection of tranquil villages. As a result, local officials and planners face great pressure to further develop the region, presenting the danger of destroying its traditional and authentic character. Local plans include the building of a new city centre that will offer amenities to tourists including galleries, entertainment, hotels, and restaurants. Planners are talking about using architecture inspired by European designs. Such developments will undoubtedly change the traditional character of Yaxi because the plans hardly incorporate the unique aspects of Yaxi's culture and traditions. The region's authentic character and also its slow pace of life are in danger as tourism is set to boom. Joining the Cittaslow movement has inadvertently put Yaxi on the map of fast places.

217. Yaxi. Cittaslow projects include events such as the Golden Flower Festival, which started in 2008. Attracting tourists is a major goal.

218. Yaxi. Bee-keeping amid rapeseed flowers.

219. Yaxi. Traditional crafts include handmade baby shoes. These are handstitched and are sold in Gaochun's old town market.

Small Town Development in South Korea

South Korea has become one of the most advanced newly industrialising countries in Asia. It is also one of the most densely urbanised countries in the world, with an urban population that has increased by more than 55 percent over the past 50 years. Yet the country also shows great disparities and imbalances between the largest metropolitan regions, such as Seoul and Busan, and its hinterland that is characterised by many small towns and rural villages. Even though the national government has recognised the importance of small towns and rural villages since the 1970s with its internationally known development program *Saemaul Udong*, the development prospects of small towns are still lagging those of the largest metropolitan areas.

Like China, South Korea has experienced significant rural–urban migration, and small towns and rural villages have experienced dramatic changes since the 1960s. South Korea's economic success has been based on the development of metropolitan growth poles. During the 1960s, spatial development policies focused on fostering Seoul and Busan as the country's twin growth poles. As a result, the working-age population migrated to these two metropoles while other cities lagged behind in their development and rural regions experienced depopulation. During the 1970s, the national government initiated its first National Development Plan, which focused on balanced urban development. The plan called for the development of additional regional centres to steer growth away from Seoul and Busan.

In addition, a comprehensive rural development programme was launched which became known as *Saemaul Udong* or the New Community Movement. This programme was quite successful in modernising rural areas and, to this day, it serves as a model for other countries.[202] During the 1970s there was also an effort to decentralise and contain urban development in and around Seoul through the establishment of new towns and the implementation of a greenbelt. Both efforts, however, were unsuccessful as development leap-frogged beyond the greenbelt and smaller settlements suburbanised and became large-scale satellite cities. During the

220. Hanok village, Jeonju, South Korea. Bibimbap is a traditional Korean dish that is part of Jeonju's culinary tradition. It is served in many restaurants in Jeonju's Hanok village, a certified Cittaslow town. In 2012 Jeonju was also designated a UNESCO City of Gastronomy.

1980s, South Korea started to develop more elaborate spatial development plans that incorporated the growth of smaller urban areas such as towns and villages. During this time, smaller cities having between 50,000 and 100,000 residents started to grow. In recent years, South Korea has focused more on the development of a diversified set of urban areas. The country's Fourth Comprehensive National Land Plan identified seven mega-regional economic zones that are linked with and complemented by supra-economic regions and by 161 "daily living spheres." In addition, a new green policy (the so-called Green New Deal) provides stimulus to all kinds of urban areas for the development of environmentally sustainable projects. The goal is to achieve a somewhat green territorial development strategy. Yet the question remains as to whether the decades-long focus on large cities as growth poles, with its resulting backwash effects, will compensate for the decline that many rural villages and small towns have experienced.

Small towns and rural villages in South Korea are subject to many significant challenges, especially the out-migration of the working-age population to the largest urban centres in the country. Unlike Japan, where depopulation in rural areas and small towns was primarily confined to mountain regions, the problem in South Korea has occurred all across the country. The South Korean population is ageing at a very rapid pace. South Korea's National Statistical Office expects a "super-aged society" by 2026. Population decline in rural areas and small towns, combined with an ageing society, leads to serious problems regarding the maintenance of public infrastructure and the availability of working human capital. South Korea's small towns are also facing a number of social changes such as the pro-liferation of international marriages because local farmers are unable to find partners and thus are increasingly marrying women from other countries.

South Korea's economic miracle has, since the 1960s, been manifested primarily in the larg-est urban centres. Policy makers and politicians hoped for a trickle-down effect, which has not materialised. However, with the efforts toward democratisation, decentralisation, and increased local autonomy which started in the 1990s, some projects (such as those associated with the Cittaslow movement) aim to contribute to small town sustainability. Governmental efforts also focus on the vitality of rural and small town environ-ments. They include a Rural Traditional Theme Village Programme which is managed by the Rural Development Administration and funds more than 140 projects to revitalise traditions and cultures and to attract urbanites as tourists. Somewhat different from those in China, these efforts illustrate a growing recognition of the value of local tradi-tions and cultures as well as the possibility of local residents initiating projects from the bottom-up.

221. Samjicheon, South Korea. Traditional hanok houses characterise many Cittaslow towns in South Korea. Hanok houses are built in the traditional vernacular form of South Korean domestic architecture, with consideration to the positioning of the house in relation to its surround-ings and climatic conditions. A young Korean couple from Seoul decided to live a more simple life in the town.

Cittaslow Towns in South Korea

South Korea is the first Asian country where a number of small towns have been certified by the Cittaslow movement. As of early 2013, there are 10 Cittaslow towns across the South Korean peninsula. They are Jeungdo Island, Cheongsando, the Yuchi District, Samjicheon village, Agyang District, Yesan-gun, Namyangju-si, Jeonju Hanok village in Jeonju, Cheongson, and Sangju. What is interesting about these towns is that they represent a diverse mix of types of smaller settlements such as villages in rural areas, small towns within the suburban belts of large cities, and historic urban neighbourhoods within medium-sized cities. Most of them, however, have a small town character and strong connections to their agricultural hinterlands, something that is very similar to European Cittaslow towns.

The Cittaslow movement was introduced to South Korea by Professor Dehyun Sohn of Hanyang University, who is the coordinator the South Korea Cittaslow Network and has a personal interest in the "slow philosophy," and whose academic work is related to tourism and regional development. He talked with town mayors and local politicians and convinced them to apply to Cittaslow. Even though they initially did not fully understand the movement, the mayors recognised the potential of focusing on local traditions and cultures, particularly for tourism. Given that South Korea has a strong tradition of top-down administration, it is somewhat surprising that the central government only later became involved. Initially, national-level ministries were suspicious of the movement, but now they recognise its potential in developing small town vitality and, in some cases, they instrumentalise the projects to advance small town and rural development.

In South Korea, economic success and modernisation took place very rapidly. Many local traditions and cultures vanished because of the rapid change from a predominantly rural and agricultural society to a highly modern, internationally connected, and globalised society. There is, however, a growing recognition of the value of history, culture, traditions, and local arts and crafts. "Slowing down" has also caught on with stressed city dwellers from Seoul. Several of the Cittaslow towns offer workshops where participants can learn how to pickle vegetables and to make traditional dishes such as *kimchi*. Other workshops that are offered

222. Hanok village, Jeonju, South Korea. This handwriting master is supported by the local government. The skill to use traditional kanji letters has almost disappeared since the simpler style known as *hangul* was introduced.

give people the opportunity to practice traditional handwriting, papermaking, or dressing in traditional costumes. Also, a number of young people have left the cities to look for a slower pace of life. They in effect have become "slow lifers."

Samjicheon village is a place where local traditions and cultures are still valued very highly. The name Samjicheon means "village of the three rivers"; the small settlement of about 500 residents is located in Changpyeong-myeon near the large city of Gwangju (population 1.4 million) in the southwestern corner of the country. Characteristic of the village are the well-preserved traditional hanok houses and the more than 3.6-km-long stone walls and the little creeks that run through the settlement. After the village was certified as a Cittaslow town, the national and provincial governments started to provide financial support for the building of a visitor centre, the restoration of the traditional gravel pathways and creeks, and the maintenance of the traditional-style hanok houses. Strict building regulations about housing styles and materials ensure that new buildings conform to the historic character, while tax credits and subventions help home builders.

A special market for local products, arts, and crafts is held every other week near the Cittaslow visitor centre and a daily local market in the newer part of the village allows farmers to sell their produce. Projects to develop the "slow" profile of Samjicheon were initially developed in top-down fashion, with a private consulting firm developing ideas. Today, however, local volunteers are in charge. Also, the Cittaslow initiative was initially funded by higher administrative units. Today their contribution has declined and local volunteers must adjust and downscale their projects. Among these are study circles, called *Talpangi Hakdang*, where people from the village and from outside can learn special crafts such as textile dyeing or sewing traditional linen burial gowns. These activities have fostered entrepreneurship in the village. Several women in town offer workshops and sell their products. In a country where local entrepreneurs and small and medium-sized businesses are still in the minority, such initiatives are critical in efforts to diversify the local economy.

The Cittaslow movement has reinvigorated small towns like Samjicheon. In South Korea where large business conglomerates (the so-called *chaebols*) have been dominant, the development of entrepreneurial opportunities for small firms has traditionally been neglected. Cittaslow projects like those in support of local markets, workshops, and restaurants create local business opportunities. The South Korean approach to small town development through the "slow philosophy" seems to be promising.

223. Hanok village, Jeonju, South Korea. Papermaking has a long tradition in South Korea. A small factory still produces paper by hand and visitors can observe the process.

224. Hanok village, Jeonju, South Korea. Signs featuring the Cittaslow snail signify the boundaries of the hanok village.

225. Samjicheon, South Korea. Traditional walls, small streams, and pebble pathways were restored to maintain and revitalise the old town centre.

Lessons for Small Town Development in Emerging Countries

As countries such as China, South Korea, and India grow and urbanise at a rapid rate and scale, the need to support sustainable development in rural villages and small towns becomes more urgent. This is starting to be recognised by policy makers and planners. Yet, as the examples of slow city development in China and South Korea show, their respective approaches differ significantly. While South Korea seems to place more emphasis on maintaining the authenticity of small towns and villages through the support of projects related to local culture, crafts, and traditions, China seems to be caught up in a process of rapid modernisation that puts small town culture, history, and heritage at great risk. Some observers argue that China's rural areas and small towns are a "vanishing world" and that many aspects associated with traditional lifestyles are rapidly disappearing.[203]

227. Near Chennai, India. Small towns near large metropolitan areas in India face many pressures, including the provision of safe housing and commercial infrastructure.

228. Mamallapuram, India. Mamallapuram is a small, tourist-oriented village in India's Tamil Nadu state. Even though the village benefits from tourism, there are still areas of great poverty.

226. Tortuguero village, Costa Rica. Small towns are home to 45 percent of the population in Costa Rica.

The examples of small towns in Europe and North America that we present in this book illustrate several lessons that are important for emerging countries. For one, countries in Europe and North America have a long tradition of local autonomy. This implies that small towns should formulate and implement projects, ideas, development goals, and visions based on what is needed and desired at the local level. There is cooperation with higher-level government authorities, but these authorities typically do not exert a strong influence on small towns. This is unlike China, for example, where higher-level authorities still have great influence on local outcomes. Central or provincial governments will often introduce projects to the local level and, thus, development takes place exogenously rather than being developed bottom-up. This does not leave much room for innovative ways to value, maintain, and protect local ways of life. Instead, new developments tend to take on a uniform, modern character, obliterating local traditional building styles and cultures.

Small town sustainability in emerging countries will become a much more important and pressing issue in the future. Efforts to improve quality of life for the local populations will have to balance goals such as modernisation and the protection of traditional

229. Mamallapuram, India. Designated as part of a tourist corridor along the coast to the south of Chennai, the town lacks the infrastructure necessary to support any significant tourism.

ways of life. It is obvious that creating balanced growth patterns across these nations will be important to their peaceful and equitable development.

230. Mamallapuram, India. Informal businesses are thriving all over countries like India. Small towns are often more dependent on them if their economic bases are not diversified.

221. Vigevano, Italy.

11

Conclusion: What Works (and What Doesn't)

The great variety in the history, morphology, and economy of small towns in the developed countries of the world means that generalisations about lessons learned must be treated with caution. Similarly, it would be naïve to suggest that any and every small town can meet the "triple bottom line" of the three Es. That, however, is an issue for national and supranational regional policies. From the perspective of individual small towns, the four salient issues with regard to long-term sustainability concern:

1. Maintenance: How to maintain the town's sociocultural attributes in the face of structural economic change, the changing patterns and dynamics of urbanisation, and the influence of global forces and interdependencies. In practice: How to foster sense of place, neighbourliness, and conviviality.

2. Progress: How to critically assess whether progress toward sustainability has been made and how to examine the types of conflicts that may exist among the three Es. In practice: Developing indicator systems and measurements that hold individuals and organisations in small towns accountable.

3. Social development: How to address poverty and inequality, ensure adequate health care facilities, educational provision, and affordable housing so that, at minimum, economic and sociocultural downward spirals do not erode community capacity and so preclude the ability to manage change in an equitable and progressive way.

4. Vision: How citizens' social values must change in order for towns to become more sustainable in a biophysical environmental sense. In practice: How to deliver educational and informational programmes to citizens, mobilise volunteer and business sectors, and develop strategic town policies around the triple bottom line.

First of all, it is clear that laissez-faire, neoliberal approaches to development do not work in the interests of small town sustainability. Changing technologies, the economic logic of scale and agglomeration, and the changing international division of labour, combined with public-sector rationalisation, preclude any real prospect of sustainability for small towns. Even places that are fortunate enough, from the perspective of employment and incomes, to be part of the post-Fordist economy need some sort of collective, progressive approach to community liveability and social well-being, if only to avoid the negative spillovers and externalities of growth. Some sort of intervention, we argue, is always necessary in order to safeguard and promote the public interest and to maintain a strategic approach to sustainability. The question then becomes: What sort of intervention? We have argued that traditional approaches to local economic development, focusing primarily on place promotion, marketing, and "smokestack chasing," do not work because they are not sustainable. Even where jobs are created through such intervention, the result is often to transform towns into "would-be" places that lose their character and identity and become dependent on "islands of McDonaldisation" and single-shot "solutions" that are subject to external control and are vulnerable to sudden disinvestment. Regional, national, and supra-national policy frameworks have also been found to be ineffective in promoting small town sustainability. Just as small towns have been somewhat neglected in academic scholarship, so they tend to be excluded from international, national, and regional policies. This is not to say that policy frameworks are ineffective or undesirable. Indeed, there is a great range of policy options that could be deployed in underpinning small town sustainability. Take, for example, the palette of policy options available in addressing the problem of the loss of independent retail outlets in small towns as a result of the increasing dominance of national and international chain stores and franchises. These include:

- Introducing impact reviews for "big box" stores that would require them to specify their economic impact on the community;
- Introducing the idea of "planning gain" to planning permissions for retail developments, whereby developers would be required to include locally owned and operated stores;
- Setting a limit on local market share for supermarket chains. A limit of 8 to 10 percent would preclude any abuse of market power;
- Capping the physical size of supermarkets;
- Requiring local authorities to develop retail plans for their area, ensuring that town centres are the primary focus for development;
- Creating community land trusts that establish community ownership of key tracts of town centre land;
- Requiring the local procurement of goods and services (or a minimum percentage of them);
- Extending local property tax relief to independent local retailers; and
- Imposing local bans or caps on franchise businesses that adopt standardised services, methods of operation, decor, uniforms, architecture, or other features virtually identical to businesses elsewhere.[204]

Economic vitality, broadly construed, is pivotal in any approach to sustainability at any scale. It is a necessary precondition for citizen engagement. If people do not have time because they have to work two or three jobs, they are not able to contribute in meaningful ways. Economic vitality is also necessary because sustainability initiatives must have investments from the public and private sector. As we saw in Chapter 6, the traditional approach to economic development hinges on smokestack

chasing, often facilitated by the dedication of land and infrastructure for an industrial park. This approach can sometimes be given a more sustainable dimension when the smokestack chasing is more selective, as illustrated by the town of Ararat, Australia (population 8,200), where an industrial precinct known as the Renewable Energy Park will manufacture turbine blades for wind energy generators. The strategic objective is for Ararat to become a major regional producer of component parts for a wide range of alternative energy technologies. Although this initiative is bringing externally controlled corporations to town, it is also focused on engaging existing businesses, stimulating new ones, and building the knowledge base and general capacity of the local community around the field of renewable energy technologies.[205]

Another example of selective smokestack chasing is provided by Hersbruck, Germany (population 12,500), where the "smokestacks" are specialised health care and fitness enterprises. A Cittaslow member, Hersbruck has developed a "healthy region" strategy that extends to 13 villages around Hersbruck and a total of 40,000 people. In this small region there are about 180 companies that are health-related in some way, including a large public health insurance company and a private skin clinic. Building on this economic framework and the recreational infrastructure of bicycle and hiking trails in the Pegnitz Valley, the town of Hersbruck has invested 21 million euros in a public-private partnership to develop a new spa, the Frankenalb Therme. Opened in December, 2004, the complex on the eastern edge of town includes a day spa, swimming baths, saunas, a wellness centre, and a health food restaurant, and is heated by boilers fuelled by wood chips. The "healthy region" theme is reinforced by a certification programme that recognises hotels which maintain allergen-free rooms and restaurants which offer menu items that are allergen-free. The town itself, meanwhile, has established a policy of having non-GMO clauses in all city contracts, including those involving school meals and leases of city land to farmers.

Elsewhere, approaches to sustainable enterprise have been framed around broader attempts to support local entrepreneurs. One example is

Faringdon, England (population 6,000), a Beacon Town where the Enterprise Gateway described in Chapter 9 nurtures new and existing businesses and provides them with essential infrastructure. An independent, nonprofit entity, the Gateway provides desk space (from desk-sharing to small offices), free seminars, and short, practical workshops on key business topics. Local entrepreneurs can use the Gateway for as little as an hour to meet clients, or spend a day working at a networked computer, or they can rent office space for a month at a time. The Gateway runs courses as diverse as health and safety, self-employment for people over 50, exporting, marketing, and exploiting the Web. Many of the companies that have set up in the Gateway are in the field of information technology, but also include new media, marketing, software development, and consultancy businesses.[206]

In Wolverton, England (population 12,492), another Beacon Town, the emphasis is on *social* entrepreneurship. A strategic alliance of businesses, volunteers, and government agencies – Wolverton Unlimited – has developed a support programme for local entrepreneurs, the Social Advisory Group for Entrepreneurs (SAGE). SAGE is made up of local people skilled at asking the right questions to challenge and support small enterprise. Ideas that have been put forward to SAGE include the Wolverton Community Market; Back to Earth (which gives communities space to grow their food and for outdoor education); Community Repaint (where surplus household paint is collected, sorted and reused by charities); bicycling promotion; a community café; and a community newspaper.[207]

Still another example demonstrates the potential of networks in promoting small town sustainability. The Business in the Community (BitC) movement is a national network of more than 750 member companies in the United Kingdom, and has a 20-year record of connecting businesses with their communities. In the past few years, BitC has collaborated with the Action for Market Towns network to encourage and support business engagement. BitC members provide support in a number of ways. These include strategic support (offering expertise in business planning and strategic development); technical expertise (where

employees of BitC members volunteer to help bring a local project to fruition); *pro bono* support (such as advising on accounting or other financial and professional matters); and mentoring (providing a business partner to act as a sounding board and professional adviser in business matters).[208]

These examples point to an important success factor in small town sustainability: Citizens and policy makers must proactively develop strategic decisions about the nature and character of urban planning and economic development projects in their towns. Residents must take action and become involved. Business owners need to be engaged. And policy makers need to recognise that they have room for strategic actions even if global economic forces seem to flow against them.

Insights from Emerging Countries

As Chapter 10 illustrates, small town development in emerging countries such as China and India can be critical to achieving balanced urban development patterns and greater equity among places. However, the rapid pace and large scale of urbanisation patterns in these emerging market economies puts small town sustainability at great risk. The most important goal of small town development is probably the modernisation of infrastructures and the provision of an economically viable lifestyle so as to retain residents and avoid depopulation from rural–urban migration. Another important goal should be the protection and maintenance of traditions, cultures, values, and heritage.

These two goals often clash as rural villages and small towns are struggling to keep up with the rapid pace of development and deal with the often overpowering dominance of higher level authorities and those mainly interested in financial gains. The case of South Korea's Slow City movement shows that small towns can achieve this balance if they empower their residents to take action and develop projects. When local residents are empowered to contribute in meaningful ways, the ideas and projects that are developed will incorporate local traditions and heritage. The danger lies, however, in the urgency of small town development needs as large-scale projects (often in tourism) promise short-term gains and success, yet with limited social, economic, and environmental sustainability. Lessons for emerging countries are therefore found in participatory models of citizen engagement and in projects that appreciate local history and culture.

China's central government places great emphasis on the goal of achieving a "harmonious society." Such a goal implies a sustainable balance between the growing coastal megacities and the countryside: the rural villages and small towns in the remaining hinterland. As Asian countries are struggling with rural–urban migration, they need to recognise the historical importance of small towns as commercial, cultural, and social nodes in a national network of cities, as well as their function as conveyers of urban–rural interactions. Approaches like the Slow City movement help highlight the importance of small towns and rural villages and they hold great promise for the future.

Will Small Towns Make a Difference?

Will all or any of the small town initiatives we have described make a difference? Will these small communities be able to reverse trends such as global warming, socioeconomic inequities, and economic decline? Will they be able to sustain and expand their sustainability efforts? There are significant barriers to small town sustainability, and whether their efforts can unleash significant changes and turn around unsustainable trends is uncertain. Financial constraints, national and international inertia in developing laws and regulations, political unwillingness, economic crises, and other types of setbacks are only a few of the reasons why small towns might be in a difficult position.

However, the variety of examples and the far-reaching networks and collaborations illustrated in this book are signs of hope. Small towns can become model communities for collaborative and networked approaches that take a systems perspective. The Swedish *Eko Kommun* movement originated from study circles that met in people's living rooms in small towns such as Övertoneå, and is now applied in many communities across the globe. Such movements have the power to spark grassroots action, connect agents of change, and create knowledge transfer.

To maintain and enhance positive impacts, small towns need to monitor and evaluate their success. Sustainability indicators and measurement systems are one way to hold individuals and organisations accountable and to monitor progress. Cittaslow's 54-point criteria list is one example of useful sustainability indicators, but the movement has yet to recertify a town. Britain's Clone Town index measures trends on the opposite end. Australia's Small Towns: Big Picture programme is a creative approach to involve country-town residents in the development of indicators, and is a good example of how to connect public participation and assessment.

Small towns also need to be aware of the potential barriers to change. Because their limited administrative and financial capacities may inhibit great investments, they must carefully think about how to finance sustainability initiatives. Networks and collaborations help with knowledge transfers and allow small towns to learn from each other without investing heavily in expensive consultants, studies, and reports. Many small towns can also rely on a strong culture of volunteerism. Local business people and citizens care about their towns and want to give back. Harnessing this type of human capital will be essential.

Critical Success Factors

In more general terms, and in the longer run, small town sustainability clearly depends on approaches based on a platform of intersecting and mutually reinforcing local initiatives. Specifically, small town sustainability must rest on a combination of:

- Building on local comparative advantages;
- Promoting a local sense of place (history, culture, and regional cultural landscapes);
- Promoting rhythm and seasonality;
- Promoting local products;
- Promoting outdoor activity – places and channels for encounters and places for people-watching;
- Promoting "third places";
- Taking care of the physical fabric of the town (including historic preservation, improving pedestrian access, establishing open green spaces with more trees, fewer streets and hard surfaces, and the consolidation of cars and parking);

- Promoting eco-friendly behaviours (composting, recycling, etc.) and investing in renewable energy systems and environmentally sensitive infrastructure (eco-friendly schools and kindergartens, public transportation, etc.);
- Being attentive to the needs of locals *as well as* newcomers *and* visitors;
- Finding sustainable ways to make long-term investments in the community's social, economic, and environmental infrastructure;
- Creating awareness of local sustainability issues and initiatives;
- Involving local business leaders *and* community groups *and* local government; and, finally,
- Tracking and measuring progress toward sustainability.

A key requirement here is that of congruency: pursuing initiatives that are complementary or mutually reinforcing. As illustrated by Figure 21 (page 27), there are tensions and potential conflicts between each of the three principal dimensions of sustainability; congruence occurs when initiatives are co-located within the tri-polar field that represents sustainability.

As we have suggested throughout this book, such an approach has to be "bottom-up" rather than "top-down." As such, small town sustainability is likely to be facilitated most effectively by peer-to-peer networks, sharing best practices while building on individual towns' experiences, resources, and priorities. Perhaps the most innovative of the current networks is the Cittaslow movement. The Cittaslow charter embraces the environmental, sociocultural, and economic dimensions of liveability and social well-being, while the Cittaslow approach is specifically designed to assist towns in establishing a set of congruent initiatives. Congruency is achievable because, although goals and initiatives are concretely defined through a uniform set of criteria, there is an inherent flexibility in the multiple ways in which Cittaslow principles can be interpreted and applied by various interest groups. Similarly, the Cittaslow framework recognises international, regional, and local differences in the economic, ecological, and sociocultural attributes of small towns, thus providing another dimension of flexibility.

The success of networks and movements such as Cittaslow is important not only for the quality of life in small towns themselves, but also for regional and national well-being. Small towns account for a significant fraction of the total population in many regions and are also deeply integrated with regional economies and regional landscapes. It follows that, in the long run, territorial cohesion and balanced regional development are highly dependent on sustaining the constellations of small towns that underpin and anchor both city regions and deep rural areas.

Notes

Chapter 1

1. George Ritzer, *The Globalization of Nothing*, Thousand Oaks, CA, Pine Forge Press, 2004.
2. Walter Benjamin, "The Work of Art in the Age of Mechanical Reproduction," in: H. Zohn (trans.), *Illuminations: Essays and Reflections*, New York, Schocken, 1969 [1936], pp. 217–252.
3. Andrew Simms, "The gaudy sameness of clone towns," *New Statesman*, January 24, 2005, p. 26.
4. *Congressional Quarterly Researcher*, "Slow Food Movement," 17 (4), 2007.
5. Campaign for Real Ale: http://www.camra.org.uk/; accessed : March 6, 2013.
6. Andrew Simms, et al., *Re-imagining the High Street: Escape from Clone Town Britain*, London, New Economics Foundation, 2010.
7. Daniel Defoe, *A Tour Thro' the Whole Island of Great Britain, Divided into Circuits or Journies*, London, G. Strahan, W. Mears, R. Francklin, S. Chapman, R. Stagg, and J. Graves, 1724.
8. Winchester City Council: http://www.winchester.gov.uk/GeneralM.asp?id=SX9452-A7832FF7andcat=5808; accessed April 12, 2008.
9. David Harvey, *Spaces of Hope*, Berkeley, CA, University of California Press, 2000; see also Paul L. Knox, "Creating ordinary places: Slow cities in a fast world," *Journal of Urban Design*, 10, 2005, pp. 1–11.
10. United Nations Centre for Human Settlements (UNCHS), *Global Report on Human Settlements*, 2001, p. 38.
11. *Ibid.*, p. 4.
12. Department for Communities and Local Government, State of the English Cities, *Liveability in English Cities*, London, 2006, p. 15.
13. K. E. Stein, et al., *Community and Quality of Life,* Washington, D.C., National Academies Press, 2002, p. 32.
14. Ray Oldenburg, *The Great Good Place*, New York, Marlowe, 1999, p. 16.
15. "Last orders," *The Guardian*, March 23, 2007; http://www.guardian.co.uk/britain/article/0,,2041087,00.html; accessed March 7, 2013.
16. Scott Campbell, "Green cities, growing cities, just cities? Urban planning and the contradictions of sustainable development," *Journal of the American Planning Association*, 3, 1996, pp. 296–312.
17. World Commission on Environment and Development, *Our Common Future* (Bruntland Report), Oxford, Oxford University Press, 1987, p. 40.
18. Suzanne Vallance, "The Sustainability Imperative and Urban New Zealand. Promise and Paradox," PhD dissertation, Lincoln University, NZ, 2007.

Chapter 2

19. Association for the Taxation of Financial Transactions to Aid Citizens: http://www.attac.org/?lang=en; accessed March 7, 2013.
20. The European Union's CIVITAS programme in Graz: http://www.civitas-initiative.org/city_sheet.phtml?id=29andlan=en; accessed March 7, 2013.
21. Lifestyles of Health and Sustainability: http://www.lohas.com/. Japan's Consumer Marketing Research Institute: http://www.jmrlsi.co.jp/english/index.html; accessed March 7, 2013.
22. Julie Guthman, "Fast food/organic food: Reflexive tastes and the making of 'yuppie chow'," *Social and Cultural Geography*, 4, 2003, pp. 45–58.
23. Fairtrade Labeling Organisations International: http://www.fairtrade.net/faq_links.html?andno_cache=1; accessed March 7, 2013.
24. http://www.fairtrade.org.uk/get_involved_fairtrade_towns.htm; accessed March 7, 2013.
25. Carl Honoré, *In Praise of Slowness*, San Francisco, HarperSanFrancisco, 2004, pp. 14–15.
26. Slow Food International: http://www.slowfood.com; accessed March 7, 2013.
27. Carlo Petrini, *Slow Food: The Case for Taste*, New York, Columbia University Press, 2001, p. 8.
28. Slow Food International: http://slowfood.com/international/11/biodiversity?-session=query_session:42F942811b6b60FBF6jrk2CF8540; accessed March 20, 2013.
29. North Carolina Small Towns Initiative: http://www.ncruralcenter.org/smalltowns/initiative.htm; accessed March 7, 2013.
30. Northern Periphery Small Town Network: http://www.northernperiphery.net/main-projects.asp?intent=detailsandtheid=31; accessed March 7, 2013.
31. AlpCity programme: http://www.alpcity.it/; accessed March 7, 2013.
32. Sustaining Small Expanding Towns: http://www.susset.org/susset/index.html; accessed March 20, 2013 .
33. World Health Organisation, Healthy Cities Programme: http://www.euro.who.int/healthy-cities; accessed March 7, 2013.
34. Mark Roseland, "Dimensions of the eco-city," *Cities*, 14, 1997, pp. 197–202.
35. Town of Okotoks: http://www.okotoks.ca/; accessed March 7, 2013.
36. Dongtan Eco-City: http://www.worldarchitecturenews.com/index.php?fuseaction=wanappln.projectview&upload_id=2137; accessed March 20, 2013.
37. Masdar's zero-carbon city: http://www.masdar.ae/en/#masdar; accessed March 20, 2013.
38. Ministry of Economy, Trade and Industry, *Eco-Towns in Japan. Implications and Lessons for Developing Countries and Cities.* Osaka, Global Environment Centre Foundation, 2005.
39. See http://www.transitionnetwork.org/; accessed March 20, 2013.
40. Lebensqualität durch Nähe: http://www.lqn-info.de/neu/startseite.php; accessed March20, 2013.
41. Action for Market Towns: http://www.towns.org.uk/index.php; accessed March 7, 2013.
42. Beacon Towns: http://mt.net.countryside.gov.uk/cgi-bin/item.cgi?id=2840andd=11andh=24andf=46anddateformat=%25o%20%25B%20%25Y; accessed April 12, 2008.
43. Heike Mayer and Paul L. Knox, "Slow cities: Sustainable places in a fast world," *Journal of Urban Affairs*, 28, 2006, pp. 321–334; Heike Mayer and Paul L. Knox, "Pace of Life and Quality of Life: The Slow City Charter," in: Joseph Sirgy, Rhonda Phillips, and Don Rahtz (eds.), *Community Quality-of-Life Indicators: Best Cases III*, Blacksburg, VA, International Society for Quality-of-Life Studies, 2007, pp. 20–39.
44. Hydrogen Cities Charter: http://www.foet.org/ongoing/hydrogen-orvieto.html; accessed March 7, 2013.

Chapter 3

45. Sarah James and T. Lahti, *The Natural Step for Communities: How Cities and Towns Can Change to Sustainable Practices*, Gabriola Island, BC, New Society Publishers, 2004.
46. *Ibid.*, p. 24; see also American Planning Association, Policy Guide on Planning for Sustainability, 2000: http://www.planning.org/policy/guides/pdf/sustainability.pdf; accessed March 20, 2013.
47. Scott Campbell, "Green cities, growing cities, just cities? Urban planning and the contradictions of sustainable development," *Journal of the American Planning Association*, 3, 1996, pp. 296–312.
48. Mark Martin, "Small town, global issues: Climate change, energy costs at the heart of utility district's vote on coal-fired power," *San Francisco Chronicle*, December 10, 2006, p. B-1.
49. Jenna Russell, "Clothesline rule creates flap," *The Boston Globe*, March 13, 2008.
50. William Yardley, "Victim of climate change, a town seeks a lifeline," *The New York Times*, May 27, 2007.
51. Intergovernmental Panel on Climate Change, Climate Change

2007: Synthesis Report, 2007; accessed March 7, 2013 from http://www.ipcc.ch/pdf/assessment-report/ar4/syr/ar4_syr.pdf

52. Eric Schlosser, *Fast Food Nation: The Dark Side of the All-American Meal*, New York, Houghton Mifflin, 2002.

53. United Nations Human Settlements Programme, "Kenya Small Towns: Mobilizing Voluntary and Community Action for Environmental Planning and Management," 2008; accessed March 20, 2013 from http://ww2.unhabitat.org/programmes/uef/cities/summary/kenyasma.htm.

54. Dolores Hayden and J. Wark, *A Field Guide to Sprawl*, New York, W. W. Norton, 2004, p. 56.

55. Tegan K. Boehmer, S. L. Lovegreen, D. Haire-Joshu, and R. C. Brownson, "What constitutes an obesogenic environment in rural communities?" *American Journal of Health Promotion*, 20, 2006, pp. 411–421.

56. James and Lahti, *The Natural Step, op.cit.*, p. 30.

57. Heather Voisey, C. Beuermann, L. A. Sverdrup, and T. O'Riordan, "The political significance of Local Agenda 21: The early stages of some European experience," *Local Environment*, 1, 1996, pp. 33–50.

58. John Bailey, "Lessons from the pioneers: Tackling global warming at the local level," 2007, p. 4; accessed March 20, 2013 from http://www.ilsr.org/lessons-pioneers-tackling-global-warming-local-level/

59. See http://www.usmayors.org/climateprotection/list.asp; accessed March 20, 2013.

60. Bailey, "Lessons from the pioneers," *op.cit.*

61. James and Lahti, *The Natural Step, op.cit.*

62. See SEkom: http://www.sekom.nu/index.php/in-english; accessed March 20, 2013.

63. James and Lahti, *The Natural Step, op.cit.*.

64. Robertsfors Kommun, "Robertsfors municipality: Sustainable development plan for the Robertsfors municipality," 2005, p. 24; accessed March 28, 2008 from http://www.esam.se/images/stories/pdf/robertsfors_sustainable_development_plan_2005.pdf

65. For more information about ECOLUP, see http://www.ecolup.info/docs/indexeco.asp?id=7207anddomid=629andsp=Eandaddlastid=andm1=7205andm2=7207; accessed April 12, 2008.

66. M. Reichenbach-Klinke, "Das Experiment von Fraunberg," *deutsche bauzeitung*, 05, 2007, pp. 32–34.

67. Werkstatt Stadt, "Ökologische Neubausiedlung: Viernheim "Am Schmittsberg," 2007; accessed March 18, 2013 from http://www.werkstatt-stadt.de/ipros/03_suche/drucken.php?projekt=81

68. Beth Daley, "Small N.H. city takes on global warming challenge," *The Boston Globe*, December 16, 2007.

69. Peter Newman and I. Jennings, *Cities as Sustainable Ecosystems: Principles and Practices*, Washington, D.C., Island Press, 2008.

Chapter 4

70. Paul L. Knox, "Creating ordinary places: Slow cities in a fast world," *Journal of Urban Design*, 10, 2005, pp. 1–11.

71. Mark Girouard, *Cities and People. A Social and Architectural History*, New Haven, CT, Yale University Press, 1985, p. 69.

72. William Cronon, *Nature's Metropolis: Chicago and the Great West*, New York, W. W. Norton, 1991.

73. Paul L. Knox and Linda McCarthy, *Urbanization*, Upper Saddle River, NJ, Prentice Hall, 2005.

74. Martin Heidegger, *Poetry, Language, Thought*, New York, Harper and Row, 1971.

75. Christian Norberg-Schulz, *Genius Loci: Towards a Phenomenology of Architecture*, New York, Rizzoli, 1980.

76. Peter Madsen and R. Plunz, (eds.), *The Urban Lifeworld. Formation, Perception, Representation*, London, Spon Press, 2001.

77. Raymond Williams, *The City and the Country*, London, Chatto and Windus, 1973.

78. Knox, "Creating ordinary places."

79. Kathleen E. Stein, et al., *Community and Quality of Life*, Washington, D.C., National Academies Press, 2002.

80. Robert Sack, *Homo Geographicus*. Baltimore, Johns Hopkins University Press, 1997, p. 10.

81. H. V. Morton, *A Traveler in Italy*, New York, Dodd, Mead, 1964, p. 527.

82. *Ibid*, p. 164.

83. This is the subject of structuration theory. See Anthony Giddens, *Central Problems in Social Theory*, London, Macmillan, 1979; Anthony Giddens, *The Constitution of Society: Outline of the Theory of Structuration*, Cambridge, UK, Polity Press, 1984; Anthony Giddens, *Modernity and Self Identity: Self and Society in the Late Modern Age*, Cambridge, UK, Polity Press, 1991; and C. G. A. Bryant and D. Jary (eds.), *Giddens's Theory of Structuration: A Critical Appreciation*, London, Routledge, 1991.

84. Giddens, *Constitution of Society, op.cit.*

85. Elizabeth Wilson, "The rhetoric of urban space," *New Left Review*, 209, 1995, p. 151.

86. Virginia Postrel, *The Substance of Style*, New York, HarperCollins, 2003, pp. 110–111.

87. B. Joseph Pine and James Gilmore, *The Experience Economy*, Boston, Harvard Business School Press, 1999; James Gilmore and B. Joseph Pine, *Authenticity: What Consumers Really Want*, Boston, Harvard Business School Press, 2007.

Chapter 5

88. International Making Cities Livable: http://www.livablecities.org/; accessed March 18, 2013.

89. Kevin Lynch, *Image of the City*, Cambridge, MA, MIT Press, 1960; Christopher Alexander, *A Pattern Language: Towns, Buildings, Construction*, New York, Oxford University Press, 1977; Christopher Alexander, *The Timeless Way of Building*, New York, Oxford University Press, 1979.

90. Robert Delevoy, quoted in Nan Ellin, *Postmodern Urbanism*, Oxford, Blackwell, 1996, p. 10.

91. Ferdinand Tönnies argued that two basic forms of human association could be recognised in all cultural systems (Tönnies, *Community and Society*, 1887). The first of these, *Gemeinschaft*, he related to an earlier period in which the basic unit of organisation was the family or kin-group, with social relationships characterised by depth, continuity, cohesion, and fulfillment. The second, *Gesellschaft*, was seen as the product of urbanisation and industrialisation that resulted in social and economic relationships based on rationality, efficiency, and contractual obligations among individuals whose roles had become specialised. See also Chapter 7, p. 134.

92. Bernard Rudofsky, *Architecture Without Architects. An Introduction to Non-Pedigreed Architecture*, New York, Museum of Modern Art, 1964.

93. Jacques Ribaud, quoted in Ellin, *Postmodern Urbanism*, p. 31.

94. Colin Rowe, "Collage city," *Architectural Review*, August 1975, pp. 65–91.

95. Quoted in Bernard Tschumi, *Architecture and Disjunction*, Cambridge, MA, MIT Press, 1994, p. 227

96. Paul L. Knox, *Metroburbia, USA*, New Brunswick, NJ, Rutgers University Press, 2008.

97. Peter Katz (eds.), *The New Urbanism: Toward an Architecture of Community*, New York, McGraw-Hill, 1994.

98. Knox, *Metroburbia*; David Harvey, "The new urbanism and the communitarian trap: On social problems and the false hope of design," *Harvard Design Magazine*, Winter/Spring, 1997, pp. 68–69; Paul W. Clarke, "The ideal of community and its counterfeit construction," *Journal of Architectural Education*, 58, 2005, p. 44.

99. Richard Sennett, "The Search for a Place in the World," in: Nan Ellen (ed.), *Architecture of Fear*, New York, Princeton Architectural Press, 1997, pp. 61–72.

100. Mark Hinshaw, "The case for true urbanism," *Planning*, June 2005, pp. 26–27.
101. Mathew Carmona, Tim Heath, Taner Oc, and Steve Tiesdell, *Public Places, Urban Spaces. The Dimensions of Urban Design*, Oxford, Architectural Press, 2003, p. 7.
102. Rob Krier and Christoph Kohl, *The Making of a Town: Potsdam Kirchsteigfeld*, London, Papadakis Publishing, 1999.
103. Kathleen James-Chakraborty, "Kirchsteigfeld – A European perspective on the construction of community," *Places*, 14, 2001, p. 60.
104. Ludger Basten, "Perceptions of urban space in the periphery: Potsdam's Kirchsteigfeld," *Tijdschrift voor Economische en Sociale Geografie*, 95, 2004, p. 96.
105. Nan Ellin, *Integral Urbanism*, London, Routledge, 2006, p. 7.
106. Edward Relph, "Temporality and the Rhythms of Sustainable Landscapes," in: Tom Mels (ed.), *Reanimating Places. A Geography of Rhythms*, Aldershot, UK, Ashgate, 2004, p. 113.
107. See, for example, Scottish Government, Planning in Small Towns. Planning Advice Note 52, 1997; http://www.scotland.gov.uk/Publications/1997/04/pan52; accessed March 18, 2013.
108. Gordon Cullen, *Townscape*, London, Architectural Press, 1961.
109. Edmund Bacon, *Design of Cities*, New York, Penguin, 1974.
110. Peter Smith, "Urban Aesthetics," in: B. Mikellides (ed.), *Architecture and People*, London, Studio Vista, 1980, pp. 74–86.
111. Pierre Von Meiss, *Elements of Architecture: From Form to Place*, London, E and FN Spon, 1990.
112. Stephen Owen, "Classic English hill towns: Ways of looking at the external appearance of settlements," *Journal of Urban Design*, 12, 2007, p. 110.
113. Paul Zucker, *Town and Square. From the Agora to Village Green*, New York, Columbia University Press, 1959.
114. Jan Gehl, *Life Between Buildings. Using Public Space*, 3rd edition, Copenhagen, Arkitektens Forlag, 1996, p. 131.
115. *Ibid.*, p. 24.
116. *Ibid.*, p. 23.

Chapter 6

117. Centre for Community Enterprise. Expertise and Resources for Community Economic Development, 2008; January 21, 2008 from http://www.cedworks.com/index.html
118. George A. Erickcek and H. McKinney, "'Small cities blues:' Looking for growth factors in small and medium-sized cities," *Economic Development Quarterly*, 20, 2006, pp. 232–258.
119. See http://www.ers.usda.gov/publications/EIB4/EIB4_lowres.pdf, accessed March 18, 2013.
120. Martin Fackler, "In Japan, rural economies wane as cities thrive," *The New York Times*, December 5, 2007.
121. Andrew Simms, Petra Kjell, and Ruth Potts, *Clone Town Britain*, London, New Economics Foundation, 2005; Andrew Simms, et al., *Re-imagining the High Street: Escape from Clone Town Britain*, London, New Economics Foundation, 2010.
122. See, for example, Paul E. Peterson, *City Limits*, Chicago, Chicago University Press, 1981. Also, J. Logan and H. Molotch, *Urban Fortunes: The Political Economy of Place*, Berkeley, CA, University of California Press, 1988; and D. Imbroscio, *Reconstructing City Politics: Alternative Economic Development and Urban Regimes*, Thousand Oaks, CA, Sage, 1997.
123. Jonathan Davies, "Can't hedgehogs be foxes, too? Reply to Clarence N. Stone," *Journal of Urban Affairs*, 26, 2004, pp. 27–33.
124. David Bell and Mark Jayne, *Small Cities: Urban Experience Beyond the Metropolis*, Abingdon, UK, Routledge, 2006, p. 2.
125. George Ritzer, "Islands of the living dead: The social geography of McDonaldization," *American Behavioral Scientist*, 47, 2003, pp. 119–136.
126. David Imbroscio, *Reconstructing City Politics*, Thousand Oaks, CA, Sage, 1997.
127. Bill McKibben, *Deep Economy: The Wealth of Communities and the Durable Future*, New York, Times Books, 2007, p. 2.
128. John P. Kretzmann and J. McKnight, *Building Communities from the Inside Out: A Path toward Finding and Mobilizing a Community's Asset*, Evanston, IL, Northwestern University, Center for Urban Affairs and Policy Research, 1993, p. 25.
129. Bell and Jayne, *Small Cities, op.cit.*, pp. 1–18.
130. *Ibid.*, p. 6.
131. Ash Amin, A. Cameron, and R. Hudson, "The Alterity of the Social Economy," in: Andrew Leyshon, R. Lee, and C. Williams (eds.), *Alternative Economic Spaces*, London, Sage Publications, 2003, p. 36.
132. See http://ec.europa.eu/enterprise/entrepreneurship/crafts.htm; accessed March 18, 2013.
133. See http://www.craft3.org/About; accessed March 18, 2013.
134. Andreas Otto, "Downtown Retailing and Revitalization of Small Cities: Lessons from Chillicothe and Mount Vernon, Ohio," in: B. Ofori-Amoah (ed.), *Beyond the Metropolis: Urban Geography As If Small Cities Mattered*, Lanham, MD, University Press of America, 2007, pp. 245–268.
135. Dennis Rondinelli, "Towns and small cities in developing countries," *Geographical Review*, 73, 1983, p. 387.
136. Jane Jacobs, *The Economy of Cities*, London, Penguin Books, 1969.

Chapter 7

137. Michael Polanyi, *Personal Knowledge: Towards a Post-Critical Philosophy*, Chicago, University of Chicago Press, 1962, p. 210.
138. *Ibid.*, p. 211.
139. Ivan Illich, *Tools for Conviviality*, Berkeley, CA, Heyday Books, 1973, p. 11.
140. *Ibid.*, p. 12.
141. Monica Hesse, "You can take it with you: Marketing to those on the go," *The Washington Post*, September 5, 2007, p. C01.
142. Katherine L. Cason, "Family mealtimes: More than just eating together," *Journal of American Dietetic Association*, 106, 2006, pp. 532–533.
143. Marktforschungs- und Beratungsinstitut psychonomics AG, "Zwischen Hamburgern und Frankfurtern – Eine Typologie von Fastfood-Nutzern," 2007; accessed February 26, 2008 from http://www.psychonomics.de/fastfood-studie-psychonomics.pdf
144. Jane Jacobs, *The Death and Life of Great American Cities*, New York, Vintage Books, 1961.
145. See http://www.pageflakes.com/buzzoffcampaign; accessed March 18, 2013.
146. Ferdinand Tönnies, *Gemeinschaft und Gesellschaft. Grundbegriffe der reinen Soziologie*, Darmstadt: Wissenschaftliche Buchgesellschaft, 2005 [1887].
147. William G. Flanagan, *Urban Sociology: Images and Structure*, 2nd ed., Boston, Allyn and Bacon, 1995, p. 45.
148. Louis Wirth, "Urbanism as a way of life," *The American Journal of Sociology*, 44, 1938, pp. 1–24.
149. Barry Wellman and B. Leighton, "Networks, neighborhoods, and communities: Approaches to the study of the community question," *Urban Affairs Quarterly*, 14, 1979, pp. 363–390.
150. Robert D. Putnam, *Bowling Alone: The Collapse and Revival of American Community*, New York, Simon and Schuster, 2000, p. 19.
151. *Ibid.*
152. Cornelia Flora Butler and Jan Flora, *Rural Communities: Legacy and Change*, Boulder, CO, Westview Press, 1992.
153. *Ibid.*, p. 65.
154. Hersbruck is also described in Heike Mayer and P. L. Knox, "Slow cities: Sustainable places in a fast world," *Journal of Urban Affairs*, 28, 2006, pp. 321–334.
155. See http://www.a-e-r.org/de/presse/2007/2007032201.html; accessed March 18, 2013.

156. See http://www.sextantio.it/macro.asp?id=3andlg=en; accessed March 18, 2013.
157. Susan Clifford and A. King, "Losing Your Place," in: S. Clifford and A. King (eds.), *Local Distinctiveness: Place, Particularity and Identity*, London, Common Ground, 1993, p. 14.
158. *Ibid.*, p. 15.
159. Carlo Petrini, *Slow Food Nation: Why Our Food Should Be Good, Clean, and Fair*, New York, Rizzoli, 2005, p. 165.
160. *Ibid.*, p. 166.
161. Mindi L. Schneider and C. A. Francis, "Marketing locally produced foods: Consumer and farmer opinions in Washington County, Nebraska," *Renewable Agriculture and Food Systems*, 20, 2005, pp. 252–260.
162. Maria Fonte, "Slow Food's Presidia: What do small producers do with big retailers?" 2005; accessed March 18, 2013 from http://www.rimisp.org/FCKeditor/UserFiles/File/documentos/docs/pdf/0496-003721-fontemariaslowfoodspresidia.pdf
163. Ulrich Beck, *Was ist Globalisierung?* Frankfurt a. M., Suhrkamp Verlag, 1997.

Chapter 8

164. Allen Eaton, *Handicrafts of the Southern Highlands*, New York, Russell Sage Foundation, 1937; M. Patten, *The Arts Workshops of Rural America*, New York, Columbia University Press, 1936; E. White, *Highland Heritage*, New York, Friendship Press, 1937.
165. Carlo Cuesta, D. Gillespie, and L. Padraic, "Bright stars: Charting the impact of the arts in rural Minnesota," 2005; accessed March 18, 2013 from http://www.mcknight.org/stream_document.aspx?rRID=3169andpRID=3168
166. B. Joseph Pine and James Gilmore, *The Experience Economy*, Boston, Harvard Business School Press, 1999; R. Florida, *The Rise of the Creative Class and How It's Transforming Work, Leisure, Community and Everyday Life*, New York, Basic Books, 2002.
167. Charles Landry, *The Creative City: A Toolkit for Urban Innovators*, London, Earthscan Publications, 2000, p. 6.
168. Jeremy Nowak, "Creativity and neighborhood development: Strategies for community investment," 2007, p. 1; accessed March 18, 2013 from http://www.trfund.com/resource/downloads/creativity/creativity_neighborhood_dev.pdf
169. Ann Markusen and Amanda Johnson, "Artists' centers: Evolution and impact on careers, neighborhoods and economies," 2006, p. 92; accessed March 18, 2013 from http://www.hhh.umn.edu/img/assets/6158/artists_centers.pdf
170. Charles Landry, *Culture at the Heart of Transformation: Swiss Agency for Development and Cooperation (SDC) and the Arts Council of Switzerland*, Zurich, Pro Helvetia, 2006.
171. Landry, *Creative City*; Florida, *The Rise of the Creative Class*; P. Wood and C. Taylor, "Big ideas for a small town: The Huddersfield creative town initiative," *Local Economy*, 19, 2004, pp. 380–395.
172. Maureen Rogers, "Social sustainability and the art of engagement – the Small towns: Big picture experience," *Local Environment*, 10, 2005, pp. 109–124.
173. Florida, *The Rise of the Creative Class*.
174. Ron Boschma and M. Fritsch, "Creative class and regional growth: Empirical evidence from eight European countries," *Economic Geography*, 85, 2009, pp. 391-423. The eight countries studied were Denmark, Finland, Germany, Netherlands, Norway, Sweden, Switzerland, and the United Kingdom.
175. Christopher Dreher, "Be creative or die," 2002; accessed March 18, 2013 from http://dir.salon.com/story/books/int/2002/06/06/florida/index.html
176. Jamie Peck, "Struggling with the creative class," *International Journal of Urban and Regional Research*, 29, 2005, pp. 740–770.
177. Allen Scott, "Creative cities: Conceptual issues and policy questions," *Journal of Urban Affairs*, 28, 2006, pp. 1–17.
178. For more information, see http://www.european-creative-industries.eu/; accessed March 18, 2013.
179. Roger Diener, J. Herzog, M. Meili, P. de Meuron, and C. Schmid, *Die Schweiz – ein städtebauliches Portrait*. Basel, Boston, Berlin, Birkhäuser, 2006.
180. David McGranahan and T. Wojan, "Recasting the creative class to examine growth processes in rural and urban counties," *Regional Studies*, 41, 2007, pp. 197–216.
181. David McGranahan and T. Wojan, "The creative class: A key to rural growth," 2007, p. 21; accessed March 18, 2013 from http://webarchives.cdlib.org/sw1vh5dg3r/http://ers.usda.gov/
182. Pamela Podger, "With bold museum, a Virginia city aims for visibility," *The New York Times*, December 29, 2007; accessed March 18, 2013 from http://www.nytimes.com/2007/12/29/us/29roanoke.html?ref=arts
183. Ann Markusen, "Cultural planning and the creative city," paper presented at the annual meeting of the American Collegiate Schools of Planning, Cincinnati, 2006.
184. Edward Relph, *The Modern Urban Landscape*, Baltimore, The Johns Hopkins University Press, 1987.

Chapter 9

185. Andrew Simms, J. Oram, A. MacGillivray, and J. Drury, *Ghost Town Britain*, London, New Economics Foundation, 2002; J. Oram, M. Conisbee, and A. Simms, *Ghost Town Britain II: Death on the High Street*, London, New Economics Foundation, 2003.
186. David Harvey, *Social Justice and the City*, London, Arnold, 1973.
187. Market Towns Team, *Beacon Town: Newmarket, Suffolk*, Cheltenham, The Countryside Agency, 2005.
188. Andrew Isserman, E. Feser, and D. Warren, "Why some rural communities prosper while others do not," 2007; accessed March 18, 2013 from http://extension.missouri.edu/ceed/reports/WhyRuralCommunitiesProsperIsserman.pdf
189. Mark Steil, "Small town pharmacies struggle," March 28, 2008; accessed March 18, 2013 from http://minnesota.publicradio.org/display/web/2008/03/24/pharmacy/?rsssource=1
190. John Fitzgerald, "A chilling call to St. Paul: School superintendents speak out about Minnesota's failed funding system," 2008; accessed March 18, 2013 from http://www.mn2020.org/assets/uploads/article/supsurvey.pdf
191. For the top 100 communities in 2010, see http://www.americaspromise.org/About-the-Alliance/Press-Room/100-Best-Press-Materials.aspx; accessed March 18, 2013.
192. Andrew Hargreaves, "Building communities of place: Habitual movement around significant places," *Journal of Housing and the Built Environment*, 19, 2004, p. 46.
193. Institute for Criminal Policy Research, *Anti-Social Behaviour Strategies: Finding a Balance*, Bristol, UK, The Policy Press for the Joseph Rowntree Foundation, 2005.
194. Market Towns Team, *Beacon Town: Thirsk, North Yorkshire*, Cheltenham, The Countryside Agency, 2005.
195. Market Towns Team, *Beacon Town: Faringdon, Oxfordshire*, Cheltenham, The Countryside Agency, 2005.
196. Robert D. Putnam, "The prosperous community: Social capital and public life," *The American Prospect*, 13, 1993, pp. 35–42.

Chapter 10

197. David Satterthwaite, *Outside the large cities: The demographic importance of small urban centres and large villages in Africa, Asia and Latin America*. London, UK: International Institute for Environment and Development, 2006.
198. Bingqin Li and Xiangsheng An, *Migration and small towns in China: Power hierarchy and resource allocation*. International Institute for Environment and Development (IIED), Human Settlements Group, 2009.

199. Laurence Ma and Ming Fan, (1994). Urbanisation from below: The growth of towns in Jiangsu, China. *Urban Studies*, 31, 1994, pp. 1625-1645.
200. Hualou Long, Yansui Liu, Xiuqin Wu, and Guihua Dong, Spatio-temporal dynamic patterns of farmland and rural settlments in Su-Xi-Chang region: Implications for building a new countryside in coastal China. *Land Use Policy*, 26, 2009, pp. 322-333.
201. Li and An, *Migration and small towns in China, op. cit.*
202. Mike Douglass, *The Saemaul Undong: South Korea`s rural development miracle in historical perspective.* Singapore: National University of Singapore, 2013.
203. Matthias Messmer and Hsin-Mei Chuang, *China`s vanishing worlds: Countryside, traditions and cultural spaces.* Bern: Bentili Verlag, 2012.

Chapter 11

204. Andrew Simms, P. Kjell, and R. Potts, *Clone Town Britain*, London, New Economics Foundation, 2005.
205. Maureen Rogers and R. Walker, "Sustainable enterprise creation: Making a difference in rural Australia and beyond," *International Journal of Environmental, Cultural, Economic and Social Sustainability*, 1, 2005, pp 1–9. Available online at http://www.latrobe.edu.au/csrc/publications/sustEnterprise.pdf; accessed March 18, 2013.
206. Market Towns Team, *Beacon Town: Faringdon, Oxfordshire*, Cheltenham, The Countryside Agency, 2005.
207. Market Towns Team, *Beacon Town: Wolverton, Milton Keynes,* Cheltenham, The Countryside Agency, 2005.
208. Market Towns Team, *Beacon Towns: The Story Continues,* Cheltenham, The Countryside Agency, 2005.

Key References

Agger, Ben, *Speeding Up Fast Capitalism: Cultures, Jobs, Families, Schools, Bodies*, Boulder, CO, Paradigm Publishers, 2004.

Andrews, Cecile, *Slow Is Beautiful: New Visions of Community, Leisure, and Joie de Vivre*, London, New Society, 2006.

Ayegman, Julian, *Sustainable Communities and the Challenge of Environmental Justice*, New York, NYU Press, 2005.

Barrientos, Stephanie and **Catherine Dolan** (eds.), *Ethical Sourcing in the Global Food System*, London, Earthscan, 2006.

Beatley, Timothy, *Green Urbanism: Learning from European Cities*, Washington, D.C., Island Press, 2000.

Beatley, Timothy, *Native to Nowhere: Sustaining Home and Community in a Global Age*, Washington, D.C., Island Press, 2004.

Beck, Ulrich, *Risikogesellschaft: Auf dem Weg in eine andere Moderne*, Frankfurt a. M., Suhrkamp Verlag, 1986.

Beck, Ulrich, *Was ist Globalisierung?* Frankfurt a. M., Suhrkamp Verlag, 1997.

Beck, Ulrich, *Cosmopolitan Vision*, Cambridge, UK, Polity Press, 2006.

Beck, Ulrich, **Giddens, Anthony**, and **Scott Lash**, *Reflexive Modernisierung: Eine Kontroverse*, Frankfurt a. M., Suhrkamp Verlag, 1996.

Bell, David and **Mark Jayne**, *Small Cities: Urban Experience Beyond the Metropolis*, New York, Routledge, 2006.

Bell, David and **Gill Valentine**, *Consuming Geographies. We Are Where We Eat*, London, Routledge, 1997.

Benedikt, Michael, "Reality and authenticity in the experience economy," *Architectural Record*, 189, 2001, pp. 84–85.

Berce-Bratko, Branka, *Can Small Urban Communities Survive?* Burlington, VT, Ashgate, 2001.

Breheny, Michael, "Counter-urbanisation and Sustainable Urban Forms," in: J. Brotchie, E. Blakely, P. Hall, and P. Newton (eds.), *Cities in Competition*, Melbourne, Longman Australia, 1995.

Brennan, David and **Lorman Lundsten**, "Impacts of large discount stores on small US towns: Reasons for shopping and retailer strategies," *International Journal of Retail and Distribution Management*, 28, 2000, pp. 155–161.

Campbell, Scott, "Planning: Green Cities, Growing Cities, Just Cities," in: D. Satterthwaite (ed.), *Sustainable Cities*, London, Earthscan, 1999, pp. 251–273.

Daniels, Thomas, "Small town economic development: Growth or survival?" *Journal of Planning Literature*, 4, 1989, pp. 413–429.

Davidson, Sharon and **Amy Rummel**, "Retail changes associated with Wal-Mart's entry into Maine," *International Journal of Retail and Distribution Management*, 28, 2000, pp. 162–169.

Duany, Andres and **Elizabeth Plater-Zyberk**, "The second coming of the American small town," *Wilson Quarterly*, 16, 1992, pp. 3–51.

Eriksen, Thomas, *Tyranny of the Moment: Fast and Slow Time in the Information Age*, London, Pluto Press, 2001.

Evans, Peter, *Livable Cities: Urban Struggles for Livelihood and Sustainability*, Berkeley, CA, University of California Press, 2002.

Flora, Cornelia Butler and **Jan Flora**, *Rural Communities: Legacy and Change*, Boulder, CO, Westview Press, 1992.

Garhammer, Manfred, "Pace of life and enjoyment of life," *Journal of Happiness Studies*, 3, 2002, pp. 217–256.

Garrett-Petts, W. F., *The Small Cities Book: On the Cultural Future of Small Cities*, Vancouver, BC, New Star Books, 2005.

Gaytan, Marie, "Globalizing resistance: Slow food and new local imaginaries," *Food, Culture, and Society*, 7, 2004, pp. 97–116.

Gehl, Jan, *Life Between Buildings: Using Public Space*, Copenhagen, Arkitektens Forlag, 1996.

Gleick, James, *Faster: The Acceleration of Just About Everything*, New York, Pantheon Books, 1999.

Goldsmith, Edward and **Jerry Mander** (eds.), *The Case Against the Global Economy and a Turn Towards Localization*, London, Earthscan, 2001.

Goodno, James, "Pitching in: Some small towns are going into the retail business," *Planning*, April, 2005, pp. 40–41.

Gräf, Holger, *Kleine Städte im neuzeitlichen Europa*, Berlin, Berliner Wissenschafts-Verlag, 2000.

Greenberg, Michael, "Neighborhoods: Slow places in a fast world?" *Society*, 38, 2000, pp. 28–32.

Guy, Clifford, "Outshopping from small towns," *International Journal of Retail and Distribution Management*, 1, 1990, pp. 3–14.

Hallsmith, Gwendolyn, *The Key to Sustainable Cities: Meeting Human Needs, Transforming Community Systems*, London, New Society Publishers, 2003.

Hallsworth, Alan and **Steve Worthington**, "Local resistance to larger retailers: The example of market towns and the food superstore in the UK," *International Journal of Retail and Distribution Management*, 28, 2000, pp. 207–216.

Hibbard, Michael and **Lori Davis**, "When the going gets tough: Economic reality and the cultural myths of small-town America," *Journal of the American Planning Association*, 52, 1986, pp. 419–428.

Illich, Ivan, *Tools for Conviviality,* Berkeley, CA, Heyday Books, 1973.

Jacobs, Jane, *The Death and Life of Great American Cities*, New York, Vintage Books, 1961.

Jacobs, Jane, *The Economy of Cities*, London, Penguin Books, 1969.

James, Sarah and **Torbjörn Lahti**, *The Natural Step for Communities: How Cities and Towns Can Change to Sustainable Practices*, Gabriola Island, BC, New Society Publishers, 2004.

Jenks, Mike and **Nicola Dempsey** (eds.), *Future Forms and Design for Sustainable Cities,* London, Architectural Press, 2005.

Knox, Paul, "Creating Ordinary Places: Slow Cities in a Fast World," *Journal of Urban Design*, 10, 2005, pp. 3-13.

Knox, Paul and **Heike Mayer**, "Europe's internal periphery. Small towns in the context of reflexive polycentricity", in *The Cultural Political Economy of Small Cities*, Bas van Heur and Anne Lorentzen (eds.), London: Routledge, 2011, pp. 142-157.

Kretzmann, John and **John McKnight**, *Building Communities from the Inside Out: A Path toward Finding and Mobilizing a Community's Asset,* Evanston, IL, Northwestern University, Center for Urban Affairs and Policy Research, 1993.

Labrianidis, Lois, *The Future of Europe's Rural Peripheries*, Aldershot, Hampshire, UK, Ashgate, 2004.

Lafferty, William (ed.), *Sustainable Communities in Europe*, London, Earthscan, 2001.

Landry, Charles, *The Creative City: A Toolkit for Urban Innovators,* London, Earthscan, 2000.

Levine, Robert and **Ara Norenzayan**, "The pace of life in 31 countries," *Journal of Cross-Cultural Psychology*, 30, 1999, pp. 178–205.

Leyshon, Andrew, **Lee, Roger**, and **Colin C. Williams**, *Alternative Economic Spaces*, London, Sage Publications, 2003.

Li, Bingqin and **Xiangsheng An,** *Migration and small towns in China: Power hierarchy and resource allocation,* International Institute for Environment and Development (IIED), Human Settlements Group, 2009.

Markusen, Ann and **Amanda Johnson**, "Artists' centers: Evolution and impact on careers, neighborhoods and economies", 2006, retrieved March 13, 2008, from http://www.hhh.umn.edu/img/assets/6158/artists_centers.pdf

Mayer, Heike and **Paul L. Knox**, "Small town sustainability: prospects in the second modernity," *European Planning Journal*, 18, 2010, pp. 1545-1565.

Mayer, Heike and **Paul L. Knox**, "Slow Cities: Sustainable Places in a Fast World" *Journal of Urban Affairs*, 28, 2006, pp. 321-334.

McKibben, Bill, *Deep Economy: The Wealth of Communities and the Durable Future*, New York, Times Books, 2007.

Mels, Tom (ed.), *Reanimating Places. A Geography of Rhythms*, Burlington, VT, Ashgate, 2004.

Messmer, Matthias and **Hsin-Mei Chuang**, *China`s vanishing worlds: Countryside, traditions and cultural spaces.* Bern: Bentili Verlag, 2012.

Newman, Peter and **Isabella Jennings**, *Cities as Sustainable Ecosystems: Principles and Practices*, Washington, D.C., Island Press, 2008.

Nijkamp, Peter and **Adriaan Perrels**, *Sustainable Cities in Europe*, London, Earthscan, 1994.

Ofori-Amoah, Benjamin, *Beyond the Metropolis: Urban Geography as if Small Cities Mattered*, Lanham, MD, University Press of America, 2007.

O'Riordan, Timothy, *Globalism, Localism, and Identity*, London, Earthscan, 2001.

Owen, Stephen, "Classic English hill towns: Ways of looking at the external appearance of settlements," *Journal of Urban Design*, 12, 2007, pp. 93–116.

Pacione, Michael, "Urban livability: A review," *Urban Geography*, 11, 1990, pp. 1–30.

Pal, John and **Emma Sanders**, "Measuring the effectiveness of town centre management schemes: An exploratory framework," *International Journal of Retail and Distribution Management*, 25, 1997, pp. 70–77.

Parkins, Wendy and **Geoffrey Craig**, *Slow Living*, Oxford, Berg, 2006.

Paterson, Elaine, "Quality new development in English market towns," *Journal of Urban Design*, 11, 2006, pp. 225–241.

Peck, Jamie, "Struggling with the creative class," *International Journal of Urban and Regional Research*, 29, 2005, pp. 740–770.

Petrini, Carlo, *Slow Food: The Case for Taste*, New York, Columbia University Press, 2001.

Petrini, Carlo, *Slow Food Nation: Why Our Food Should Be Good, Clean, and Fair*, New York, Rizzoli, 2005.

Polanyi, Michael, *Personal Knowledge: Towards a Post-Critical Philosophy,* Chicago, University of Chicago Press, 1962.

Portney, Kent, *Taking Sustainable Cities Seriously: Economic Development, the Environment, and Quality of Life in American Cities*, Cambridge, MA, MIT Press, 2003.

Powe, Neil, **Hart, Trevor**, and **Tim Shaw** (eds.), *Market Towns. Roles, Challenges, and Prospects*, London, Routledge, 2007.

Putnam, Robert, *Bowling Alone: The Collapse and Revival of American Community*, New York, Simon and Schuster, 2000.

Rogers, Maureen, "Social sustainability and the art of engagement – the small towns: Big picture experience," *Local Environment*, 10, 2005, pp. 109–124.

Roseland, Mark, *Eco-City Dimensions: Healthy Communities, Healthy Planet*, Gabriola Island, BC, New Society Publishers, 1997.

Roseland, Mark, *Towards Sustainable Communities,* Gabriola Island, BC, New Society Publishers, 1998.

Satterthwaite, David, *Outside the large cities: The demographic importance of small urban centres and large villages in Africa, Asia and Latin America*. London, UK: International Institute for Environment and Development, 2006.

Shuman, Michael, *The Small-Mart Revolution: How Local Businesses Are Beating the Global Competition,* San Francisco, Berrett-Koehler Publishers, 2006.

Thrift, Nigel, "Cities without modernity, cities with magic," *Scottish Geographical Magazine*, 113, 1997, pp. 138–149.

Tönnies, Ferdinand, *Gemeinschaft und Gesellschaft. Grundbegriffe der reinen Soziologie*, Darmstadt, Wissenschaftliche Buchgesellschaft, 2005 [1887].

Tsouros, Agis (ed.), *Healthy Cities in Europe*, London, Routledge, 2008.

Vaz, Teresa De Noronha, **Morgan, Eleanor**, and **Peter Nijkamp**, *The New European Rurality: Strategies for Small Firms*, Burlington, VT, Ashgate, 2006.

White, Stacey Swearinger and **Cliff Ellis**, "Sustainability, the environment, and new urbanism: An assessment and agenda for research," *Journal of Architectural and Planning Research*, 24, 2007, pp. 125–143.

Williamson, Thad, **Imbroscio, David**, and **Gar Alperovitz**, *Making a Place For Community: Local Democracy in a Global Era*, New York, Routledge, 2003.

Internet Resources

International Networks
Aalborg Commitments: http://www.aalborgplus10.dk/
Cittaslow Germany: http://www.cittaslow-deutschland.de/
Cittaslow UK: http://www.cittaslow.org.uk/
Cittaslow International:
     http://www.cittaslow.net/ECOLUP: http://www.ecolup.info
International Council for Local Environmental Initiatives:
     http://www.iclei.org/
International Making Cities Liveable:
     http://www.livablecities.org/
Lebensqualität durch Nähe:
     http://www.lebensqualitaet-durch-naehe.de
Project for Public Spaces: http://www.pps.org/
Slow Food International: http://www.slowfood.com/

European Networks
AlpCity: http://www.alpcity.it/
European Council for the Village and Small Town:
     http://www.ecovast.org/
European Healthy Cities Network:
     http://www.euro.who.int/healthy-cities
Pro Helvetia's Creative Cities Project: http://www.sdc.admin.ch/
     en/Home/Projects/Creative_Cities_in_Albania
SmallTownNetworks: http://www.highland.gov.uk/
     businessinformation/economicdevelopment/regeneration/
     smalltownnetworks.htm
SusSET (Sustaining Small Expanding Towns):
     http://www.britnett-carver.co.uk/susset/

Australia
Keep Australia Beautiful: Sustainable Cities:
     http://www.kab.org.au/01_cms/details.asp?ID=4
Small Towns: Big Picture: http://www.latrobe.edu.au/
     smalltowns/connections/stbp.htm
Sustainable Cities Programme:
     http://www.environment.gov.au/settlements/sustainable-
     cities.html

Germany
Shrinking Cities/Schrumpfende Städte:
     http://www.shrinkingcities.com/

Japan
Japan for Sustainability: http://www.japanfs.org/index.html
Japan's Eco-City Contest: http://www.japanfs.org/db/1430-e

New Zealand
New Zealand Urban Design Protocol: http://www.mfe.govt.nz/
     issues/urban/design-protocol/index.html

North America
Arkansas' DeltaMade: http://www.arkansasdeltamade.com/
Centre for Community Enterprise: http://www.cedworks.com/
Cool Mayors for Climate Protection:
     http://www.coolmayors.org/
Economic Gardening in Littleton, Colorado:
     http://www.littletongov.org/bia/economicgardening/
HandMade in America: http://www.handmadeinamerica.org/
International Centre for Sustainable Cities (ICSC):
     http://icsc.ca/what-is-a-sustainable-city.html
Michigan's Cool Cities Initiative: http://www.coolcities.com/
National Trust Main Street Center:
     http://www.mainstreet.org/
North Carolina's Small Towns Initiative:
     http://www.ncruralcenter.org/smalltowns/index.html

Paducah Artist Relocation Programme:
     http://www.paducaharts.com/
Shorebank Enterprise Cascadia: http://www.sbpac.com/
The Hometown Advantage: http://www.newrules.org/retail/
Your Town Alabama:
     http://www.yourtownalabama.org/index.html

Sweden
Sveriges Eko Kommuner:
     http://www.sekom.nu/standard.asp?id=39

The Netherlands
Alphen aan den Rijn, The Dutch test case for sustainable town
     planning: http://www.p2pays.org/ref/24/23406.htm

UK
Action for Market Towns: http://www.towns.org.uk/index.php
Fairtrade Towns: http://www.fairtrade.org.uk/get_involved/
     campaigns/fairtrade_towns/default.aspx
New Economics Foundation:
     http://www.neweconomics.org/gen/
Transition Towns: http://transitiontowns.org/Main/HomePage

Emerging countries
China's Building a New Socialist Countryside Initiative: http://
     english.gov.cn/special/rd_index.htm
Slow Cities in South Korea: http://english.visitkorea.or.kr/enu/
     SI/SI_EN_3_4_12_15.jsp
South Korea's Saemaul Undong Center: http://www.saemaul.
     net/background.asp

Other useful resources
Agenda 21: http://www.un.org/esa/sustdev/documents/
     agenda21/index.htm
ATTAC (Association pour la taxation des transactions pour
     l'aide aux citoyens): http://www.attac.org/?lang=en
LOHAS (Lifestyles of Health and Sustainability):
     http://www.lohas.com/
The Natural Step Network:
     http://www.naturalstep.org/com/nyStart/

Index of Places

Photo Credits

All photographs are by the authors, except the following: